Upstream
PRE-INTERMEDIATE

Student's Book

Virginia Evans-Jenny Dooley

Express Publishing

Contents

	Topics	Vocabulary	Reading
UNIT 1 Heroes and Villains (pp. 6-15)	• people (character & appearance)	character adjectives; appearance; personal qualities *antonyms; adjectives with prepositions*	- Characters Larger than Life (multiple choice) - Beauty is in the eye of the beholder (m/c cloze) - Literature Corner: *Scandal in Bohemia* by Conan Doyle (T/F)
UNIT 2 Lifestyles (pp. 16-25)	• jobs & places • lifestyles • the city & country	city life/country life; jobs & job qualities; describing places; parts of a town; commuting *antonyms; adjectives with prepositions; adj-n phrases*	- A City Slicker or a Country Lover? (T/F) - signs (multiple choice) - Culture Clip: Celebration: dream town USA (m/c cloze)

Self-Assessment Module 1 (pp. 26-27) – Curricular Cuts 1 (p. 28) – (History) Elizabeth's Portraits

UNIT 3 Earth Calling (pp. 30-39)	• the environment • endangered species	environmental problems & solutions; endangered animals & protected species	- The Earth in our hands (T/F) - No ordinary zoo (m/c cloze) - *RRS Ernest Shackleton* Captain's Log (multiple choice)
UNIT 4 Travellers' Tales (pp. 40-49)	• holidays • climate/weather • transport	types of holidays, sites & resorts; climate & weather; holiday equipment; means of transport *prepositional phrases*	- Looking for the ideal getaway? (multiple matching – short texts) - Literature Corner: *Gulliver's Travels* by Jonathan Swift (multiple matching – missing sentences)

Self-Assessment Module 2 (pp. 50-51) – Curricular Cuts 2 (p. 52) – (Geography) The World's Climates

UNIT 5 On Offer (pp. 54-63)	• shops and shopping • clothes/accessories	types of shops & shopping; products; clothes; describing objects; gifts; homes *prepositional phrases; antonyms*	- Checking out second-hand city (multiple choice) - signs & notices (multiple choice) - Culture Clip: Styles of Homes (multiple matching)
UNIT 6 Happy Days! (pp. 64-73)	• celebrations • festivals & events	traditional celebrations & customs; festive activities; feelings; greetings cards *verbs with prepositions*	- A Traditional Irish Wedding (T/F) - Culture Clip: Bizarre Annual Events in the UK (multiple matching)

Self-Assessment Module 3 (pp. 74-75) – Curricular Cuts 3 (p. 76) – Maths

UNIT 7 Eating out! (pp. 78-87)	• places to eat • food and drinks	restaurant-related words; the supermarket; recipes & cooking methods; tastes; cutlery, crockery & appliances; quantities; menus *verbs with prepositions*	- A Taste of Toronto (multiple matching – short texts) - Literature Corner: *Charlie & the Chocolate Factory* by Roald Dahl (comprehension questions)
UNIT 8 Fit for Life (pp. 88-97)	• sports • accidents and injuries	types of sports; sport injuries; places & equipment; personal qualities *adjectives with prepositions*	- The Last Great Race (T/F) - messages (multiple choice) - signs (multiple matching) - Literature Corner: *The Olympic Anthem* (reading for specific information)

Self-Assessment Module 4 (pp. 98-99) – Curricular Cuts 4 (p.100) – (Science) A Balanced Diet

UNIT 9 Going out! (pp. 102-111)	• entertainment • the arts • charity	types of entertainment; cinema & films; reviews; books & newspapers; TV jobs/ programmes; theatre; charity *prepositional phrases; regrets*	- Pick of the Week (multiple matching – short texts) - Graffiti – Is it Art? (open cloze) - Culture Corner: Comic Relief (completing a summary)
UNIT 10 Fast Forward (pp. 112-121)	• technology • education	teenagers & technology; gadgets; education & technology; means of communication; text messages; processes; science; faults *prepositional phrases; compound nouns; antonyms*	- All About Britain's Teenagers (multiple choice) - Culture Corner: The Education System of the UK & the USA (completing missing information in tables)

Self-Assessment Module 5 (pp. 122-123) – Curricular Cuts 5 (p. 124) – (Art & Design) Styles of painting

Songsheets 1-5 (pp. 125-130) Grammar Reference Section (pp. 132-141) American English-British English Guide (p.152)
Irregular Verbs (p. 131) Word List (pp. 142-151)

Grammar	Listening	Speaking	Writing
present simple/ continuous; stative verbs; adverbs of frequency; question words Phrasal verbs: GET	- multiple choice - multiple matching (missing sentences)	describing fictional characters; making choices; socialising; describing people *intonation – expressing surprise & concern*	- a letter giving advice *Portfolio: description of a hero/villain; classified ad; e-mail to a friend*
comparatives and superlatives; -ing/infinitive forms; specific/general preferences Phrasal verbs: PUT	- listening for detailed meaning - multiple matching (missing sentences)	introducing oneself; expressing likes/dislikes; asking for/giving directions; talking about jobs; expressing preferences; (role-play) a job interview; describing pictures *intonation – stressed syllables*	- a letter of application *Portfolio: article about where you live; description of neighbourhood; questions for a quiz*
present perfect simple/continuous; clauses of purpose Phrasal verbs: RUN	- completing missing information - multiple choice	improving one's town/city; a short talk from notes; describing pictures; reacting to news; acting out a dialogue; (role-play) at Customs	- notes *Portfolio: poster about the environment; article about a zoo; letter to a friend*
present/past participles; past simple/continuous; linkers; the definite/indefinite article; used to/would Phrasal verbs: COME	- multiple matching - listening for specific information - completing missing information	narrating experiences; expressing feelings; checking in; complaining/apologising; giving travel information; expressing disapproval; describing pictures *intonation – expressing annoyance*	- a story *Portfolio: holiday advertisement; weather forecast; factfile about your country*
modal verbs; making assumptions/requests; too/enough; order of adjectives Phrasal verbs: LOOK	- listening for specific information - listening for gist - multiple choice - mutiple matching	asking about prices; calming down; describing objects; offering/accepting gifts; asking for/buying things; (role-play) salesperson/customer *intonation – losing patience*	- a report assessing good & bad points *Portfolio: description of the best place to shop; page for a clothes catalogue; poster of school/work rules*
future forms; future continuous; question tags Phrasal verbs: BREAK	- listening for gist - listening for specific information - intonation	a short talk from notes; describing celebrations & customs; making arrangements; inviting; congratulating & thanking *intonation in question tags*	- postcard *Portfolio: article about a traditional wedding; greetings cards; e-mail to a friend*
countables/uncountables; quantifiers; indefinite pronouns; past perfect simple/ continuous Phrasal verbs: GIVE	- multiple choice - listening for specific information - multiple matching - to take notes	discussing food preferences/tastes; (role-play) eating out/ordering a meal; comparing table manners; describing pictures; *intonation – stressed syllables*	- a story *Portfolio: description of an unusual restaurant; recipe for a local dish; shopping list*
the passive; *with/by*; conditionals: type 0, 1; *if/unless*; linkers (result, addition, contrast, etc) Phrasal verbs: BRING	- listening for detailed meaning - multiple choice - multiple matching - listening for specific sounds	discussing sports; negotiating; describing pictures; expressing opinions; asking about/describing health; sympathising – giving advice; acting out dialogues *intonation – hesitating*	- a pros and cons essay *Portfolio: postcard to a friend; short communicative message; sports quiz*
conditionals: type 2, 3; wishes; relative clauses; *so/neither* Phrasal verbs: TURN	- listening for detailed meaning - multiple matching - completing missing information	discussing entertainment; suggesting/(dis)agreeing; talking about a book/TV programmes; (role-play) booking tickets; expressing preferences; describing paintings; acting out dialogues	- an informal letter reviewing a film *Portfolio: review for a school event; TV guide; interview with a graffiti artist*
clauses of concession; *all/most/some/none*; reported speech; indirect questions; causative form Phrasal verbs: TAKE	- multiple matching - to fill in gaps - listening for detailed meaning	discussing technology; short talk from notes; conducting a survey; talking about pros & cons; describing pictures; (role-play) requesting action/giving an account of an event *intonation in questions*	- a letter of complaint *Portfolio: article about teenagers in your country; text message to a friend; questions for a science quiz*

Published by Express Publishing

Liberty House, New Greenham Park, Newbury,
Berkshire RG19 6HW
Tel: (0044) 1635 817 363
Fax: (0044) 1635 817 463
e-mail: inquiries@expresspublishing.co.uk
http://www.expresspublishing.co.uk

© Virginia Evans & Jenny Dooley 2004

Design and Illustration © Express Publishing, 2004

All rights reserved. No part of this publication may be reproduced, stored in a retrieval system, or transmitted in any form, or by any means, electronic, photocopying or otherwise, without the prior written permission of the publishers.

First published 2004

ISBN 1-84466-573-9

Acknowledgements

Authors' Acknowledgements

We would like to thank all the staff at Express Publishing who have contributed their skills to producing this book. Thanks for their support and patience are due in particular to: Megan Lawton (Editor in Chief), Stephanie Smith and Michael Sadler (senior editors); Andrew Wright (editorial assistant); Brian O'Neil (senior production controller) and the Express Publishing design team; Warehouse (recording producer); and Emily Newton, Kevin Harris, Daniel Parker, Erica Thompson and Timothy Forster. We would also like to thank those institutions and teachers who piloted the manuscript, and whose comments and feedback were invaluable in the production of the book.

The authors and publishers wish to thank the following, who have kindly given permission for the use of copyright material:

Unit 3a: © 2003 the Jane Goodall Institute, www.janegoodall.org/ on pp. 30-31; *Unit 3b:* © Henry Doorly Zoo, www.omaha.org/ on p. 33; *Culture Clip 3:* RRS Ernest Shackleton © Copyright Natural Environment Research Council British Antarctic Survey 2004, www.antarctica.ac.uk/ on p. 39; *Literature Corner 7:* Charlie and the Chocolate Factory by Roald Dahl, published by Penguin Books, by permission of David Higham Associates on p. 87

Photograph Acknowledgements

Unit 1a: © everetcollection / iml image group on p. 7; *Culture Clip 3:* RRS Ernest Shackleton © Copyright Natural Environment Research Council British Antarctic Survey 2004, www.antarctica.ac.uk/ on p. 39; *Culture Clip 6:* Bognor Birdman © Spirit FM, www.spiritfm.net/ on p. 73; *Unit 7a:* Mr Greenjeans © Copyright Fabulous Savings, 2000, www.fabuloussavings.com/; Rainforest Café and Captain John's Harbour Boat Restaurant © Copyright 1997-2004, toronto.com; and The Old Spaghetti Factory © www.oldspaghettifactory.net/ on p. 79

Colour Illustrations: Stone

Music Compositions & Arrangement by Ted & Taz

While every effort has been made to trace all the copyright holders, if any have been inadvertently overlooked the publishers will be pleased to make the necessary arrangements at the first opportunity.

People of the World

Module 1
Units 1-2

- express likes/dislikes/preferences
- ask for/give directions
- act out a job interview

▶ Practise ...

- the present simple/ continuous
- adverbs of frequency
- question words
- comparative/superlative forms
- -ing/infinitive forms
- pronunciation
- intonation (expressing surprise & concern in stressed syllables)
- phrasal verbs: *get*, *put*

▶ Write ...

- a short paragraph about your favourite hero(ine) or villain
- a classified ad
- an e-mail to a friend
- an informal letter of advice
- a short article about yourself and where you live
- a short description of your neighbourhood
- a short quiz about the capital city of your country
- a letter of application

▶ Look at Module 1

- Find the page numbers for pictures 1-5.

▶ Find the unit and page number(s) for

- classified ads ☐
- an e-mail ☐
- jokes ☐
- a town map ☐
- signs ☐
- a quiz ☐
- a CV ☐

▶ Listen, read and talk about ...

- character & appearance
- habits/routines/lifestyles
- places & geographical features
- signs
- jobs/workplaces/job qualities

▶ Learn how to ...

- describe people
- talk about personal qualities
- socialise
- make choices

Culture Clips: Celebration - Dream Town USA

Literature Corner: Scandal in Bohemia

Curricular Cuts (History): Elizabeth I

1a Heroes and Villains

Lead-in

1
a. Which of the characters in the pictures are heroes/heroines and which are villains?

b. Who has got ...
- curly brown hair
- pointed ears
- a long white beard
- a black moustache
- a magic mirror
- a sharp metal hook instead of a hand
- a magic staff
- a broad-brimmed hat
- shiny black hair and rosy cheeks

Frodo Baggins has got curly brown hair.

Listening

2
a. In pairs, decide which of these adjectives best describe each character in the pictures.

mischievous & daring *Peter Pan*
cunning & dangerous
kind & caring
vain & cold-hearted
polite & considerate
evil & greedy
brave & honest

A: Who do you think is mischievous and daring?
B: I'd say Peter Pan.

b. Listen and check. Which extra character is described?

Reading

3 Look at the pictures and the title of the article. What does the title mean?

Characters Larger than life

Frodo Baggins

Saruman

In any book, cartoon or film we all love to see the heroes defeat the villains, save the world, win the girl and live happily ever after. But just between you
5 and me, don't we feel a little bit sorry for the villains as well?

Saruman, from *The Lord of the Rings*, is an all-time favourite villain, the type of villain I like. He is a tall wizard with a long
10 white beard and cold dark eyes. He wears a long white robe and carries a magic staff. Once he was a good wizard but the power of a magic ring has made him evil and greedy and now he wants
15 to rule the world. Only Frodo, the small ring bearer, can stop him.

Frodo Baggins, a Hobbit, is small, brave and honest, with bright eyes, curly brown hair and very large hairy feet! His
20 mission is to take the magic ring to Mordor where it will be destroyed. He travels with some friends and together they have to face many dangers. Gandalf a wise wizard, protects them
25 and shows them the way.

Another of my favourite heroes is Peter Pan, a mischievous, daring boy with pointed ears who can fly and never grows older. Peter and his friends, the Lost Boys, have a dangerous enemy 30 called Captain Hook.

With his black moustache, cruel laugh and a sharp metal hook instead of a hand, the cunning Captain Hook is a perfect villain. He always wears a broad- 35 brimmed hat and fine clothes. He lives with a band of pirates on his ship, the *Jolly Roger*, making plans to kidnap the Lost Boys and capture the boy he hates.

Not all villains are men. The Wicked 40 Queen in *Snow White* is one of the most cold-hearted villains ever. Beautiful but vain, the queen asks her mirror every day, "Mirror, mirror on the wall, who is the fairest of them all?" The answer 45 always pleases her, until one day the mirror replies that kind and caring Snow White is even prettier than her. The jealous queen is so angry that she dresses up as an old woman and gives 50 Snow White a poisoned apple.

Whether heroes or villains, these are the characters I admire the most. I love to watch the heroes fight the villains and eventually see good win over evil. I also 55 can't help feeling for the villains and their weaknesses; I just love to hate them! These stories are timeless and the characters are definitely larger than life.

6

StudySkills

Reading effectively

Read the text once quickly. This will help you understand what type it is, the author's purpose and its general content. Read the questions and the answers. Read the text again carefully and find the part of the text each question refers to. The information may be phrased in different words.

4 Read the text and for each question (1-4) choose the best answer A, B, C or D. Then, explain the highlighted words.

1 What is the writer's main purpose in writing the text?
  A to describe how heroes catch villains
  B to describe some well-known heroes and villains
  C to tell some well-known cartoon stories
  D to tell some well-known fairy tales

2 What does the writer say about Saruman?
  A He was not always evil.
  B He is the writer's favourite character.
  C Frodo wants to destroy him.
  D He has lost a valuable ring.

3 Which of the statements is true of Captain Hook?
  A He works on his own.
  B He has a partner called Jolly Roger.
  C He has a black beard.
  D He takes care of his appearance.

4 What is the writer's opinion of villains?
  A They are more important than the heroes.
  B He likes them more than the heroes.
  C He is happy to see them lose.
  D They are just as important as the heroes.

5 Listen and read. Say a few words about the stories and suggest another title for the text.

Speaking

6 Tell the class about your favourite film or TV hero(ine)/villain. Talk about:
  • the character's name • where he/she appears
  • character • appearance • what happens in the story

Writing

Portfolio: Use your answers from Ex. 6 to write a short paragraph for a teen magazine about your favourite hero/heroine or villain. Use the second and third paragraphs of the text as a model. Start like this:

..., from ..., is my favourite .... He/She's ....

Captain Hook

Peter Pan

The Wicked Queen

Snow White

1b Vocabulary Practice

Character

▶ Reading

1 a. What type of texts are A and B? What do you think they are about?

b. Read the texts. Which advert:

1 wants actors to advertise something?
2 asks people to apply by post?
3 only wants three people?
4 wants only male actors?

c. Underline the character adjectives in the adverts. Use them to answer the questions.

What do we call a person who ...
1 has good manners? *polite*
2 likes to hurt or upset people? *rude*
3 shows understanding of other people's needs? *caring*
4 is very proud of their looks? *good looking*
5 expects good things to happen? *optimistic*
6 cares only about himself/herself? *selfish*
7 doesn't get upset or angry? *fair friendly*
8 gives more than is usual? *generous*

StudySkills

Remembering New Words: Opposites

Learn words in pairs of opposites. This will help you remember them more easily.

2 Match the adjectives to their opposites. What prefixes do we use to form negative adjectives?

polite — dishonest
patient — impolite
honest — impatient
sensitive — insensitive
friendly — unfriendly
caring — unselfish
selfish — uncaring

A

Actors wanted for new film 'Bad Guys'.

Location: Brooklyn **Audition date:** 14th September

Characters:
☆ **Sean** – 25-30, dark complexion, tall, medium build, good looking, cruel and greedy
☆ **Stacy** – 30-36, pale complexion, medium height, slim, average looks, vain and selfish
☆ **Laura** – 26-32, fair complexion, short, average build, pretty, optimistic, caring, sensitive and honest

Send pictures and CVs to:
Michael Glover,
Chimera Filmworks
Inc. PO Box 304,
Brooklyn, New York

B

CASTING CALL
FOR TV COMMERCIAL

Location: Creative Edge Studios, Los Angeles **Seeking:** Three male actors

• **Jack:** handsome, blond hair, blue eyes, aged 18-23; friendly, patient, polite.
• **Buddy:** good-looking, dark curly hair, moustache, in early twenties; friendly, generous, easy-going.
• **Delivery Guy:** tall, strong build, in late twenties; impatient, bossy, rude.

Also seeking: male and female extras, aged 16-18.
Actual shooting date is Sunday, 28th September.

Please call Dawn Reed with any questions 703-478-0880

▶ Speaking

3 In pairs, use character adjectives to talk about people you know.

A: Have you met our new neighbour?
B: No, I haven't. What's he like?
A: He's very friendly and polite!

Appearance

4 Which words in the adverts (A & B) describe appearance/height/build?

5 Circle the odd words out. Justify your answers.

1 crooked, straight, almond-shaped, long **nose**
2 bright, blonde, green, dark **eyes**
3 well-built, spiky, curly, wavy, short **hair**
4 round, shoulder-length, oval, pretty **face**

1 The odd word out is 'almond-shaped' because this describes somebody's eyes.

8

1b

[Picture labels: Ann, Helen, 1 Joanna, 2 Sam, Peter, Tim, 3 Chris, 4 Laura, John, 5 Alex]

▶ *Listening*

6 🎧 Who is who? Look at the picture, listen and write the names: *Alex*, *Chris*, *Joanna*, *Laura* and *Sam* for people 1-5. What does each person look like?

GAME

Think of a person from the picture above. In teams, try to guess who this person is. Each team can ask five yes/no questions.

Team A S1: *Is it a man?*
   Leader: *Yes.*
Team B S1: *Has he got curly hair?*

Adjectives with prepositions

7 Underline the correct preposition. Use the adjectives to tell your partner about people you know.

1 John is **good at/on** languages.
2 She is very **good on/to** her patients.
3 He is very **friendly with/of** my parents.
4 She's **afraid for/of** dogs.
5 Pat is **jealous of/at** her sister.
6 He is **kind to/with** his parents.
7 Ann is **patient of/with** children.
8 Pete is **rude to/at** his friends.

✏️ *Writing*

Portfolio: The TV studio you work at as a secretary is looking for two actors for a new TV series. Write an advert (30-50 words), stating:

- what the advert is for
- location & audition date
- age & appearance of each character
- what types of character you want the actors to play
- contact name & phone number

Use advert A in Ex. 1 as a model.

9

1c Grammar in use

Present simple & present continuous
Grammar Reference

1 Read Ann's e-mail and find examples of:

a a fixed future arrangement
b an action happening around the time of speaking
c a timetable
d a permanent state
e a temporary situation
f a habit/routine
g an action happening now

Hi!
From: AnnB **To:** Emily
Subject: Hi!

Dear Emily,

Thanks for your e-mail. It's always great to hear from you. As for me, I'm really busy. College life **is** very exciting, but there's so much to do. I **get up** at 8 o'clock on weekdays because lectures **start at** 9:30. I spend most of my afternoons in the library as **I'm taking** six different courses this term and there's lots of reading to do! At the weekend I **do** some part-time waitressing. So, as you can see, **I'm working** very hard these days. But it's not all work and no play. Tonight **I'm having dinner** with some classmates. I can't wait!

I'd better finish here because Sarah, my flatmate, **is calling** me to come and help her. Come and visit me soon!

Ann

---

2 a. Put the verbs in brackets into the *present simple* or *present continuous*.

1 A: *Are you doing* .... (you/do) anything interesting this weekend?
   B: No, I *am studying* .... (study) for my Biology exam.
2 A: Why *are you* .... (you/be) in such a rush?
   B: Because *my train leaves* .... (my train/leave) in ten minutes.
3 A: What *do James do* .... (James/do)?
   B: *He works* .... (he/work) at the Natural History Museum in the city centre.
4 A: *Do you like* .... (you/like) your flat?
   B: Not really. Actually, I *'m looking* .... (look) for a new one at the moment.
5 A: Nina *looks* .... (look) nervous.
   B: She is. She *is seeing* .... (see) the dentist this afternoon.
6 A: *Does he want* .... (he/want) to go to the theatre this evening?
   B: He can't. He's *having* .... (have) an important business appointment.
7 A: Why *Anna isn't coming* .... (not/Anna/come) to work these days? Is she ill?
   B: No, she's on leave. She's *getting* .... (get) married next week.
8 A: How much *is the brain weigh* .... (the brain/weigh)?
   B: About 2% of your total body weight, and *it uses* .... (it/use) 20% of your body's energy.

b. Can you find any stative verbs in Ex. 2a?

Adverbs of frequency
Grammar Reference

3 Ask and answer as in the example to find out about your partner's habits.

How often...

- get up before 6 am?
- play computer games?
- watch TV?
- be on time for work/school?
- listen to classical music?
- read the newspaper?
- go to the theatre?
- go out with your friends?

| always |
| usually |
| often |
| sometimes |
| rarely |
| seldom |
| never |

A: How often do you get up before 6 am?
B: I never get up before 6 am. I usually get up at about 7:30.

▶ *Listening*

4 a. Listen and match the people to what they are doing. There is one extra picture.

A George
B Paul and Steve
C Kate and Jill
D Simon
E Miranda

b. In pairs ask and answer as in the example.

A: Is George talking on the phone?
B: No, he isn't. He's ...

10

Beauty is in the eye of the beholder

1c

How do you react when you 1) ...... at yourself in the mirror? Do you smile 2) ...... do you feel like crying? Does the idea of wearing summer clothes 3) ...... you panic, or does it excite you?
Body image has become a 4) ...... important issue in our society. 5) ...... young women and teenage girls, in particular, are greatly influenced 6) ...... the images they see in adverts, films and magazines. They go on dangerous crash diets 7) ...... they want to look like the super-thin supermodels and movie stars they see and read about. But we don't 8) ...... to copy our favourite celebrities. Thin is not always beautiful. People come in 9) ...... shapes and sizes – that's 10) ...... makes each person interesting. So, next time you look in the mirror, remember that you are special.

	A	B	C	D
1	A watch	B look	C see	D view
2	A and	B but	C or	D so
3	A feel	B get	C do	D make
4	A so	B main	C such	D very
5	A Many	B Much	C More	D Some of
6	A by	B with	C from	D about
7	A so	B that	C because	D and
8	A must	B need	C should	D ought
9	A every	B each	C all	D some
10	A what	B which	C why	D that

StudySkills

Completing a text (gap-filling)

Read the title and the text quickly to get the gist. Read the text again, one sentence at a time, focusing on the words before and after each gap. Look at the four options and choose the word that fits best. Read the completed text again to make sure that it makes sense.

▶ **Reading**

5 a. What do you think the title of the text means?

b. Read the text. Which of the following is a better alternative to the title?

1 Health is better than wealth.
2 Feel good about yourself.

c. Read and choose the correct word for each space (1-10). Compare your answers with your partner's. Listen and check.

Question words

6 In pairs, ask each other questions about your lifestyles. Use:
• what • where • when • who • how often

A: *What time do you get up?*
B: *At 7:30.*

Sentence transformations

7 Complete the second sentence so that it means the same as the first. Use no more than three words.

1 Can you describe Peter to me?
Can you tell me ...what is Peter... like?
2 Peter takes after his father.
Peter looks ...like he's father...
3 What is Peter's job?
What ...does Peter... do?
4 Peter is always late for work.
Peter ...is never... on time for work.

Phrasal verbs

8 Explain the phrasal verbs in your language. Then, complete the sentences.

off / back / get / up / on (with) / over

1 John has to get ...up... early in the morning.
2 He can't get ...over... the shock of being in the car accident.
3 How do you get ...on... with your neighbours?
4 She's happy because she's ...... her old job ...back....

Writing

Portfolio: Look at Ex. 1 again. Imagine you are Emily. Send an e-mail in reply to Ann. Write about:

• your daily routine   • any plans for the weekend
• what you are doing these days

11

1d Listening & Speaking skills

Personal qualities

1 What should a good leader be like? Circle three qualities below which you think are important. Compare your choices with your partner's.

- honest • fair • popular
- patient • sensitive • friendly
- determined • quick-thinking
- calm • humorous

A: I think a good leader should be honest, calm and determined, don't you?
B: Yes, those are important qualities. But I think he should also be fair.

▶ **Listening**

StudySkills

Listening for specific information

Read the questions and possible answers. Underline the key words. Listen carefully. Try to listen for synonyms or rephrasing. The questions follow the order of the information on the recording.

2 a. You will hear an interview with a psychologist. Read through the questions and underline the key words. Can you think of synonyms?

b. Listen and put a tick (✓) in the correct box. Do you agree with Dr Graaf?

1 Dr Graaf believes that all good leaders have
- A ☐ special personal qualities.
- B ☐ team spirit.
- C ☐ a great sense of humour.

2 Dr Graaf says that leaders have to
- A ☐ try to be more popular.
- B ☐ make difficult decisions.
- C ☐ please everybody.

3 What does Dr Graaf say about bosses?
- A ☐ They sometimes make bad choices.
- B ☐ They are sometimes in a panic.
- C ☐ They are not always liked.

4 Dr Graaf says that to be an effective leader, you must be
- A ☐ determined.
- B ☐ like a superhero.
- C ☐ respected and trusted.

Making choices

3 You want to open your own restaurant and you are looking for a partner. Which of the two people would you choose, and why? Discuss in pairs and make your decision.

Robert
easy-going
patient
reliable   **but**   shy
sensible   a bit lazy
                        stubborn

Sarah
friendly
cheerful   **but**   gets upset easily
honest   forgetful
ambitious   a bit impatient

A: Well, I think I'd choose ... because ... .
B: I'm not so sure. He/She is/gets ... and he/she can also be rather ... .
A: What about ... ? He/She's ... , etc.

FUN TIME

How do you know when you're getting old?

When the cake costs less than the candles.

12

1d

Expressing surprise and concern

▶ *Intonation*

4 🎧 Listen and repeat. Translate these sentences into your language.

1 *What's the matter?*
2 *You're joking!*
3 *What's wrong?*
4 *You can't be serious!*

▶ *Reading*

5 You are going to listen to a conversation. Read the first two exchanges in the dialogue below and guess the answers to the questions.

1 Where are Judy and Stan?
2 What do you think their relationship is?
3 Who is upset?

6 🎧 Read and complete the dialogue with sentences from Ex. 4. Listen and check. Which of the people a, b or c is Stan's neighbour? Take roles and act out a similar dialogue.

Judy: Hi, Stan. You look upset. **A** ☐
Stan: Oh, come in, Judy. I'm a bit fed up.
Judy: Why? **B** ☐
Stan: Well, it's my neighbour. He keeps complaining about my music. He says I play it too loud and he comes round nearly every day to tell me to turn it down.
Judy: **C** ☐
Stan: I'm afraid not.
Judy: How loud do you play your music?
Stan: Not that loud. I'll show you.
Judy: Stan, turn it down!
Stan: Why? What's up?
Judy: Well, is your neighbour tall with short curly brown hair, a beard and a moustache?
Stan: Yes, he looks exactly like that. Why?
Judy: Because someone who looks a lot like that is walking towards your front door right now!
Stan: **D** ☐ Here we go again.

7 🎧 In pairs, guess what happens next. Listen and check.

Socialising

8 a. Read the table and complete the exchanges.

Speaker A	Speaker B
Hello! What a nice surprise!	Hi! Nice to see you!
Hi, there. How are you?	Not bad. How about you?
Hi there. How are you doing?	Pretty good, thanks.
See you tomorrow!	Goodbye!
Bless you!	Thanks!
Thank you very much indeed!	Don't mention it.
Hello. You must be …	Yes. It's a pleasure to meet you …
I haven't seen you for ages!	Hi! You haven't changed a bit!

A: ....!
B: Thanks! I've got a terrible cold.
A: Hi! ....!
B: Hi! You haven't changed a bit.
A: Thank you very much for looking after my dog.
B: ....

b. In pairs, use the table above to act out exchanges in which you:

- greet a friend you haven't seen for a long time
- say goodbye to your colleagues when leaving the office
- greet a friend you bump into on the street
- meet someone you have heard about for the first time
- thank a friend for a special gift

13

1e Writing an informal letter giving advice

Getting started

1 Read the extracts from three teenagers' e-mails. Who is: lonely? desperate? shy?

"I've just moved to a new school and everything's different. I haven't got any firends here and I feel like I don't fit in."
Danny

"I've put on such a lot of weight recently and I just don't know what to do. I've tried all sorts of diets, but nothing seems to help."
Sally

"When I'm with a group of people, I just sit there in silence. I'm always too afraid to say anything in case I make a fool of myself."
Tom

Sally is desperate because she ... .

2 Use the phrases below to give advice to Sally, Danny and Tom.

Giving advice	Justification
• It would be a good idea to ...	• This/That way ...
• The best thing to do is ...	• This would mean that ...
• What you should do is ...	• Then, (you ...) ...
• Why don't you ...?	• If you do this, ...
• You could also ...	• By doing this, ...

A: What you should do is stop eating sweets and chocolate. That way ...
B: That's right, Sally. You could also ...

Let's look closer

3 Read the e-mail. Underline the phrases Pete uses to give his advice.

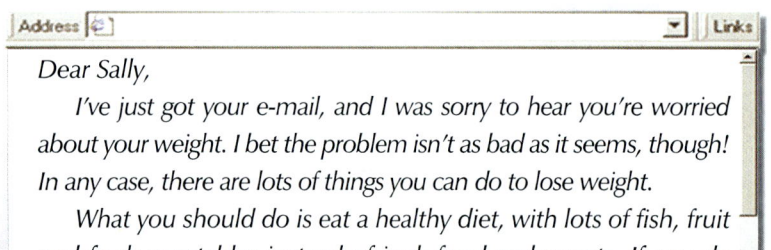

Dear Sally,

I've just got your e-mail, and I was sorry to hear you're worried about your weight. I bet the problem isn't as bad as it seems, though! In any case, there are lots of things you can do to lose weight.

What you should do is eat a healthy diet, with lots of fish, fruit and fresh vegetables instead of junk food and sweets. If you do this, you'll soon lose weight, and you'll look and feel much healthier, too. You could also exercise more and walk whenever possible rather than going by car or bus. That way you'll burn calories and get your body back in shape at the same time.

I know it's hard to do at first, but believe me, it will work! Good luck, and don't forget to let me know how you're getting on.
All the best,
Pete

4 Which of the following are opening/closing remarks for an informal letter of advice?

1 Here's what you can do.
2 I hope everything goes well.
3 I'm so sorry you feel this way.
4 I was sorry to hear about your problem.
5 I hope I've been of some help.
6 Let me know what happens.

Your turn

StudySkills

Brainstorming for ideas

Before writing, underline the key words, then brainstorm for ideas. Write your ideas down, then choose the most important ones. This helps you organise your writing.

5 a. Read the rubric and brainstorm for ideas to give as much advice as possible. Make notes in your notebook.

This is part of a letter you got from an English pen friend.

I feel very lonely in my new neighbourhood. I have no friends and I'm really depressed. Any advice?

Write your letter to your friend.

b. Answer the questions in the plan, then write your letter (80-100 words).

Plan

Dear + *(your friend's first name),*
Opening Remarks (Para 1) – *express sympathy, offer help*
Main Body (Para 2) – *give your advice, explain the results*
Closing Remarks (Para 3) – *end the letter*

Take care,/Yours,/etc
(your first name)

AMAZING FACTS!

A person's height almost doubles in the first 2-3 years of life, but it takes another 15 years to double again!

Literature Corner 1

▶ **Reading & Listening**

1 Who was Arthur Conan Doyle? Which famous detective did he create? Read the first text and check.

2 Read the first paragraph of the main text. Who do you think the person outside the door is? 🎧 Listen and read to find out.

3 Read the rest of the text and mark statements 1-6 *T* (True) or *F* (False). Then, explain the words in bold.

1 The visitor is wearing expensive clothes. .....
2 The visitor's mouth and chin are hidden by a mask. .....
3 The visitor says he is Count von Kramm. .....
4 The visitor is unsure whether to trust Watson. .....
5 Holmes does not know why the visitor has come. .....
6 Holmes realises the visitor is the King when he takes off the mask. .....

▶ **Speaking**

4 Read lines 5-15 again and, in pairs, group all the words used to describe the king under the headings:

• physical appearance • clothes
• facial features • character

Use the prompts to describe the King of Bohemia to your partner.

Arthur Conan Doyle (1859-1930)

This well known Scottish author was the **creator** of the famous **fictional** detective, Sherlock Holmes, and his loyal friend, Dr Watson. Although Doyle wrote many other pieces, including historical novels, political essays and plays, we will always remember him for his Sherlock Holmes' **mysteries**.

In *Scandal in Bohemia*, the King of Bohemia hires Sherlock Holmes to help find some letters and a photograph that might be used by a woman, Irene Adler, to **blackmail** the King and **ruin** his **reputation**.

Scandal in Bohemia

A slow and heavy step, which had been heard upon the stairs and in the corridor, **paused** immediately outside the door. Then there was a loud knock on the door.

"Come in!" said Holmes.

A very tall man entered, with the **chest** and **limbs** of a Hercules. 5
His dress was rich with a richness which would, in England, be considered **bad taste**. He was wearing a **double-breasted coat** with **fur-trimmed collar** and **cuffs**, over which he wore a deep blue **cloak lined** with **flame-coloured** silk. His boots, which went **halfway** up his legs, were also **trimmed** with fur, completing his 10 appearance of **barbaric** richness. He had a thick moustache and a straight **chin** suggesting strong **determination**, but a black mask hid the **upper** part of his face. He was carrying a hat in one hand, while his other hand was **raised**, as if he had just finished **straightening** his mask. 15

"Please take a seat," said Holmes. "This is my friend and colleague, Dr Watson. Whom have I the honour to address?"

"You may address me as Count von Kramm, a Bohemian **aristocrat**. I hope your friend is a man I can trust. If not, I prefer to speak to you alone," said our strange visitor. 20

"You can say anything in front of this man that you can say to me," Holmes replied. The Count **nodded** and continued. "You will excuse the mask; my employer wishes my true **identity** to **remain** a secret."

"If your **majesty** would like to tell us your problem," Holmes **remarked**, "I will be happy to **advise** you." 25

The Count **sprang** from his chair, **paced** nervously up and down the room, then **took off** the mask and threw it on the floor.

"You are right!" he cried. "I am the King. Why should I try to hide it?"

"Why, indeed?" said Holmes. "I knew, even before you spoke, that you were the Grand Duke of Cassel-Felstein and the King of Bohemia." 30

15

2a Lifestyles

A CITY SLICKER OR A COUNTRY LOVER?

A — fantastic scenery

"Hi! My name is Stephen and I live in a tiny flat in Brixton, south-west London. I chose to live here because there is never a **dull** moment in a city like London. I'm an art student and the **hustle and bustle** of so many people in one area is the **inspiration** for a lot of my painting. Another advantage of city life is having everything you need so **close at hand**. Living beside the Tube station means I don't need a car to get around, which saves me money. Also, there are shopping centres, art galleries and museums everywhere.

Of course, London, like any large city, has its problems, too. Londoners don't **chat** on the Tube or the bus and there is much less **community spirit** than in the country, where my parents live. In fact, they don't understand how I can **put up with** the **constant** noise and pollution, and traffic congestion. However, I see that as a small price to pay. I'm **in my element** here in the heart of this fine city. As a famous poet once said, 'He who is tired of London is tired of life.'"

Lead-in

1 Introduce yourself to the class. Talk about:

- your name • where you come from
- where you live • home • family • job

My name's ... and I'm ... years old. I come from ... but I live in .... I've got ... (brothers/sisters) .... I am a ... .

2 Use the prompts to describe the pictures (A-E) to your partner.

- A clear lake, high mountains, trees, clean air
- B busy motorway, a lot of cars, exhaust fumes, air pollution
- C bus stop, well-dressed passengers in a queue, wait to get on bus
- D a variety of expensive shops, shoppers, modern escalators
- E cosy house, pretty garden, lots of flowers and bushes

Picture A shows fantastic scenery. I can see a clear lake and high mountains. There are trees by the side of the lake and the air is fresh and clean.

Listening

3 🎧 Listen and say where each person lives. What reasons do they give for liking where they live?

Bill – Anne – John & Mary

Reading

4 Look at the title of the article and the introduction. What is the article about? Listen and check.

B — traffic congestion/air pollution
C — convenient public transport
D — large shopping centre

2a

A sleepy village surrounded by woods and rivers might suit some people, but others prefer the bright lights and fast pace of the big city. 'Down Town' spoke to Stephen and Marianna to get both sides of the story.

"Hello – or 'G'day', as we say **down under**. My name is Marianna and I live in New South Wales, Australia, on a **huge** ranch called The Rain River Land. It's a beautiful area with fantastic scenery. I live here with my husband Joe and our two children, Patrick, 11, and Abby, 8.

We have lived on this **ranch** for several years and love our **healthy** lifestyle. We have 70,000 hectares of land, so the children have lots of space to run around and enjoy the peace and quiet. The air is clean and **fresh** and we produce a lot of our own food so we are sure that what we eat is fresh. There's lots of hard work to do running a ranch, but we don't mind.

Of course, there are some negative aspects to life out here. There are often **droughts** in Australia, and sometimes we can't grow any **crops** for months. We feel **isolated** sometimes, too, especially since the nearest neighbours are almost 100km away. Another problem is that many things are not as easily available as in the city. There are no **local facilities** such as schools, supermarkets and shops, and if we are ill we have to call the flying doctor.

Although life here can be difficult, we wouldn't change it for the world."

E **peaceful neighbourhood**

StudySkills

Reading for specific information

Read the statements and underline the key words. Read the text to get the gist. Read again carefully. Look for synonyms/opposites or words/phrases with similar/different meanings to the key words in the statements.

5 Read the article and mark the statements (1-8) True **(T)** or False **(F)**. Then, explain the words/phrases in bold.

1 Stephen is a professional painter.
2 Stephen thinks using public transport is cheaper than travelling by car.
3 Stephen's parents don't like the noise of London.
4 Stephen is tired of living in London.
5 Marianna and her family have lived on the ranch for most of their lives.
6 Life on a ranch has some disadvantages.
7 Marianna doesn't have any neighbours close by.
8 Marianna wishes her life was different.

Speaking

• **Expressing likes/dislikes**

6 Read the article and list the pros and cons of living in the country/city. Use your notes and the expressions in the table to tell the class where you prefer living.

Expressing likes	• I love; I like; I really enjoy
Expressing dislikes	• I just hate; I don't like … at all; I can't stand
Being neutral	• I don't mind; I'm not really sure; It's difficult to say

S1: *I like living in the city because …*
S2: *I just hate living in …*

Writing

Portfolio: Write a short article for a teen magazine about yourself and the place you live in (50-60 words). Write:

• full name • job/studies/habits
• name of the place you live in
• reasons why you (don't) like it

17

2b Vocabulary Practice

Places

StudySkills

Learning new words: adjective-noun phrases

Learn nouns with the adjectives they go with. This will help you remember them and use them correctly.

1 Study the phrases. Can you think of any more adjectives? Use as many phrases as possible to talk about where a) you live and b) a friend lives.

I live in … . It's … with … . There is/are … .
… lives in … . It's … with … . There is/are … .

SHOP: busy, local, corner, expensive

STREET: tree-lined, narrow, congested, wide

VILLAGE: quiet, isolated, pretty, small

HOUSE: semi-detached, comfortable, traditional, terraced, spacious

TOWN: industrial, large, modern, clean

RESTAURANT: elegant, crowded, cheap, popular, fast-food

Signs

▶ *Reading*

2 Where might you see signs 1-3? What does each mean? Circle the correct explanation A, B or C.

1 (Keep dogs on lead)
   A You mustn't let your dog run free.
   B You can't have dogs in this area.
   C Only dogs can guide you in this area.

2 (Beware of bull)
   A Please help protect the bull.
   B Be careful, a bull has escaped.
   C The bull here may be dangerous.

3 (Reserved)
   A Someone bought this table.
   B You may sit at this table.
   C You can't sit at this table; it's booked.

3 Find the opposites of the adjectives in bold. In pairs, act out exchanges as in the example.

busy street; **expensive** shop; **dirty** beach; **small** town

A: What a **busy** street!
B: Yes, it isn't very **quiet**, is it?

Asking for/Giving directions

4 Work in pairs. Choose a building on the map on p. 19. Describe its position. Your partner finds the building.

• next to • on the corner • between
• opposite • in front of • behind
• to the left/right of

A: It's opposite the hospital.
B: It's the …

▶ *Listening*

5 🎧 Listen to the directions a local gives to a visitor in Oaksville. Mark the route on the map.

2b

▶ Speaking

6 **Portfolio:** Work in pairs. Starting from the train station, ask for and give directions to the bank, the museum, etc. You can record your dialogue and keep it in your *Language Portfolio*.

Asking for directions	Giving directions
Excuse me, could you tell me the way to …?	Of course / Sure. Take the first/second turning on your left/right … . / Turn into …
Excuse me. How do I get to …?	Just cross / go up / down this road/ street and … .
Do you know where … is?	It's to the left of/right of / opposite / next to … .
	Go past the … .

A: Excuse me, could you tell me the way to … ?
B: Sure! Just cross … .

Jobs & Workplaces

7 Look at the map. Where does each person work? In pairs think of more jobs and their workplaces.

Secretary   Librarian
Security guard   Dentist
Waiter   Teacher   Traffic Warden
Bank clerk   Journalist
Nurse   Sales assistant

A secretary works in an office.

Job qualities

8 Match the qualities below to the jobs in Ex. 7.

- sincere • friendly • patient • honest • caring
- calm • cheerful • responsible • careful
- organised • practical • polite

A traffic warden needs to be responsible, practical and polite.

9 Which job suits you? In pairs, ask and answer.

A: Do you think you'd be a good teacher?
B: I think so. I'm quite patient and caring. / Not really. I'm not patient enough.

GAME

Play in teams. Who could say this? In teams, guess the job.

Team A S1: Are you ready to order, sir?
Team B S1: A waiter.

✎ Writing

Portfolio: Draw a map of your neighbourhood, then write a short description (30-50 words) and present it to the class. Write about:

• buildings • streets • shops • facilities

My neighbourhood is … . There are … . The streets are … . There is a chemist opposite … and/but there is(n't) … .

2c Grammar in use

Comparatives and superlatives
Grammar Reference

▶ **Reading & Listening**

1. a. Read the title and subheadings of the quiz. What is it about?

   b. Do the quiz. Listen and check your answers.

2. Circle the comparative and superlative forms in the quiz. Then, complete the table.

QuizTime

Britain's Capital

Tourist Attractions

1. Which is the most popular tourist attraction in London?
   - A the British Museum
   - B Buckingham Palace
   - C the Tower of London

2. What is the tallest landmark in London?
   - A Big Ben
   - B the London Eye
   - C the Houses of Parliament

Shopping

3. How many shops are there in London?
   - A more than 50,000
   - B more than 20,000
   - C more than 30,000

4. Which is the busiest shopping street in London?
   - A Regent Street
   - B Oxford Street
   - C Piccadilly

5. Which is the most expensive shopping district in London?
   - A Camden
   - B Knightsbridge
   - C Chelsea

Transport

6. The London Underground is the .... in the world.
   - A fastest
   - B busiest
   - C oldest

REGULAR	COMPARATIVE	SUPERLATIVE
Adjective		
old	*older* than	the ....
busy	busier than	the ....
tall	taller than	the ....
fast	faster than	the ....
popular	more popular than	the ....
expensive	more expensive than	the ....
Adverb		
late	later	the latest
early	earlier	the earliest
carefully	more carefully	the most carefully
IRREGULAR		
good/well	better than	the best
bad/badly	worse than	the worst
little	less than	the least
much/many	....	the most

- *as ... as* is used to compare two people/things, etc, that are equal in some way. *Rome is* **as expensive as** *Paris.*

3. How are comparatives and superlatives formed? Are the rules the same in your language?

4. Choose three adjectives from the table in Ex. 2 in their comparative or superlative form and make sentences about the place you live in.

   The Town Hall is the oldest building in my town.

▶ **Speaking**

5. a. Use the adjectives to compare the countries.
   - long • high • big • small • low • short

	UK	IRELAND	USA
SIZE (sq km)	244,820	70,284	9,629,091
POPULATION	60,094,648	3,924,140	290,342,554
MOUNTAIN	Ben Nevis (1,343 m)	Carrauntoohill (1,041 m)	Mt McKinley (6,194 m)
RIVER	The Severn (290 km)	The Shannon (370 km)	The Mississippi (3,780 km)

A: Is the UK smaller than Ireland?
B: No! The UK is bigger than Ireland, but not as big as the USA.
A: Yes, the USA is the biggest of all.

b. Make a similar table for your country. Compare it to the UK and the USA.

STUDYSKILLS

Learning Grammar Structures

When you learn an English grammar structure, you can compare it to the grammar equivalent in your language. This will help you learn the new structure more easily.

2c

-ing/infinitive forms
Grammar Reference

6 Read the text. Underline the -ing forms and circle the infinitive forms. Which form do we use:

1 after adjectives with prepositions?
2 after modal verbs?
3 after verbs of preference (e.g. like, love, etc)?
4 to show purpose?

Jane never liked working in an office. She gave up her job to train as a gardener. She discovered that she was very good at gardening and could make anything grow. What she loves most is being outdoors in the fresh air, and she never gets tired of working with plants.

7 Put the verbs in brackets into the correct form.

1 A: I am planning .... (move) to the country.
   B: Really? Won't you .... (be) bored there?
2 A: Would you like .... (come) to New York with me?
   B: That would be great. I need .... (get) a visa first, though.
3 A: There is nothing I enjoy more than .... (walk) in the countryside.
   B: Me too. I hate .... (live) in the city.
4 A: Do you mind .... (travel) all the way to work every day?
   B: Well, it takes me two hours .... (drive) to work, but I don't mind at all.

8 Complete the sentences about yourself, using -ing/infinitive forms.

1 I can't stand ....
2 I hate ....
3 I could ....
4 I'm tired of ....
5 I've decided ....

Sentence transformations

9 Complete the second sentence so that it means the same as the first, using no more than three words. What grammar structures are tested?

1 It's better to avoid travelling during the rush-hour.
   It's not a good idea .... during the rush-hour.
2 There are only a few parks in this city.
   There are not .... in this city.
3 LA is one of the most expensive cities in the world.
   Very few cities in the world are .... LA.
4 He prefers London to York.
   He likes London .... York.

Phrasal verbs

10 Explain the phrasal verbs with 'put'. Use appropriate ones to replace the verbs in bold. Choose one and draw a picture.

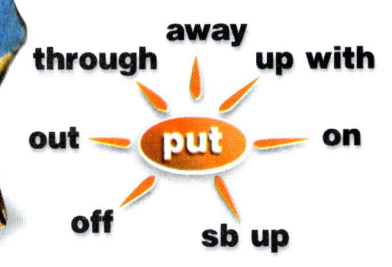

through — away — up with
out — put — on
off — sb up

1 The firefighters managed to **extinguish** the fire.
2 Can you **connect me** to Mr Smith, please?
3 He has **gained** 10 kilos since he moved here.
4 They **postponed** moving house until May.

Adjectives with prepositions

11 Fill in: *with*, *to*, *from*, *of*, *for*. Use the adjectives in bold to make sentences about the place you live in.

1 New York is very **different** .... Los Angeles.
2 The square is **crowded** .... people.
3 London is **famous** .... its nightlife.
4 The town centre is **full** .... cheap restaurants.
5 Are you **familiar** .... this area?
6 This town is **familiar** .... me. I used to live here.

Writing

Portfolio: Collect information to write a short quiz about the capital city of your country (35-50 words).

2d Listening & Speaking skills

Comparing places

1 a. You are going to listen to two friends talking about Budapest. Before you listen, look at sentences 1-6 and, in pairs, try to guess whether they are true or false.

		True	False
1	The best way to travel around is by car.	☐	☐
2	Traffic can be very heavy.	☐	☐
3	You can buy lovely gifts.	☐	☐
4	Eating out doesn't cost much.	☐	☐
5	Public transport is not expensive.	☐	☐
6	Summers are cool.	☐	☐

▶ *Listening*

b. Listen and tick (✓) the sentences as True or False. Were your guesses correct?

2 Listen again and make notes about Budapest under the headings below. Make similar notes about the place you live in. Compare the two places.

• traffic • shopping • restaurants • public transport • weather

Traffic in Budapest is as heavy as in my town.

Expressing preferences

3 a. In pairs, use the table and the prompts to form dialogues as in the example. You can use your own ideas.

Asking about specific preference	Expressing specific preference
• Do you want + full infinitive ... *Do you want to go to the theatre?* • Do you fancy + -ing form ...? *Do you fancy eating out?* • Would you like + full infinitive ... *Would you like to go to a party tonight?*	• I'd prefer + full infinitive/ noun *I'd prefer to watch a film.* • I'd rather + bare infinitive (+ than + bare infinitive) *I'd rather order take-away (than eat out).*

• see a film/go dancing
• play golf/play football
• eat Chinese food/eat Indian food
• have dinner with.../have an early night
• go to a football match/go to a rugby match
• eat out/get a take-away

A: *Do you fancy seeing a film tonight?*
B: *Not really. I'd rather go dancing.*

b. Study the table. Then, use the headings to talk about your preferences.

Entertainment
Food

General Preference
• I prefer + noun + *to* + noun → *I prefer vegetarian food to meat.*   • I prefer + (-ing form) + *to* + (-ing form) → *I prefer walking to driving.*   • I prefer + full infinitive + *rather than* + bare infinitive → *I prefer to play tennis rather than play golf.*

Means of Transport
Sports

I prefer going out with my friends to playing computer games.

▶ *Intonation*

4 Match the words, then listen and underline the stressed syllables.

A	B
local	transport
traffic	spirit
community	centre
public	facilities
city	congestion

Job interviews
▶ *Reading*

5 Who might say the sentences (1-5) below: an employer or a prospective employee?

1. *Please have a seat.*
2. *I've got a degree in British History.*
3. *Did you have any trouble finding us?*
4. *What work experience have you had?*
5. *Could you tell me what your qualifications are?*

6 a. Complete the interview with sentences from Ex. 5. Listen and check.

A: Good afternoon, Ms Harris. **a** ☐
B: No, not at all.
A: **b** ☐
B: Thank you.
A: I understand you are applying for the position of Tour Guide.
B: Yes, that's right.
A: **c** ☐
B: Certainly. **d** ☐ Oh, and I speak four languages.
A: I see. **e** ☐
B: I worked for two years as a tour guide at the Tower of London, and as a clerk in the Tourist Information Centre at Victoria Station for three years.

b. Do you think Ms Harris will get the job? Why (not)? Listen and find out.

c. Take roles and act out the dialogue. You can change the ending.

StudySkills

Role-playing

Role-play is effective if you use your imagination. Think of the situation, the setting, who you are, how you feel, what gestures you might use, etc.

▶ *Speaking*

7 **Portfolio:** Look at the job advert. Take roles and act out a job interview. Use the dialogue in Ex. 6 as a model. Record your dialogues.

WANTED: Experienced Head Chef for well-known French restaurant.
The right person must have NVQ Level 3, speak fluent French and have at least 2 years' experience preparing French food. 40-hour week, including weekends. Excellent pay.
To arrange an interview, call 01743 281978.

Describing pictures

8 a. Look at the picture and complete the text.

This picture shows a businessman. He is
1) .... the driver's seat
2) .... a car. He must be
3) .... his way to work because he is wearing a suit and a tie. He is driving 4) .... shaving while he is looking 5) .... the mirror.
He must be late 6) .... he looks stressed.

b. Now look at the picture in Ex. 6 and describe it to your partner. Think about:

- where they are
- what they are wearing
- what they are doing
- how they feel

FUN TIME

Is your boss furious because you're leaving next month?

Yes, he thought it was this month.

23

2e Writing a letter of application

Getting started

1 What information do you think we should include in a letter of application for a job? Think about: *age, qualifications*, etc.

2 a. Which beginnings/endings would be appropriate?

A
Dear Sir/Madam,
Yours faithfully,

B
Dear Tom,
Best wishes,

C
Dear Mr Smith,
Yours sincerely,

b. What is the difference between A and C?

Let's look closer

3 Read the rubric, then read the letter and match the paragraphs to the headings.

A Age/Qualifications   C Reason for writing
B Availability   D Experience/Personality

- You are looking for a part-time job. You saw an ad asking for a part-time sales assistant and you want to apply for the job. Write your letter.

Dear Sir/Madam,
▶1 I would like to apply for the position of Part-time Sales Assistant which I saw advertised in the Guardian.
▶2 I am a seventeen-year-old student. I have ten GCSEs including Maths and English. At the moment I am studying for my 'A' Levels.
▶3 I have no actual work experience. However, I would enjoy working with the public as I like meeting people. I am friendly and polite as well as responsible and hard working so I think I am suitable for the post.
▶4 I hope you will consider me for the position. I am able to attend an interview at any time.
Yours faithfully,
Deborah Riley
Deborah Riley

Your turn

4 a. Read the rubric. Imagine you are a DJ. Fill in the CV with your personal information.

- You saw this advertisement in *The Weekly News* and you want to apply for the position.

DJ WANTED for busy Latin American club. Experience necessary. Must have a pleasant personality. Knowledge of Spanish preferred. Would suit a young, energetic person.
Contact: Mr Wade, PO Box 1287

CURRICULUM VITAE

PERSONAL DETAILS
Name/Surname: ....
Address: .... Tel.: ....
Date of birth: .... Nationality: ....

EDUCATION
Qualifications: ....
Languages: ....

WORK EXPERIENCE (*most recent first*)
....

PERSONAL QUALITIES
....

b. Which of the following are opening/closing remarks?

1 I am writing to apply for the post advertised in ...
2 I look forward to hearing from you in due time.
3 I would be happy to attend an interview at any time convenient to you.
4 I am writing with regard to your advertisement in ...

5 Answer the questions in the plan. Use your answers and your CV to write the letter of application in Ex. 4a (80-100 words).

Plan

- *Who will you address your letter to?*

Introduction (Para 1) *reason for writing? for what position? where was it advertised?*

Main Body (Paras 2-3) *age? qualifications? current job? previous experience? personal qualities?*

Conclusion (Para 4) *closing remarks?*

- *How will you sign off?*

AMAZING FACTS!
Flying around the moon is the same distance as flying from New York to London and back.

Culture Clip 2

Celebration - Dream Town USA

Close your eyes and imagine the perfect town, with pretty houses and tree-lined streets **0)** *around* a clear blue lake. Now, open your eyes and head **1)** .... the town of Celebration in Florida, USA, **2)** .... the Walt Disney Company has, once again, turned a dream into reality.

3) .... houses in Celebration have garages at the back, so the streets are clear of parked cars. Fences are low and backyards are small **4)** .... people can talk to their neighbours. Children play happily in the parks and playgrounds. Parents let them go off by themselves without **5)** .... their safety. The town's facilities, **6)** .... include a school, medical centre, fitness centre, bank and post office, combine modern technology with the traditional style of a small 1950s town.

If you can't put up with life in the fast lane, take a break and **7)** .... a visit to Celebration. Who knows – you might even decide to **8)** .... !

▶ Reading & Listening

1 Look at the title and the pictures. What is *Celebration*? Where is it?

2 How are these words and phrases related to the text? Read and check.

- pretty houses
- tree-lined streets
- clear blue lake
- small backyards
- parks
- playgrounds
- medical centre
- fitness centre
- bank
- post office

There are pretty houses in Celebration.

3 Read the text again and choose the best answer A, B, C or D.

0	**A** around	**B** on	**C** at	**D** about
1	**A** at	**B** over	**C** for	**D** in
2	**A** what	**B** there	**C** that	**D** where
3	**A** All the	**B** Both of	**C** Each and every	**D** The most
4	**A** that makes	**B** as urges	**C** so that	**D** such as
5	**A** caring for	**B** looking into	**C** worrying about	**D** protecting from
6	**A** who	**B** these	**C** which	**D** whose
7	**A** have	**B** give	**C** do	**D** pay
8	**A** remain	**B** live	**C** leave	**D** stay

4 🎧 Listen and read to answer the questions 1-3.

1. Why should someone visit Celebration?
2. What do you think the writer's aim is?
3. Where might you see such a text?

▶ Speaking

- Is there a town like *Celebration* in your country? Describe it.

- Talk to your partner about your ideal town. Think about:
  • name • location • what to see and do

  My ideal town would be called .... It would be in/near, etc, ... There would be ... and ... .

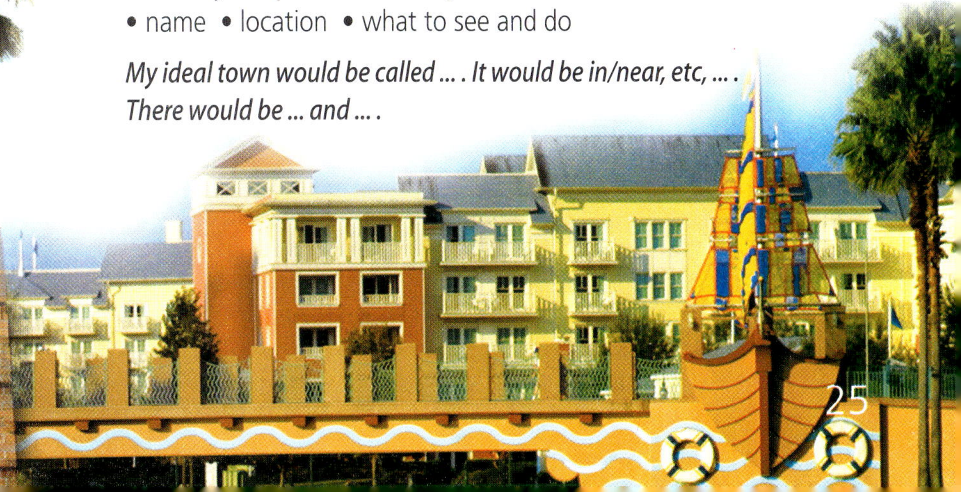

Self-Assessment Module 1

Vocabulary & Grammar

1 Fill in the missing word.

1 What does Paul look .... ?
2 Bob always tells the truth. He's ....
3 To get to the bank, take the first turning .... your left.
4 Ken is .... He never gets angry or upset.
5 What time .... the TV programme start?
6 She likes the hustle and .... of London.
7 Sarah and Jane aren't getting .... lately. They argue all the time.
8 We hate city life. We can't put .... with the noise.
9 London is more expensive .... Athens.
10 That was .... worst film ever.

(10 marks)

2 Circle the correct item.

1 Harry works as a traffic ....
   A assistant   B warden   C director
2 Jenny has curly blonde hair and .... cheeks.
   A pointed   B rosy   C bright
3 Teachers need to be .... with their students.
   A confident   B responsible   C patient
4 Jane likes eating at .... restaurants.
   A elegant   B terraced   C corner
5 "Where does he .... from?" "England."
   A come   B get   C is
6 James always thinks of others. He's very ....
   A careful   B friendly   C caring
7 Tony has good manners. He is very ....
   A caring   B patient   C polite
8 I don't fancy going out. I'd rather .... in.
   A stay   B staying   C to stay
9 Ian doesn't mind .... long hours.
   A to work   B work   C working
10 Mark's car is as .... as Anne's.
   A older   B old   C oldest

(10 marks)

Use of English

3 Complete the second sentence so that it means the same as the first. Use up to three words.

1 Tom takes after his grandfather.
  Tom .... his grandfather.
2 Jane is gaining weight.
  Jane .... on weight.
3 No place in the world is as beautiful as this.
  This is .... place in the world.
4 I never forget to visit my aunt on Saturdays.
  On Saturdays I always .... visit my aunt.
5 I prefer travelling by train to travelling by bus.
  I prefer .... by train rather than travel by bus.

(10 marks)

4 Fill in the correct preposition.

1 I'm not familiar .... this area. I've never been here before.
2 She is jealous .... her sister because she lives on a huge ranch in Australia.
3 The city is crowded .... tourists.
4 Pat is very patient .... her students.

(8 marks)

Communication

5 Complete the exchanges.

a Thank you.
b I'd rather order pizza.
c Bless you!
d Hi, there. How are you?
e Take the first turning on your right.

1 A: Excuse me – how do I get to the bank?
  B: ....
2 A: Do you fancy eating out tonight?
  B: ....
3 A: ....
  B: Not bad. How are you?
4 A: ....
  B: Thanks!
5 A: ....
  B: Don't mention it.

(10 marks)

26

Self-Assessment Module 1

Listening

6 You will hear a radio programme about Barcelona. For each question, put a tick (✓) in the correct box.

1 Visitors to Barcelona should not go
  A ☐ in the middle of summer.
  B ☐ when there is a festival on.
  C ☐ in winter.

2 The best way to get around the city is
  A ☐ on a moped.
  B ☐ by taxi.
  C ☐ on the Metro.

3 Barcelona is
  A ☐ a city with modern and old features.
  B ☐ a completely modern city.
  C ☐ a very old city.

4 What does the speaker say about La Rambla?
  A ☐ It is full of cars.
  B ☐ It is Barcelona's best-known street.
  C ☐ It is a famous food market.

5 What can you see in Maremagnum?
  A ☐ a cathedral
  B ☐ a bird market
  C ☐ lots of shops and cafés

6 The Sagrada Família cathedral
  A ☐ doesn't take long to visit.
  B ☐ is not completed.
  C ☐ is difficult to climb up.

(12 marks)

Reading

7 Read and choose the correct word for each space.

Get the picture? How 1) .... do you go to the hairdresser's with a new hairstyle in 2) .... but then lose your nerve because you aren't sure what it will 3) .... like? Don't you wish you could try out new hairstyles before you decide 4) .... one you want? Well, with today's computer software you can choose 5) .... over 200 hairstyles in a 6) .... minutes and see how they look on you – without touching a single hair! All you need is a digital picture of yourself. The software is easy to 7) .... and you can see both the front-view and the side-view of the hairstyles. Try them out on screen and see which one you like 8) .... . It's the 9) .... way to see if a hairstyle really 10) .... you, before the scissors go to work.

1	A usually	B rarely	C seldom	D often
2	A head	B mind	C hand	D eye
3	A seem	B feel	C look	D appear
4	A this	B a	C that	D which
5	A from	B of	C for	D off
6	A some	B lot	C few	D little
7	A use	B make	C see	D try
8	A best	B much	C well	D very
9	A easily	B easiest	C easier	D ease
10	A fits	B matches	C suits	D goes

(20 marks)

Writing

8 You have moved to a new neighbourhood. Write a letter to an English-speaking friend, saying:
- what there is to see and do there.
- what you like/dislike about it.
- how different it is from your old neighbourhood.

(20 marks)
(Total = 100 marks)

Now I can...
- introduce myself
- talk about
  – character & appearance
  – habits/routines/lifestyles
  – jobs/workplaces/job qualities
- express my likes/dislikes/preferences
- ask for/give directions
- act out a job interview
- write
  – a short paragraph about my favourite hero(ine) or villain
  – a classified ad
  – an e-mail to a friend
  – an informal letter of advice
  – a short article about myself and where I live
  – a short description of my neighbourhood
  – a letter of application

...in English

27

CURRICULAR CUTS — History

1 a. What do you know about Elizabeth I?

   b. Look at portraits A and B. Describe them.

2 🔊 Listen and read. Number the portraits in the order you hear them.

3 Read and list the symbols in the portraits. Explain what they symbolise. Then explain the words in bold.

A

4 Which of the following adjectives best describe Elizabeth in each painting?
   • strong • innocent • demanding • ambitious • determined

Fact File

1533 – Elizabeth born to Henry VIII's second wife	1554 – Elizabeth **imprisoned** by her half sister, Mary	1558 – Mary dies, Elizabeth becomes Queen	1588 – English navy **defeats** the Spanish Armada	1603 – Elizabeth dies, James I becomes King

Elizabeth's Portraits

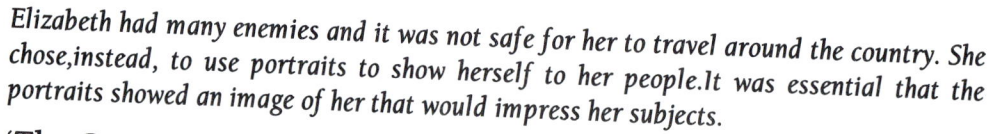

Elizabeth had many enemies and it was not safe for her to travel around the country. She chose, instead, to use portraits to show herself to her people. It was essential that the portraits showed an image of her that would impress her subjects.

'The Coronation Portrait'

This portrait shows Elizabeth just after the **coronation**. The picture shows her as a young, beautiful, innocent girl with pink cheeks and long hair. Her rich gold **gown**, jewels and fur show her **wealth**. She is also wearing the **crown** and holding the **Orb and Sceptre** to show her royal **authority**. The message of the picture is that although she is young and beautiful, she has the **power** to **rule** the country.

'The Armada Portrait'

This portrait celebrates the **victory** of England over the Spanish Armada. In the painting Elizabeth's right hand rests on a **globe**. This symbolises that England is a **global** power. On her right there is a **crown**. The pictures behind her show the English navy in bright sunshine, and ships of the Spanish Armada being destroyed in a storm.

B

5 **Project:** Do some research using the Internet, school textbooks, encyclopaedias, etc, then draw Elizabeth's family tree. Present it to the class.

28

The Blue Planet

Module 2
Units 3-4

▶ **Before you start ...**

Who's your best friend? What does he/she look like? What is he/she like?

▶ **Look at Module 2**

- Where are pictures 1-5 taken from?

▶ **Find the unit and page number(s) for**

- banners ☐
- holiday advertisements ☐
- a poster ☐
- diary entries ☐
- newspaper headlines ☐
- an extract from a novel ☐

▶ **Listen, read and talk about ...**

- environmental issues
- animals & adoption schemes
- illegal imports
- types of holidays & means of transport
- holiday experiences
- climate/the weather
- packing tips

▶ **Learn how to ...**

- give a short talk
- express surprise
- express your feelings
- check in at a hotel
- complain & apologise
- give travel information
- express (dis)approval/annoyance/surprise
- react to news

▶ **Practise ...**

- the present perfect
- the present perfect continuous
- clauses of purpose
- the past simple/continuous
- linkers *(but, because, when, and, so, then, as)*
- the definite/indefinite article
- *used to/would*
- present/past participles
- intonation (expressing annoyance)
- phrasal verbs: *run, come*

▶ **Write / Make...**

- an environmental poster
- an article about a zoo
- a letter to a penfriend
- a holiday advertisement
- a note
- a weather forecast
- a short factfile about your country
- a story

Culture Clips: RRS Ernest Shackleton

Literature Corner: Gulliver's Travels

Curricular Cuts (Geography): The World's Climates

29

3a Earth Calling

Lead-in

1 a. How much/many of the following does your town/city have? Tell the class.

- traffic • smoke from factories
- homeless people • recycling centres
- trees/plants • stray animals
- dirty parks/rivers/beaches/streets
- bottle banks • clean-up campaigns
- bins • wildlife parks

> too much/many, (not) enough, quite a few/lot, no, any

There is too much traffic in my town.
There aren't enough bins in the streets.

b. Which three things would you change to improve the place you live in? Tell your partner.

• I'd like to see more/less/fewer ... • It would be good if there was/were ... • There should/shouldn't be ...
• I'd make sure that ...

Reading

StudySkills

Focusing on layout

Before you read a text, look at its layout (headings, pictures, etc). The layout of a text can often help you guess what it is about before you begin to read. This will help you understand the text more easily.

2 a. Look at the text. What type of text is it? Why was it written? What do the title and the quotation mean? What do you expect to read?

b. Read the text and complete the sentences. Explain the highlighted words.

1 Roots help plants to be ....
2 Although shoots appear tiny and weak, they ....
3 .... started *Roots & Shoots* in ....

The Earth in OUR HANDS
ROOTS AND SHOOTS PROGRAMME

"Hundreds of thousands of roots and shoots, hundreds of thousands of young people around the world, can break through walls. We CAN change the world."
Dr Jane Goodall
(environmentalist, humanitarian and biologist)

4 The programme includes activities such as ....
5 To take part in the programme you need to be ....

Speaking

3 a. Listen and read the text. Make notes under the following headings.

- who founded it and when • what it is
- how many members it has • who can join

b. Work in pairs. Use your notes to talk about the *Roots & Shoots* programme.

3a

How do plants grow?

In nature, the roots of a plant grow **underground** and cover a large area. This way they keep the plant strong and healthy. Shoots are young plants that have **come up** through the earth to find the sunlight that they need to **survive**. Shoots may seem small and **fragile**, but they can break open brick walls. Their strength is quite amazing.

What is *Roots and Shoots*?

Inspired by her belief that every individual can make a difference, Dr Jane Goodall decided in 1991 to form a young people's environmental group of 16 local schoolchildren in East Africa. Its name was *Roots and Shoots* and the members organised recycling programmes and cleaned up local parks, rivers and beaches. They also helped old people and **the homeless** in their neighbourhood as well as protecting **the natural habitat** of local animals. Today, *Roots and Shoots* has over 3,000 groups in more than 68 countries **worldwide** which are actively involved in Dr Jane Goodall's projects.

How can you become a member of *Roots and Shoots*?

Any young person, between preschool and university, can join the *Roots and Shoots* programme. If you want to start your own *Roots and Shoots* group, simply find other young people in your neighbourhood who want to **participate**, and an **adult** to be the group leader. Then, contact the Jane Goodall Institute for a membership form.

Jane Goodall's *Roots and Shoots* programme is **living proof** that if we want to make our world a better place for everyone, we just need to work together.

Join *Roots and Shoots* now!
http://www.janegoodall.org

Become a Member
of the Jane Goodall Institute

We work on projects such as recycling rubbish, cleaning parks and
(1) _____, and helping the elderly.
To become a member, fill out the registration form on the
(2) _____.

ANNUAL MEMBERSHIP

☐ Student/Senior $ 20.00
☐ Individual $ 35.00
☐ Other $ ☐ (please fill in amount)
☐ (3) _____ $ 50.00 (per group)
☐ Roots & Shoots $ (4) _____ (international group)
☐ Roots & Shoots $ (5) _____
☐ Renewing your Membership? (tick if yes) ☐

Listening

4 🎧 You will hear someone talking about membership of the Jane Goodall Institute. Listen and fill in the missing information.

Writing

Portfolio: In groups, make a poster to submit to *Roots and Shoots'* annual competition for the best environmental poster.

31

3b Vocabulary Practice

Environmental issues

1 Fill in: *from, to, about*.

1. PREVENT your neighbourhood ... becoming a rubbish tip
2. THINK ... the air you breathe.
3. Rainforests belong ... us all
4. SAVE US ... extinction

2 a. Match the slogans in Ex. 1 to the problems below.

rubbish
air pollution
deforestation
endangered species

b. Work in pairs. Match the sets of verbs to the problems in Ex. 2a. Then discuss as in the example.

- cut down – plant → ....
- throw away – recycle → ....
- hunt – adopt → ....
- destroy – protect → ....

A: I think deforestation is an important issue today.
B: It is, indeed. Instead of cutting down trees, we should plant new ones.

Preservation

▶ Listening

3 a. You will hear a person talking about what we can do to protect our environment. Before you listen, read the notes and try to guess the missing words.

b. Listen and fill in the gaps (1-6). Which title best matches this speech?

a **We Can Make a Difference**   b **Help Save Animals**

At home
- Recycle everything you can.
- Grow some of your own food.
- Plant 1) .... and bushes in your garden.

Transport
- Ride your bike or 2) .... instead of driving.
- Use public transport.
- Drive sensibly: don't waste petrol.

At work
- Print things on 3) .... paper.
- Print or copy on both sides of the paper.
- Use the 4) .... instead of the lift.

Shopping
- Don't buy food which is wrapped in 5) ....
- Buy locally grown food and products.
- Don't buy products which come from 6) .... animals.

▶ Speaking

4 Use the notes in Ex. 3 and the table below to give a short talk about what we can do to help preserve our environment.

Introducing	• I'd like to talk about ... • I'd like to present ... • Today's subject is ... • I'm going to talk about ...
Listing	• First / Secondly / Third, ... then ... • Also, ... • Finally ...
Concluding	• To sum up, ... • In brief, ... • In conclusion, ... • Finally ...

I'd like to talk about how we can help preserve our environment. So here's a list of things we can all do. First, ...

32

3b

Animals

5 a. List the animals below under these categories: *mammal*, *bird* or *reptile*. Which can you see in the pictures on p. 33?

- goose • sheep • tiger
- cobra • parrot • hen
- monkey • giraffe • dog
- polar bear • deer • cat
- whale • jaguar • goat
- crocodile • python
- horse • leopard
- panda • donkey
- peacock • orangutan

b. Which of the animals above are: *domestic? wild?*

▶ Reading

6 Read the title and think of questions you might want to ask about the zoo. Listen and read to check if you can answer them.

7 a. Read the text and choose the best answer (A-D) for each space (1-10). Then explain the highlighted words.

StudySkills

True Friends

Look out for words that look or sound similar to words in your language (i.e. true friends). They help you understand the text.

b. Are there any words in the text that look/sound similar in your language?

▶ Speaking

8 a. Make notes, then give your partner two reasons why people should visit the Henry Doorly Zoo.

No ordinary zoo

How would you like to visit a rainforest, explore the bottom of an ocean and still be home **0)** *in* time for dinner? Well, if you live in Omaha, USA, you can! The Henry Doorly Zoo in Omaha is like no **1)** .... zoo. There are **2)** .... of wild and endangered animals here but they live in an environment exactly **3)** .... their own.

The zoo includes the world's largest indoor rainforest, known **4)** .... the *Lied Jungle*. You can cross rope bridges, walk through caves and admire wonderful waterfalls. Leopards and pythons move through the bushes, monkeys jump from tree to tree and birds **5)** .... above your head. The zoo is home **6)** .... many species including bears, giraffes, deer, jaguars, and pumas.

Next **7)** .... the Lied Jungle is the *Kingdom of the Seas Aquarium*. Here you can see penguins sliding off ice cliffs **8)** .... the cold water below. **9)** .... a walk along the 25-metre glass tunnel which runs through a big tank, with a wide variety of fish swimming around you.

The zoo is open **10)** .... day of the year except Thanksgiving, Christmas and New Year's Day.

For detailed information visit the Henry Doorly Zoo website http://www.omahazoo.com

0	A on	B in	C at	D for
1	A such	B every	C any	D other
2	A much	B more	C many	D lots
3	A like	B as	C same	D to
4	A as	B like	C such	D for
5	A move	B cross	C fly	D pass
6	A for	B of	C to	D in
7	A in	B to	C by	D with
8	A under	B in	C into	D on
9	A Do	B Go	C Make	D Take
10	A most	B all	C every	D each

b. Imagine you are at the Henry Doorly Zoo. In pairs, act out a dialogue about what you can see, what you are doing and how you feel.

✎ Writing

Portfolio: Collect information about a zoo in your country. Write an article for your school magazine (50-80 words). Write:

- the name of the zoo • where it is • what you can see there
- your recommendation

33

3c Grammar in use

Present perfect
Grammar Reference

▶ *Reading & Listening*

1. a. What is the text on the right: a directory? a poster? a sign?

   b. Scan the text. What do these figures refer to: 10%? 2,000? 0.3°C – 0.7°C? 80%?

2. a. Listen and read. In pairs, ask and answer comprehension questions.

   b. Underline the present perfect verb forms. How is the present perfect formed?

Yet/Already - For/Since

3. The students of Southsea School are planning a clean-up day. In pairs, ask and answer questions.

   Things to be done:
   - invite other schools to take part ✓
   - organise people into groups ✗
   - advertise the event on the radio ✓
   - buy equipment (gloves, rubbish bags) ✗
   - hand out leaflets ✓
   - make posters ✗

   A: Have they invited other schools to take part?
   B: Yes, they've **already** done that. Have they organised people into groups?
   A: No, they haven't done that **yet**.

4. Use the prompts to make sentences about yourself.

   - be • visit • travel • talk • phone
   - meet • change • speak • write

   FOR...
   - three days • five months
   - a year • a long time

   SINCE...
   - last week • August • 2001
   - I was seven

   I've been a member of WWF **for** a year.

HAVE YOU EVER THOUGHT ABOUT IT?

THE BAD NEWS:
- Up to now, we have destroyed 10% of the Amazon rainforest.
- Some 2,000 species of Pacific Island birds have become extinct.
- Any waste paper you threw away six months ago has only just broken down.
- Average temperatures have risen between 0.3°C and 0.7°C.

THE GOOD NEWS:
- Bald eagle populations have increased in the last 15 years.
- Access to clean water for people in the Third World has increased to 80% since the 1970s.
- The ozone layer has started to heal.

Never/Ever

5. Tell your partner three things you have never done.

   I've never adopted an animal.

▶ *Speaking*

6. Use the prompts and your own ideas to ask and answer.

   - go to a zoo?
   - look after a sick animal?
   - watch a wildlife documentary?
   - win a competition?

   - when/be/on holiday
   - last summer/year/month
   - last Sunday/Monday, etc
   - while/be/at school, etc

   A: Have you ever been to a zoo?   B: Yes, I have.
   A: When was that?   B: Last summer.

GAME

Choose a leader. He/She says how (s)he feels. In teams guess why. Each team can ask three questions.

upset   happy   excited
thrilled   sad   angry

Leader: I'm happy.
Team A S1: Have you passed your exams?
Leader: No, I haven't.

34

Present perfect continuous
Grammar Reference

7 a. Underline the verb forms in the speech bubbles. Find an example of an action which continued for some time in the past with results visible in the present.

Tom, have you been fighting again? You've lost your front teeth!

No, Mum. They're in my pocket.

b. Use the verbs *work*, *run*, *paint*, *fix*, *play*, *fight* to ask questions.

1. Pat's out of breath.
   Has she been playing basketball?
2. Bill's face is covered in paint.
3. Ann's tired.
4. Timmy's clothes are dirty.
5. Bob has got a black eye.
6. Steve's hands are covered in oil.

8 a. Read the sentences. Find examples of an action which started in the past and continues up to the present with emphasis on the duration.

He has been typing letters since 9 am.
She has been living here for four years.
He has been typing letters all day.

b. Use the verbs and the time words to make sentences about yourself. Use the present perfect continuous.

• learn • study • write
• watch • play • live

• for • since • all day

I've been learning English for three years.

Clauses of purpose
Grammar Reference

9 a. Read the examples. How is purpose expressed?

- We can adopt an animal **so that** it can have proper care.
- We should join an environmental group **to/in order to/so as to** help protect endangered species.
- We took the cat to the vet **for** a vaccination.

b. Expand the sentences, using clauses of purpose.

1. government / pass laws / factories causing pollution / pay / heavy fines. *The government must pass laws so that factories causing pollution will pay heavy fines.*
2. we / adopt / an endangered animal / help / protect / wildlife
3. they / write to / WWF / ask for / information about / voluntary work
4. they / give out free tickets / everyone / go / concert
5. they / start / campaign / raise money

Sentence transformations

10 Complete the second sentence so that it means the same as the first, using no more than three words.

1. I last went to London Zoo when I was ten years old.
   I haven't been to London Zoo .... ten years old.
2. Michael started working as a zookeeper in 1998.
   Michael .... as a zookeeper since 1998.
3. I think you should adopt an animal.
   Why .... adopt an animal?
4. I prefer lions to hippos.
   I like lions .... hippos.

Phrasal verbs

11 Explain the phrasal verbs, then complete the sentences. Choose three phrasal verbs and draw pictures to illustrate them.

away — on — **run** — out of — over — into

1. We .... Mary while we were in the zoo.
2. We have .... sugar. Can you buy some?
3. We almost .... a deer while we were driving.
4. Most cars .... unleaded petrol nowadays.

Writing

Portfolio: You have taken part in a special 'Plant a tree' day. Write a letter to your English pen-pal telling him/her all about it. In your letter you should:

- say when and where the event took place.
- say how you liked it.
- ask if he/she has taken part in a similar event.

35

3d Listening & Speaking skills

Protecting animals

1 a. Why would you adopt an animal? Number the reasons in order of importance (1-5). Compare your list to your partner's.

- [a] to learn more about that animal
- [b] to help pay for its food and daily care
- [c] to get free gifts
- [d] to help pay for any medical attention it needs
- [e] to make it feel good

▶ **Listening**

b. Listen to an interview about an animal adoption scheme and put a tick (✓) in the correct box.

1 What was the reason for starting the animal adoption scheme?
  A ☐ The zoo didn't have enough money.
  B ☐ The zoo wasn't in good working order.
  C ☐ The zoo couldn't keep the animals.

2 The animal adoption scheme
  A ☐ hasn't been successful.
  B ☐ was started quite recently.
  C ☐ needs over 100 applicants.

3 The £30 adoption fee
  A ☐ pays for most of the animal's food and medicine.
  B ☐ pays for all of the animal's food and medicine.
  C ☐ is all spent on the animals.

4 The radio presenter thinks that
  A ☐ the scheme costs too much money.
  B ☐ the animals aren't worth £30.
  C ☐ £30 is a reasonable price.

5 If you adopt an animal, every month you get
  A ☐ a free T-shirt.
  B ☐ an adoption certificate.
  C ☐ information about the animal.

6 If you want to adopt an animal,
  A ☐ you must go to the zoo.
  B ☐ you must fill out a form.
  C ☐ you must call the radio station.

c. Would you ever consider adopting an animal? Why (not)? Tell the class.

Describing pictures

2 Look at picture A and complete the sentences.

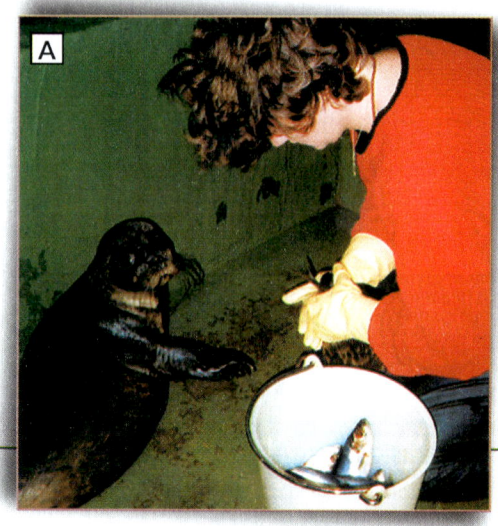

In this photograph there is a ....
The photograph was probably taken at a ....
The woman is wearing ....
Next to her there is ....
She is trying to ....
I think the seal is ....
The woman could be ....
I think she likes ....

3 a. Describe picture B to your partner. Talk about:

• people • place • activities • people's feelings

b. Look at picture B again and answer the questions.

1 How do the people in the picture feel towards the dolphins? Why do you think so?
2 Are you in favour of or against zoos? Why?

3d

Illegal imports

▶ *Reading*

4 Look at these signs. What items are travellers not allowed to bring into Britain/the EU?
e.g. ivory

PASSENGERS IN POSSESSION OF PROHIBITED FOODS RISK UP TO SEVEN YEARS' IMPRISONMENT AND/OR A HEAVY FINE

SOUVENIR ALERT
THINK BEFORE YOU BUY

5 a. Read these sentences. Who might say them and in what situation?
- Can you open your suitcases, please?
- Anything to declare?
- What's this, sir?
- Do you have anything else like this?
- Please come with me.

b. Listen and read. What illegal items did the man have?

c. Take roles and act out the dialogue.

A: Anything to declare?
B: No. I don't think so.
A: I see. Can you open your suitcases, please?
B: Yes, of course.
A: What's this, sir?
B: It's an ivory chess set. It's a gift for my uncle.
A: Don't you know it's illegal to bring products made of ivory into Britain?
B: No, I didn't know that.
A: It's against the law to bring any products made from endangered animals into the country. Do you have anything else like this?
B: Er ... well, yes – I bought a snakeskin belt for my daughter and a crocodile skin purse for my mother.
A: I see. Please come with me, sir.

6 In pairs, guess what happens next. Listen to the rest of the dialogue and check.

7 **Portfolio:** Imagine you are at Customs, coming back from a holiday. In pairs, take roles and act out a dialogue between yourself and the Customs officer. Record your dialogue.

StudySkills

Intonation

Listen to the speaker's intonation and mark the stressed syllables. Practise pronunciation and stress. Record yourself to see if you sound natural.

Reacting to news

▶ *Intonation*

8 Listen and repeat. Record yourself and check your intonation.

Positive
• Wow! • At last!
• How fantastic • How wonderful!
• That's great (news)! • Really?
• Well done! / Way to go!

Negative
• How terrible! • What a shame!
• That's shocking! • That's awful!
• That's too bad! • Oh, no!

9 In pairs, use expressions from Ex. 8 to react to the news about the headlines.

No cars in city centre

Oil slick kills fish

Fire destroys huge area of rainforest

£10,000 raised for WWF

More people growing own vegetables

A: It says here that a fire has destroyed a huge area of rainforest in the Amazon!
B: That's sad!

37

3e Writing notes

Getting started

1 Read the theory box, then read the note and complete the blanks. Find examples of omitted words.

> Notes are messages we write in various situations *(to remind, inform, thank, apologise, etc)*. They must be short and provide all the information needed without being chatty. We usually omit words such as **personal pronouns** *(I, you, etc)*, **articles** *(a/an, the, etc)*, **auxiliaries** *(am, have, etc)* and **greetings** like *Dear, Yours, etc*. We can use the imperative, informal linkers (e.g. *so* instead of *therefore*), participles, and abbreviations.

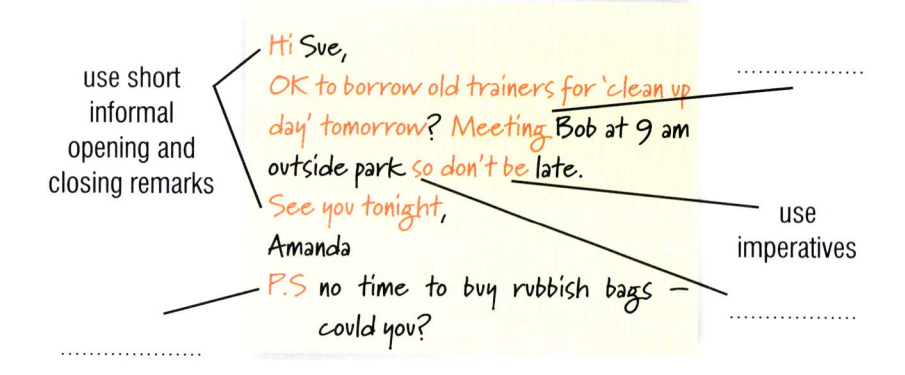

use short informal opening and closing remarks

Hi Sue,
OK to borrow old trainers for 'clean up day' tomorrow? Meeting Bob at 9 am outside park so don't be late.
See you tonight,
Amanda
P.S. no time to buy rubbish bags — could you?

use imperatives

Let's look closer

2 Read the notes below and find examples: of informal greetings/endings; omitted personal pronouns, articles and auxiliaries; imperatives, and participles.

[1] JESS!!!
Letter from Greenpeace arrived this morning. Put it on your desk. Should reply ASAP.
xxx Sandra

[2] Just a quick note to let you know about the wildlife documentary.
Filming next week at Currumbin Sanctuary. Please phone them for details, e.g. exact date, time, address, etc. Give me a call when you find out.
Thanks a million,
Jack
PTO for contact name and number

[3] Good morning Fred.
Had to call the vet–panda's sick again. Clean out monkeys' cages and bath the elephants. Done everything else.
See you at 6,
George
PS Vet said he would be here at 10am.

3 Match the highlighted abbreviations in the notes above to their meanings (1-5).

1 please turn over (the page) ....
2 and so on ....
3 for example ....
4 I've just remembered something ....
5 as soon as possible ....

4 Make sentences 1-8 shorter.

1 I would like to thank you for your help.
2 It's a great idea.
3 You should come and visit us.
4 I will see you soon.
5 I am leaving for Rome, therefore I can't be at the meeting.
6 John was not feeling well so he went home.
7 Can you tell me where and when it is?
8 Bob is coming at 9:00. Please, try not to be late.

Your turn

5 Read the rubric, underline the key words and answer the questions in the plan. Then, write your note (35-45 words).

> A colleague has invited you to take part in a 'clean-up the beach' day. Write a note and:
> - agree to help
> - ask for more information (e.g. date, time and place)
> - find out what you need to bring with you.

Plan

♦ Who is the note to? How will you start?
♦ What points/information do you have to include?
♦ Is there anything else to say?
♦ How will you end the note?

Amazing Facts!

Recycling just one glass bottle saves enough energy to light a 100 watt bulb for four hours.

38

Culture Clip 3

RRS Ernest Shackleton

▶ **Reading & Listening**

1 What can you see in the pictures? What do you think the *RRS Ernest Shackleton* is?

2 a. What type of text is this? What is the purpose of such texts? Read the text quickly to find which birds/animals are mentioned.

b. Read again and answer questions 1-4. Then, explain the highlighted words.

1 Why are they in the Antarctic?
   A to spend Christmas there
   B to do research on the wildlife
   C to save the penguins and whales
   D to carry out some experiments

2 What was their most memorable Christmas experience?
   A looking at the icebergs
   B singing Christmas carols to the penguins
   C seeing the blue whales
   D having 24 hours of sunshine

3 Why were some of the crew disappointed?
   A They were far from the station.
   B They didn't have any Christmas presents.
   C They couldn't reach their presents.
   D They couldn't enjoy the games.

4 Which of the following is the best title for the text?
   A Visiting the Antarctic
   B The Behaviour of Penguins
   C An Antarctic Christmas Holiday
   D Memories from a Scientific Expedition

3 Listen and read, then ask and answer comprehension questions.

S1: How long have they been at sea?
S2: Two months. Where are they ...?

▶ **Speaking**

4 What endangered animals are there in your country? Are there organisations that look after them?

23rd December We have almost reached the Antarctic after two months at sea. Although it is summer here and there are 24 hours of sunshine, it's still freezing and there are huge icebergs everywhere. One of our tasks while we are here, is to check the numbers, movement and feeding behaviour of the penguin colonies. We do this by capturing them and putting electronic tags on them. We have to be very careful so that no penguin is hurt.

24th December Today we sang Christmas carols to our new friends. They clapped their flippers to show they liked the singing. We also saw a family of blue whales – they must have heard our singing. What an amazing sight! The whale calves swam alongside their mothers. It was a touching scene and one we shall never forget.

25th December Happy Christmas! The crew traditionally exchange presents on these trips. Some of them were disappointed, though, because their presents were underneath food supplies and other equipment. We had expected to reach the Antarctic research station earlier but recent bad weather has delayed us. Anyway, Christmas dinner was delicious. We had roast turkey and Christmas pudding.

26th December Today we played games on the deck such as sticking our heads in buckets of freezing water. Thinking about it now, this was crazy and dangerous! Soon, we are going to reach our base station. Then we can start our research on the penguins. After we have done that, we can begin our albatross project. Checking the weight of albatross chicks is the job of Juan, a biologist from the University of Barcelona.

4a Travellers' Tales

Lead-in

1. a. Tell the class as many types of holidays (*package holiday, beach holiday, sailing,* etc) as you can in one minute.

   b. Look at the adverts on p. 41. What types of holidays do they advertise?

Listening

2. 🎧 Listen to a radio advert. What types of holidays are advertised?

Reading

StudySkills

Reading for specific information (multiple matching)

Underline the key words in the descriptions and questions. Read the text(s) and try to find sentences/phrases that match the underlined key words. The matching sentences/phrases are usually rephrased.

3. The people in pictures 1-4 live in the USA and are all trying to choose a holiday.

   - Read the texts and underline the key words.
   - Then, read the adverts and underline anything that matches up with what the people want.
   - In pairs, decide which of the holidays (A-F) is the most suitable for the people (1-4).

4. Listen and read. Explain the words in bold. Then, in pairs, ask and answer comprehension questions.

   A: How many nights is the holiday in St Petersburg?
   B: Three. Where ...?

Speaking

5. a. Match the verbs to the prompts.
   enjoy, see, stay in, visit, go on, experience

   - luxurious hotels • local cuisine
   - beachfront hotels • tropical rainforests
   - guided tours • traditional food
   - stunning wildlife • famous landmarks
   - great museums • white-water rafting
   - rare birds • rich history

   b. Look at the adverts on p. 41. Which holiday would you choose to go on? Use the phrases in Ex. 5a to discuss in pairs.

   A: The African safari seems the most exciting to me because you can see stunning wildlife. What about you?
   B: I'd go for ....

✍ Writing

Portfolio: Write your own holiday advertisement for an interesting place in your country. Write:

- name of place • type of holiday • length of stay
- activities • prices • contact number

---

1 Danny and Lisa have been married for ten years and are planning a special holiday. They both like exotic places and wildlife photography. They are looking for an unforgettable holiday full of surprises.

2 Eric wants to go somewhere special to celebrate his 50th birthday this year. He is interested in ancient history. He would like to go abroad, but he is terrified of flying!

3 Nick is 26 and he likes his holidays to be action-packed. He's very fit and active and loves the outdoors. He dreams of visiting exotic locations.

4 Julia is a busy architect and has to be back at work within a week. She's looking for a glamorous, well-organised holiday with the chance to see some beautiful architecture.

40

Looking for the IDEAL getaway?

Sightseeing in St Petersburg [A]

Three nights at the luxurious Astoria hotel. Russian culture and **professionally** guided tours. Don't miss the chance to visit this city's most famous **landmarks** and some of the world's greatest museums.

$1,460 per person (all inclusive)

Mediterranean Fun [B]

The Coral Beach Resort in Marbella, Spain offers relaxing 2-week **breaks** for all the family. **Beachfront** hotels with swimming pools, cafés, restaurants, watersports **facilities** and great nightlife! Sun and fun for everyone!

Adults $2,500
Children $1,600
(14 nights, incl. flights)

Amazon Adventure [C]

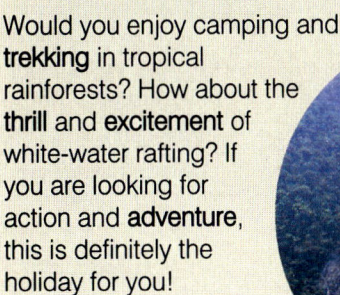

Would you enjoy camping and **trekking** in tropical rainforests? How about the **thrill** and **excitement** of white-water rafting? If you are looking for action and **adventure**, this is definitely the holiday for you!

$1,700 per person
(6 days incl. flights)

Natural Poland [D]

Babiogorski National Park offers a dramatic **setting** for a fantastic holiday for the less **adventurous**! Family-style **accommodation**. **Bird-watching enthusiasts** won't be disappointed – there are about 120 species of birds here and **early risers** are sure to **catch a glimpse** of something **unusual**.

$1,170 per person
(7 nights all inclusive)

African Safari [E]

Fabulous 12-day jeep safari in Kenya. See Africa's **stunning** wildlife in its **spectacular natural habitat**. Get a taste of real African **culture** with its **traditional** food, and enjoy the **incredible** sunsets.

$6,130 per person
(incl. flights)

Historical Mexico [F]

Experience the rich history of the Yucatan Peninsula **in style** aboard the Expreso Maya Luxury Train. Visit Chichen Itza and the Adivino Pyramid on this 5-day, **once-in-a-lifetime** trip.

$1,250 per person

Try these holiday suggestions from
Vesta Travel Co. Tel: 0626-555-0708

4b Vocabulary Practice

Packing

- suitcase
- toothpaste
- compass
- jumper
- credit card
- penknife
- sunscreen
- torch
- shoulder bag
- scissors
- binoculars
- hiking boots
- camera
- maps and guide books
- passport
- shirt
- sandals
- jacket
- first-aid kit
- soap
- T-shirt

1 Look at the items in the pictures. Which would you put in your suitcase? shoulder bag?

▶ Reading

2 Do you think you pack smartly? Listen and read to find out.

3 Read again. Which of the items in the pictures are mentioned in the text?

How to Pack Smartly

1 Take comfortable, easy-to-clean clothes. Don't take too much – for a week you should take 2-3 shirts and pairs of trousers, 1-2 pairs of shoes (hiking boots for a walking holiday and sandals for a beach holiday), a jacket or a jumper, a swimming costume and lots of underwear.
2 Don't forget the necessities. Take toothpaste, sunscreen, insect repellent and a small first-aid kit.
3 Put your shoes in plastic bags inside your suitcase so they don't dirty your clothes.
4 Keep your passport with you at all times.
5 Do not carry any sharp objects such as penknives, nailfiles or scissors in your hand luggage. Put them in your suitcase.
6 Put any breakable items such as cameras or binoculars in your hand luggage.

Weather

4 What is the weather like in your country in each season? Tell the class.

spring summer autumn winter

- warm • hot • dry • cold • mild
- rainy • snowy • cool • windy
- sunny • wet • foggy

Talking about the weather
• it's usually ... , but ...
• (e.g. summer) is (often usually) ...
• it's / it isn't often very (e.g. dry) in ...
• it rarely (e.g. snows) ... in ...

Autumn in my country is always wet and foggy but spring is usually mild.

▶ Listening

5 Listen to the weather forecast for Mexico City for tomorrow. What is the weather going to be like?

Means of transport

6 Fill in: *catch, drive, miss, get, take* or *ride* in the correct form.

1 He got held up in traffic, and as a result he .... his plane!
2 He .... the 8 o'clock train to Liverpool and met Steve there.
3 He .... his bike to school when he was a child.
4 He always .... his wife to work.
5 He .... the Tube as it was faster than driving.
6 He helped the old lady .... on the bus.

Prepositional phrases

7 a. Fill in: *on, in* or *by*.

1 travel .... bike/motorcycle/ bus/car/taxi/ boat/lorry/plane
2 go .... foot
3 travel .... a bus/plane/ train/ coach/ ship/boat
4 get .... a taxi/car/helicopter

b. Where do you usually go on holiday? How do you travel? Tell your partner.

I usually spend my holidays abroad. I never travel by plane.

Present/Past participles

8 a. Study the table.

- We use **-ed participles** to describe **how we feel**.
  *I felt **excited** when we landed in Rome.*
- We use **-ing participles** to describe what **something/somebody is like**.
  *Flying to Madrid was **exciting**.*

b. Use appropriate participles and the prompts to talk about travel experiences. Think about:

trip, flight, service/hotel, local people, museums, nightlife, etc

amused – amusing	interested – interesting
excited – exciting	fascinated – fascinating
satisfied – satisfying	thrilled – thrilling
bored – boring	disappointed – disappointing

A: How was ...?/What was the ... like?
B: It was ...
A: How did you feel about ...?
B: I felt ...

Expressing feelings

9 Portfolio: Use the adjectives and prompts to act out dialogues, as in the example. Record your dialogues.

StudySkills

Intonation

Use suitable intonation to show your feelings. This helps the listener to understand you better.

Upset Angry Fed up Exhausted Disappointed Pleased Excited

1 book / holiday
2 someone / steal my purse
3 hotel / overcharge me
4 find out / no running water
5 finish / packing suitcases
6 airline find / my missing luggage
7 get / best room in hotel
8 lose / passport

A: You look excited.
B: I am. I've booked my holiday!
A: That's good/great.

A: What's wrong? You look upset.
B: I am. Someone's just stolen my purse.
A: Oh dear. / I'm sorry.

Writing

Portfolio: Listen to the weather forecast in Ex. 5 again. Then, write a short weather forecast for your city for tomorrow.

4c Grammar in use

Past simple and past continuous
Grammar Reference

1 Read the text. Identify the tenses (1-8). Find examples of:

> We **1) reached** the hotel at 11:30 last night. It **2) was raining** heavily at the time and we were tired, so we **3) checked** in and **4) went** straight to our room. It was past midnight. My sister **5) was having** a shower while I **6) was unpacking** my suitcase. I **7) was putting** my clothes in the wardrobe, when suddenly, I **8) heard** someone trying to unlock our door.

a actions which happened immediately one after the other in the past
b an action which happened in the past
c an action which was in progress at a stated time in the past
d an action which was in progress when another action interrupted it
e two simultaneous actions in the past which were in progress.

2 Put the verbs in brackets into the *past simple* or *past continuous*.

- A: Where 1) .... (you/be) at 5 o'clock yesterday?
  B: I 2) .... (cook) dinner while Tony 3) .... (work) in the garden.
- A: When 4) .... (you/see) Sue?
  B: While I 5) .... (wait) at the bus stop yesterday morning.
- A: What 6) .... (happen) to Rob?
  B: He 7) .... (crash) his car while he 8) .... (drive) to work.

Linkers
Grammar Reference

3 Join the columns.

1 It was a really busy year for Tim — **but**
2 On the big day, he got up very early — **because**
3 He packed his suitcase, had breakfast and — **when**
4 He reached the airport 2 hours before his flight — **and**
5 There was plenty of time before he would board the plane — **so**
6 His heart was beating fast — **then**
7 He was opening the front door — **as**

a he felt a bit anxious about missing his flight.
b he was looking forward to his holiday in Malta.
c when he was about to check in, he realised he didn't have his passport.
d he reached home. Would he be able to find it?
e he heard the phone ring.
f he drove to the airport.
g he decided to drive home and get the passport.

▶ *Speaking*

4 Talk about a bad experience you had while on holiday.

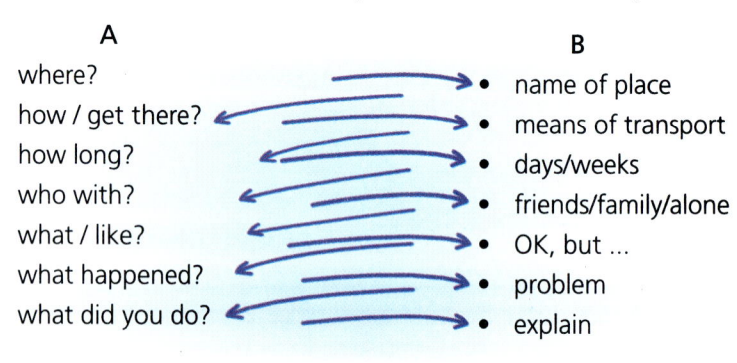

A	B
where?	name of place
how / get there?	means of transport
how long?	days/weeks
who with?	friends/family/alone
what / like?	OK, but ...
what happened?	problem
what did you do?	explain

5 Use the prompts to make sentences about yourself.

- yesterday • last month • in 2000 • last Monday
- two days ago • so • when • while • then

StudySkills

Linking ideas & sentences

Avoid writing short sentences. Use appropriate linkers to join two sentences together. It makes your writing more interesting.

GAME

Play in pairs. You narrate a story, your partner mimes it. The class votes for the best story and mime.

I was walking down the street when I slipped on a banana skin. (partner pretends to be walking, then slipping.)

Definite/Indefinite articles
Grammar Reference

▶ **Reading**

6 a. Skim the text. Does it give personal or factual information?

b. Read the text and fill in *a, an* or *the* where necessary. How do we use articles?

c. Listen and read, then tell your partner as many things about Argentina as you can remember.

Argentina is 1) .... second largest country in 2) .... South America. 3) .... Atlantic Ocean lies east of Argentina. 4) .... country is bordered by Bolivia, Brazil, Chile, Paraguay and Uruguay. 5) .... Buenos Aires is 6) .... capital. It lies along 7) .... Rio de la Plata, which means 'silver river'. The official language is 8) .... Spanish. In 1816 Argentina became 9) .... independent country.
Land: Argentina is shaped a lot like 10) .... long triangle. It is wide in 11) .... north and narrow in 12) .... south. 13) .... Andes Mountains run all the way down Argentina's long western border.
Products: 14) .... country produces beef, corn and wheat.
People: Argentina has 15) .... population of 35 million people. About 16) .... third of them live in Buenos Aires.

Used to/would
Grammar Reference

7 Which sentence expresses: a *past habit*? a *past state*? Where can we use *would* ?

1 I **used to live** in the country when I was young.
2 In summer they **used to hire** a boat and go fishing.

▶ **Listening**

8 a. Kate is talking about her summer holidays when she was six. Listen and tick (✓) the things she used to do. Then make sentences.

1	☐	go bird-watching
2	☐	lie on beach
3	☐	go swimming
4	☐	have picnics on the beach
5	☐	make sandcastles
6	☐	hike

Kate used to/would go bird-watching with her father.

b. In pairs, ask and answer.

A: *Did you use to go bird-watching when you were six?*
B: *No, I didn't. I used to/would ... .*

Sentence transformations

9 Complete the second sentence so that it means the same as the first, using the word in bold.

1 We haven't stayed at a hotel for years. **since**
It's years .... at a hotel.
2 There were two swimming pools at the hotel. **had**
The .... swimming pools.
3 John had an accident on his way to the office. **had**
John was on his way to the office .... an accident.
4 The hotel room was too small for Tom's family. **enough**
The hotel room wasn't .... Tom's family.

Phrasal verbs

10 Explain the phrasal verbs, then fill in the correct particles.

round   across   up   come   into   out

1 While in Prague, he came .... some great shops.
2 His last book came .... last month.
3 Don't call – just come .... at about 10:00.
4 She came .... a fortune when her aunt died.

✏️ *Writing*

Portfolio: Write a short factfile about your country like the one in Ex. 6.

45

4d Listening & Speaking skills

Checking in

▶ *Reading*

1 Where are the people in the picture? What are they doing?

2 Which of these sentences may be said by a receptionist?

1 *How may I help you?*
2 *I'm afraid I can't find the booking.*
3 *I demand to see the manager.*
4 *Just a moment, sir.*
5 *You mean there's absolutely nowhere to stay?*

3 a. Read the dialogue and complete sentences 1-5. Then read out the dialogue in pairs.

1 The dialogue is between Mr .... and ....
2 There's no room .... for the Martins.
3 A travel agent made .... two months ago.
4 There are no vacancies in the hotel because ....
5 Mr Martin is very ....

b. What do you think happened next? Listen and check. In pairs, think of a different ending.

A: Good evening, sir. How may I help you?
B: My name is Peter Martin. My wife and I have a reservation for a double room for tonight.
A: Just a moment, sir. I'm afraid I can't find the booking, sir. When did you reserve the room?
B: It was booked through my travel agent two months ago.
A: I'm afraid there's no record of a booking and the hotel is completely full. There's a festival on in the town and there are no rooms available anywhere.
B: You mean there's absolutely nowhere to stay? What are we going to do?
A: Well, I could try ringing around a few other places, but I don't think there's much hope.
B: Look here! My wife and I have been travelling all day. We're exhausted. I demand to speak to the manager!

Complaining and apologising

4 a. Listen and read. Underline the phrases which suggest apology.

- A: I'd like to complain about the TV. It's not working.
  B: I'm so sorry, sir. I'll get someone to see to it immediately.

- A: Excuse me, I think you gave me the wrong change.
  B: Oh dear. I *do* apologise, sir.

b. **Portfolio:** Work in pairs. Imagine you are at a hotel and you are having some problems. Use the table and your own ideas to act out similar exchanges. Record your dialogues.

Complaining	Apologising
• I'd like to complain about ...	• I'm so/terribly sorry (for)
• Excuse me, but ...	• I (do) apologise for

- room not clean
- room service slow
- no hot water
- no towels

FUN TIME

I'd like a room for the night, please.

Single, sir?

Yes, but I'm engaged to be married.

46

Giving travel information

▶ **Listening**

5 a. You are going to listen to a holiday rep talking to some new guests at their hotel. What might she tell them?

b. Listen and fill in the missing information.

STUDY SKILLS

Predicting

Before you listen, think about the topic. Predict words/phrases related to the topic. This improves your listening comprehension.

Name: Jane Clarkson
Company: Sun Tours

Meals
Breakfast: 7:30-9:30am – in 1) ....-ground floor
Lunch: 12:00-2:00pm restaurant – 2) .... floor
           packed lunches available – order 3) .... day before
Dinner: 7:30-9:30pm restaurant – variety of 4) ....
           dishes

Pool
Opening hours: 7am - 5) ....pm
Sunbeds available
Snack bar - 6) .... and snacks

6 Imagine you are a holiday rep. Tell the guests how they can spend the day. Talk about:

• meals • day trips available • shopping • beaches
• evening entertainment • where to go for help/advice

Expressing (dis)approval

7 Imagine you are filling in a hotel assessment form. In pairs, use the spidergram and the useful language to ask and answer, as in the example.

hotel facilities: swimming pool, tennis court, sports centre, laundry service, dry-cleaning service, children's playground, babysitting service, fast-food snack bar, room service

Asking	Expressing (dis)approval
• What do you think of ...?	• It's fine/excellent.
• How do you find ...?	• It's (not) good/very good (indeed).
• How is ...?	• It's poor/disappointing/awful.

A: What do you think of the room service?
B: Oh, it's very good indeed. Don't you think so?

Expressing annoyance

▶ **Intonation**

8 Listen and repeat. In pairs, make up short exchanges.

1 How dare you speak to me like that?
2 What are you talking about?
3 This is outrageous!
4 You're joking!
5 You're kidding!

A: I insist that you leave now.
B: How dare you speak to me like that?

Describing a picture

9 a. **Portfolio:** Describe the picture to your partner. Think about:

• where the people are
• what they are wearing
• what they are doing
• why they are there
• how they feel

Record your monologue.

b. What is your favourite type of holiday? Why? Tell your partner.

47

4e Writing a story (1st person narrative)

Getting started

1 What can a story be about (*adventure, mystery,* etc)? What tenses can you mostly use?

Let's look closer

2 a. Read the rubric. What can your story be about?

- A local magazine has asked its readers to send in short stories with the title *'A Trip to Remember'*. The best story wins a two-week holiday to Thailand.

b. Listen to the sounds. Can you guess the story? Read and check.

It was very windy **when** I set off for the airport last Monday morning. The sky was full of dark clouds **and** soon it started raining heavily. What a great way to start a holiday!

While I was driving to the airport, the storm got worse. Suddenly, a huge flash of lightning struck a tree. It came crashing down just metres in front of my car. The fallen tree completely blocked the road, **so** I was stuck. I tried to call the emergency services on my mobile, **but** the line was dead.

I was positive that I'd miss my plane, **so** I turned on the radio and tried to get used to the idea. Soon there was a loud knock at the window. To my surprise it was a young man in leather clothes, "Need a ride?" he said. My plane was leaving in an hour **so** I didn't think twice. I grabbed my bags, climbed carefully onto the motorcycle **and** shouted urgently, "To the airport please!"

It was my first time on a motorcycle **so** I was terrified. The young man drove so fast that I kept my eyes tightly shut all the way. Suddenly, the motorcycle came to a halt. "We're here!" he said. I looked at my watch **and** saw that I was just in time for my flight. The young man wished me a nice trip, **then** quickly sped away.

As soon as my plane took off, I breathed a huge sigh of relief. I could now relax and enjoy my holiday.

3 Read the story and put the events in the order they happened.

..... I turned on the radio.
..... He drove me to the airport.
1 I set off for the airport.
..... The plane took off.
..... Lightning struck a tree.
..... A man knocked at the window.
..... A tree blocked the road.

Linkers/Time Expressions

4 Which of the words in bold: – *join similar ideas? – refer to time? – join contrasting ideas? – show consequence*? Use them to make sentences of your own.

Adjectives & adverbs

5 Underline the adjectives in the story. Replace them with synonyms.

6 Complete the phrases 1-6 with the adverbs used in the story. How are they formed? Make sentences using the phrases (1-6).

1 .... blocked
2 climbed ....
3 shouted ....
4 drove ....
5 .... shut
6 .... sped away

Your turn

7 Underline the key words in the rubric. Answer the questions in the plan, then, write your story.

- A travellers' magazine has asked its readers to send in short stories entitled: *"The Most Exciting Holiday of My Life"* (80-100 words)

StudySkills

Sequence of events

When writing a story, present the events in the order they happened. This helps readers follow the story easily.

Plan

Introduction
(Para 1) When/Where did the story happen? Who was/were the main characters?

Main Body
(Paras 2-3) What happened? (events in sequence and the climax event)

Conclusion
(Para 4) What happened in the end? How did you feel?

Amazing Facts!

In English, all continents have names that start and finish with the same letter (*Africa, America, Asia, Australia, Europe*).

Literature Corner 4

GULLIVER'S TRAVELS

Jonathan **Swift** (1667-1745) was Dean of St Patrick's Cathedral, Dublin, but he is better remembered today as one of the finest **satirists** in the English language.

His works include *A Tale of a Tub* (1704) and *A Modest Proposal* (1729), but *Gulliver's Travels* (1726) is Swift's **masterpiece**. In this satire, Swift makes fun of politics and some of the important people of his time. In each of its four parts the hero, Lemuel Gulliver, goes on a **voyage**, but he ends up **shipwrecked** on a strange island. In Part One, Gulliver is **thrown into** the sea during a storm. He reaches **dry land** in Lilliput where he meets the **tiny** Lilliputians.

On 5th November, which was the beginning of summer in those parts, the **seamen** suddenly saw a **rock** close to the ship; but the wind was so strong that we were pushed onto it. Six of the **crew**, including myself, let down the boat into the sea and tried to get away from the ship and the rock. [1] In about half an hour the boat was **overturned** by a sudden strong wind from the **north**. What happened to the men in the boat, as well as those who **escaped** on the rock, or were left in the ship, I cannot say; but I imagine they were all lost. [2] I often let my legs drop, and could not feel the bottom; but when I was able to **struggle** no more, I found myself in **shallow waters**; and by this time the **storm** was much calmer. I walked for **nearly** a mile before I got to the shore, which I guessed was at about eight o'clock in the evening. I then walked on for another half a mile, but could not find any sign of houses or people. I was extremely tired, and with the **heat** of the weather I needed to sleep. [3] I slept better than I remembered ever having done in my life, and when I awoke, it was just daylight. I tried to get up, but was not able to for, as I was laid on my back, I found my arms and legs were strongly **fastened** on each side to the ground; and my hair, which was long and thick, tied down in the same way. I could only look upwards; the sun began to grow hot, and the light **hurt** my eyes. [4] In a little time I felt something **alive** moving on my left leg, which, moving **gently** forward over my **chest**, came almost up to my **chin**; looking downwards as much as I could, I **realised** it was a **human creature** not six inches high, with a **bow and arrow** in his hands.

▶ Reading & Listening

1 What do you know about *Gulliver's Travels*? Read the information on the left, then answer these questions.

a What kind of novel is *Gulliver's Travels*?
b How many parts has it got?
c Who is the main character?

2 a. Read the extract and match the sentences (A-E) to the gaps (1-4). There is one extra sentence which does not match any gap. Then, explain the words in bold.

A As for me, I swam, and was pushed forward by the wind and **tide**.
B I **lay down** on the grass, which was very short and soft.
C We **rowed** about nine miles, till we were able to row no more.
D **Puzzled**, I tried to discover what this strange sound might be.
E I heard noise around me; but in the position I was in, I could see nothing but the sky.

b. Listen and read. In pairs, ask and answer comprehension questions.

3 🎧 What do you think will happen next? In pairs, make up a dialogue between Gulliver and the Lilliputian standing on his chest. Listen and see if your guesses were correct.

49

Self-Assessment Module 2

Vocabulary & Grammar

1 Fill in the missing word.

1 .... Rio de la Plata is a river in Argentina.
2 .... round and see me whenever you like.
3 He joined the club in .... to learn to play tennis.
4 How long have you .... working here?
5 Have you .... been to France?
6 While shopping, I came .... a nice vase.
7 He got up early in .... to avoid the traffic.
8 He was sleeping .... the phone rang.
9 We went on a guided .... of the museum.
10 She ran .... Mrs Smith outside the bank.

(10 marks)

2 Circle the correct item.

1 We managed to catch a .... of the president of the company as she was leaving.
   A look   B sight   C glimpse

2 Snakes and crocodiles are ....
   A mammals   B reptiles   C species

3 This part of the country has a hot dry ....
   A climate   B weather   C temperature

4 Many species of animals have become ....
   A hunted   B dead   C extinct

5 As a child, he .... love watching cartoons.
   A am used to   B used to   C would

6 Spain is .... by Portugal and France.
   A edged   B joined   C bordered

7 He ran .... a friend of his on his way to work.
   A into   B out of   C over

8 He usually .... the train to work.
   A rides   B travels   C takes

9 She was very .... when she heard the bad news.
   A exhausted   B fed up   C upset

10 We .... our holiday a month ago.
   A saved   B reserved   C booked

(10 marks)

Use of English

3 Complete the second sentence so that it means the same as the first. Use up to three words.

1 It's been six months since I saw Jack.
  I haven't .... six months.
2 When I was at university, I spent most of my time studying.
  I .... spend most of my time studying when I was at university.
3 This is the first time I have been to Spain.
  I .... to Spain before.
4 I moved to London ten years ago.
  I .... in London for ten years.
5 Mary is still doing her homework.
  Mary .... doing her homework yet.

(10 marks)

4 Fill in the correct preposition.

1 That book belongs .... me.
2 Bob loves working .... animals.
3 It is not too late to save many animals .... extinction.
4 Our car broke down so we went the rest of the way .... foot.

(8 marks)

Communication

5 Complete the exchanges.

a Anything to declare?
b Excuse me – this isn't what I ordered.
c How dare you speak to me like that?
d Really? That's great news!
e It's very good.

1 A: The council has opened a recycling centre.
  B: ....
2 A: ....
  B: I'm sorry, sir. I'll change it immediately.
3 A: Go away!
  B: ....
4 A: ....
  B: No. I don't think so.
5 A: What do you think of the sports centre?
  B: ....

(10 marks)

50

Self-Assessment Module 2

Listening

6 🎧 You will hear a radio interview about a beached whale. For each question, put a tick (✓) in the correct box.

1. Mr Ian Saunders
   - A ☐ is the interviewer.
   - B ☐ works in the area.
   - C ☐ is the person who found the whale.

2. Why was the whale on the beach?
   - A ☐ because it wanted to sunbathe
   - B ☐ because it was too heavy to swim out to sea
   - C ☐ because a wave had carried it onto the shore

3. The whale is
   - A ☐ under 4 years old.
   - B ☐ a young female humpback whale.
   - C ☐ a fast swimmer.

4. Who is Jake Henner?
   - A ☐ a teacher
   - B ☐ a vet
   - C ☐ an employee at the Wildlife Protection Agency

5. What did Jake Henner do until help arrived?
   - A ☐ He kept the whale cool and dry.
   - B ☐ He tried to move the whale back into the sea.
   - C ☐ He made sure the whale was wet.

6. The blow hole of a whale needs to be
   - A ☐ wet and uncovered.
   - B ☐ dry and uncovered.
   - C ☐ dry and covered.

(12 marks)

Reading

7 Read the holiday brochure and decide if each statement (1-5) is True *(T)* or False *(F)*.

Yukon Adventure Holidays

Looking for the perfect place for a holiday? Then come to the Yukon, in north-western Canada, where we have package holidays to please everyone.

From October to March you can choose one of our 'winter wonderland' holidays. These include skiing, snowmobiling and dogsledding. From March to August we have organised hiking or mountain climbing activities, as well as canoeing or white water rafting down some of the most beautiful rivers in the Yukon Valley. All of our adventure package holidays include guides and instructors to help you enjoy activities you have never tried before. Accommodation ranges from four-star hotels to log cabins or camping grounds.

For more information check out our website: www.yukonholidays.com or call us toll free at 1-800-YUKON.

1. Package holidays are available all year round. ......
2. You can travel by dogsled in July. ......
3. You can do watersports in the Yukon. ......
4. You can only stay at campsites. ......
5. Phone calls to the company are free of charge. ......

(20 marks)

Writing

8 Your teacher has asked you to write a short story with the title: *A holiday I'll never forget*. Write about: where/when the holiday was, who you were with, what happened, what happened in the end and how you felt.

(20 marks)
(Total = 100 marks)

Now I can...

- talk about
  - environmental issues
  - types of holidays & means of transport
  - the climate/weather
  - my holiday experiences
- express
  - my feelings
  - (dis)approval, annoyance & surprise
- complain & apologise
- write
  - an article about a zoo
  - notes
  - a letter to a penfriend
  - a weather forecast
  - a holiday advertisement
  - a short factfile about my country
  - a story

...in English

CURRICULAR CUTS
Geography

2

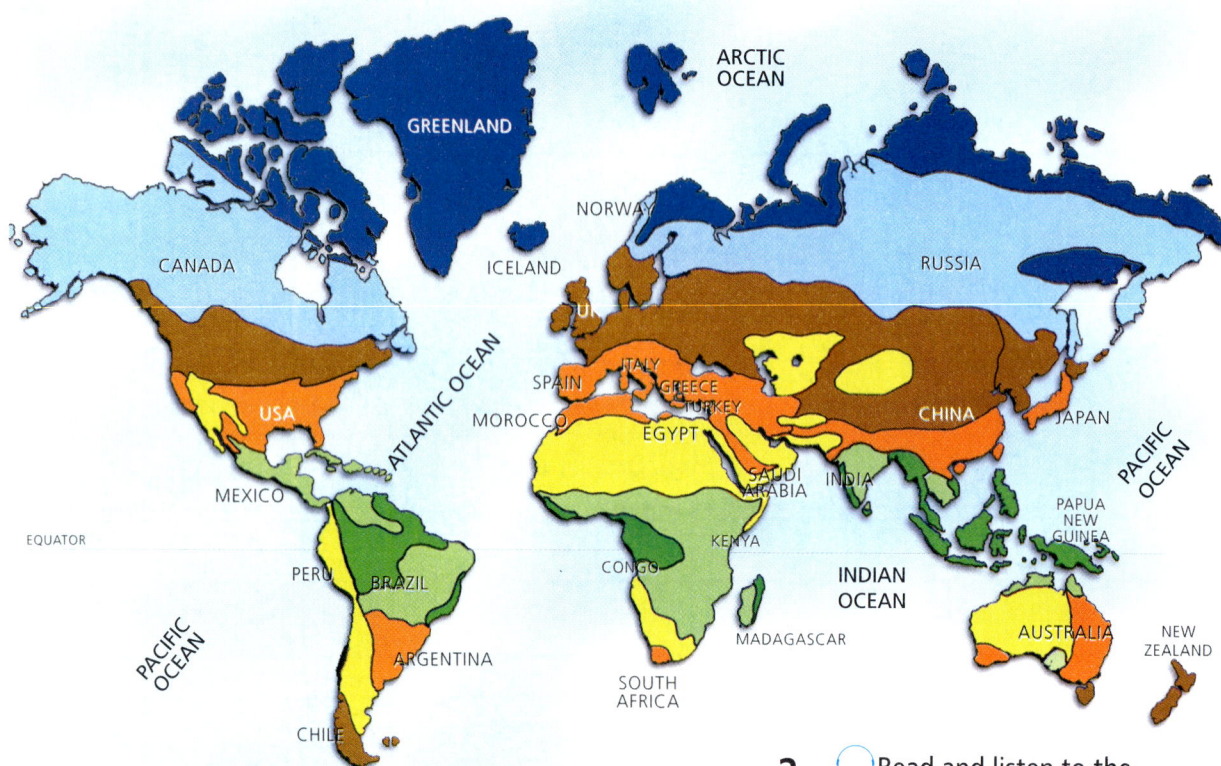

1 Look at the map and the text. How are they related? How many climate zones are there?

The World's Climates

A *Equatorial:* At or near the **equator**. No change in seasons. Hot and wet all year round. High **temperatures** and regular **rainfall** in all months.

B *Tropical:* Two seasons, wet and dry. High temperatures and lots of rain during the wet season.

C *Desert:* Very hot during the day, but at night the temperature **drops** to about 0°C. Very little rainfall. Warm and dry winds.

D *Mediterranean:* Hot, dry summers and **mild**, rainy winters. Some rain in the summer in the **form** of **thunderstorms**.

E *Temperate:* Mild summers and **cool** winters. It rains all year round. It can often be **cloudy** and **foggy**.

F *Subarctic:* Short, cool summers and very long, cold winters. Some rain during the summer. Snow is **common** during autumn and winter.

G *Tundra:* Temperature does not often **rise** above 0°C. **Freezing** even in the summer. Long, **bitterly cold** winters. Below the surface the **ground remains frozen** all year round.

2 🎧 Read and listen to the text and mark the statements True *(T)* or False *(F)*. Then explain the words in bold.

1 It rains all year round at the equator. .....
2 It's always hot in the desert. .....
3 Winters in subarctic areas are shorter than summers. .....
4 It is extremely cold in the tundra regions. .....

3 In pairs, talk about the climate in various countries marked on the map.

A: What's the climate like in Italy?
B: Italy has a Mediterranean climate, so it's hot and dry in summer.
A: Yes, and it rains in winter.

4 **Project – Portfolio:** What is the climate like in your country? Collect information from an atlas, encyclopaedias, the Internet etc, then write a short text about it.

52

Moments in Life

Module 3
Units 5-6

▶ **Before you start ...**
- Have you ever been to a zoo? Describe your visit.
- How did you spend your holiday last year? Talk about it.

▶ **Look at Module 3**
- Where are pictures 1-5 taken from?

▶ **Find the unit and page number(s) for**
- a poem ☐
- notices on shop windows ☐
- a report ☐
- a page from a clothing catalogue ☐
- greetings cards ☐
- a formal invitation card ☐
- a diary entry ☐
- a cartoon strip ☐

▶ **Listen, read and talk about ...**
- shops and products
- clothes and prices
- objects
- celebrations and customs

▶ **Learn how to ...**
- buy second-hand things
- ask about prices
- make requests
- express impatience
- calm someone down
- offer and accept gifts
- express your feelings
- congratulate and thank
- make arrangements
- invite, accept and refuse invitations

▶ **Practise ...**
- modals (*have to, must, can/can't, mustn't, may, had to, was able to, could*)
- making assumptions (*must, can't, may*)
- *too / enough*
- order of adjectives
- *will, going to*, the present simple after time words, the future continuous
- question tags
- intonation (losing patience/calming someone down/in question tags)
- phrasal verbs: *look, break*

▶ **Write / Make ...**
- a short paragraph about the perfect place to pick up bargains in your country
- a page for a clothing catalogue
- a poster of Dos and Don'ts for your school/work place
- a report assessing the good and bad points of a department store
- an article about a traditional wedding in your country
- greetings cards
- an e-mail to a friend to invite him/her to a dinner party
- a postcard

Culture Clips: Styles of Homes in the USA; Bizarre Annual Events in the UK

Curricular Cuts (Maths)

53

5a On Offer

Lead-in

1 Where can you buy the items in the pictures? What else can you buy from these shops? Tell your partner.

- department store • charity shop
- electrical store • antique shop
- second-hand shop

You can buy a camera at a(n) ...

2 Why do you think people go to second-hand shops? Use the prompts to discuss in pairs.

- pick up bargains • variety of items
- antiques • help people in need
- great/unusual/rare/cheap items

A: I believe people go to second-hand shops because they can pick up bargains. What do you think?
B: I agree. You can also find ... .

Reading

3 Look at the title and the subheadings of the text. What do you expect to read?

4 a. Read the text and for each question (1-5) choose the best answer A, B, C or D.

b. Listen and read, then explain the highlighted words.

golf bag
camera
fan
lamp
gramophone
mobile phone
carpet

1 This text was written mainly to explain
  A why second-hand items are great bargains.
  B how second-hand sales raise money for charity.
  C where you can go to buy second-hand things.
  D which items second-hand shops specialise in.

2 What does the writer say about car boot sales?
  A You probably wouldn't want the things on sale there.
  B They are a fun way to spend a holiday weekend.
  C Schools hold them to exchange toys and games.
  D A wide range of things may be found on sale there.

3 The writer says that second-hand shops
  A often sell only one particular type of thing.
  B always sell things that have been carefully checked.
  C are usually surprisingly good.
  D never give you a refund after you buy something.

4 What does the writer say about charity shops and bazaars?
  A They are good places for poor, homeless people to shop.
  B They are good because shopping there helps poor people.
  C They sell things that are worth almost nothing.
  D They give second-hand items to people in poor countries.

5 Which of the following might the writer agree with?

A First decide what you want to buy, then find the place that specialises in it.

B City centres offer the best second-hand shopping.

C Second-hand shopping takes a bit longer, but it's worth it.

D Do your second-hand shopping at weekends, Christmas and on Bank Holidays.

Checking out second-hand city

5a

Do you love to go shopping, but seem to spend all your hard-earned cash on just one or two items? If so, why not consider hunting around for cheaper, second-hand options? With a little time and patience, it's possible to find some great bargains. Take a look at the shopping alternatives we've come up with which are not only lighter on your pocket, but also lots of fun!

Car Boot Sales
People bring unwanted things that they dig out of their attics and garages to a car boot sale. There, in a large car park or on a school playing field, they sell them or swap them with other traders for something else. Anything from children's toys to sports equipment can turn up at these sales, which are usually held at weekends or on Bank Holidays.

Second-Hand Shops
Good second-hand shops can be full of surprises and are often the perfect place to pick up a bargain! Many specialise in certain items such as rare books, designer clothes and antique furniture. Always check things carefully before you buy them as it may be difficult to exchange them or get a refund later.

Charity Shops
People donate used clothes, shoes, toys and other miscellaneous items to charity shops where you can usually buy them for next to nothing! The money often goes to help people who are hungry, homeless or who live in poor developing countries.

Christmas Bazaars
These are wonderful places to buy handmade gifts, Christmas decorations and second-hand items. The beauty of these bazaars is that all the money raised usually goes to charity, so you can shop till you drop knowing that it's all for a good cause! The only problem is they are only held in December!

So, next time you're in the mood to shop, instead of using your credit card, head for 'second-hand city'. You won't be disappointed!

Listening

5 🎧 Listen to the dialogue and answer the questions.

1. Where does it take place?
2. Who are the speakers?
3. What does the man want to do?
4. What is the final price?

Speaking

6 Work in pairs. Imagine you are at a second-hand shop. Take roles and act out similar dialogues to the one in Ex. 5. Use the prompts.

chess set

Salesperson	Customer
Good morning. ... help you?	Yes, I'm interested in ... .
There you are. ... good condition.	How much ...?
... worth £... but I'll let you ... for £...	OK. I'll take it.

7 Are there any shops/events similar to the ones mentioned in the text in your area? Tell the class. Talk about:
name – place – goods – when open/held

Writing

Portfolio: Use your answers from Ex. 7 to write a short paragraph about the perfect place to pick up bargains in your town (40-60 words).

... is a great place to ... . There you can find ... . It is open/held ... .

55

5b Vocabulary practice

Shops and products

▶ *Reading*

1   a. Match the notices (A-G) to the appropriate shops (1-12). Which words helped you decide? What else can you buy in each shop (1-12)?

   b. Which of these shops can you find in your neighbourhood?

A **GREAT SAVINGS ON OFFICE EQUIPMENT** everything under **£3**

B *Half Price!* Deluxe Swiss Chocolates **£2.99**

C **Don't miss it! TV Sale** 24-inch TVs **20% OFF**

D **Special Offer!** fresh cream cakes only 65p each — offer ends soon

E **40% OFF** Quality 2-seater sofas now only **£299** order now while stocks last!

F **LOOK!** 5 kg potatoes £2 1 kg tomatoes 60p

G **Major reductions on a selection of elegant designer watches** original price £325 now £199

1	fishmonger's	5	greengrocer's	9	jeweller's
2	electrical store	6	dry cleaner's	10	baker's
3	confectioner's	7	stationer's	11	newsagent's
4	butcher's	8	chemist's	12	furniture shop

Asking about prices

▶ *Speaking*

2   Look at the prices on notices A-G. In pairs, ask and answer.

> £1 = one pound   50p = fifty pence   £1.50 = one (pound) fifty

A: Look! They've got tomatoes on special offer at the greengrocer's.
B: Really? How much are they?
A: They're only 60p a kilo.
B: That's a bargain!

Prepositional Phrases

3   Fill in: *by, for, on* or *in*. Then, use the completed phrases to make sentences about your shopping habits.

1   Could I pay .... **cheque** as I have no cash with me?
2   That's new stock but there are some items .... **sale**.
3   I wonder if this house is .... **sale**.
4   We bought our fridge .... **credit**.
5   You won't believe it; Tim paid for his car .... **cash**.

Clothes

4   In pairs, think of as many clothes and accessories as possible.

StudySkills

Remembering new words

Try to learn vocabulary in groups of words. Making connections between words helps you learn new words easier.

5   a. Read the clothes catalogue on p. 57 and list words under the headings below.

   • clothes   • materials
   • accessories

   b. Which of these items would you buy for: a beach party? a wedding? a job interview? a skiing holiday?

For a beach party, I'd buy a pair of sandals, ...

SUMMER SALE
Unbeatable value for the whole family!

All Under € 50,00
Selection of elegant silver dress rings

€ 41,00
Designer sunglasses
Choose from a wide range of styles and sizes

Special Offer € 12,50 → € 28,00
Women's black leather high-heeled shoes
Sizes 3-8

Men's black leather lace-up shoes
Sizes 7-11

€ 20,50
Men's quality white cotton shirts & ties
Sizes: M/L/XL

€ 5,00
woollen gloves
Selection of colours

€ 27,60
Unisex full-length waterproof nylon anorak
Sizes: S/M/L
Yellow/black or red/black

€ 69,00
Women's suit
100% pure wool
Sizes: S/M/L
Dry clean only

€ 98,50
Men's suits
Wool & polyester mix
Sizes: L/XL
Black/grey/navy blue
Dry clean only

Special Offer € 46,75
Unisex red & white sports jacket with free baseball cap
Sizes: S/M/L/XL
Cotton/acrylic mix
Machine washable
FREE baseball cap

€ 9,00
Men's swimming trunks
All colours and sizes in stock

€ 14,00

€ 24,50
Boys' baggy-style denim jeans
Boys' cotton shirts
Sizes: S/M/L/XL
Selection of colours

€ 9,00
Men's shorts
Sizes: S/M/L/XL
Black/navy blue/red

€ 5,00
Unisex T-shirts
Sizes: S/M/L/XL
Selection of colours and designs

€ 3,00
Women's rubber beach sandals
All sizes
Selection of colours

GAME

Play in teams. Describe a piece of clothing. Take turns to guess what the piece of clothing is.

Leader: They're woollen and we wear them to keep our hands warm.
Team A S1: Gloves.

6 Match the opposites, then, in pairs, ask and answer.

plain	short	old-fashioned	casual
long	bright	formal	loose/baggy
dull	fancy	tight	trendy

A: Well, what do you think of this dress?
B: It's a bit too plain. Why don't you try something fancier?

7 Underline the correct word. You can use your dictionaries.

1 The shoes **match/suit** your dress.
2 Can I **try/wear** this dress on?
3 This dress **fits/suits** you perfectly.
4 Blue really **goes with/suits** you.

▶ Listening

8 Match the exchanges, then listen and check. Where might you hear them?

1 ☐ Where's the menswear department?
2 ☐ Could I try these sandals on, please?
3 ☐ Can I try this on?
4 ☐ How much is this shirt?
5 ☐ I think you've overcharged me for these sunglasses.

a Of course. The fitting rooms are over there.
b It's £15, down from £20.
c Certainly. What size?
d Really? Could I check your receipt, please?
e It's on the third floor, sir.

Writing

Portfolio: Find pictures of clothes and accessories and make a page for a clothes catalogue like the one in Ex. 5. Present it to the class.

5c Grammar in use

Modals (present forms)
Grammar Reference

1 Match the modals (1-4) to their uses (a-d).

> In England ...
> 1 most school children **have to** wear a school uniform.
> 2 you **don't have to** tip taxi drivers.
> 3 you **can't/mustn't** drive a car until you are 17.
> 4 you **can** drive for a year with an international licence.

- a ☐ expresses obligation
- b ☐ gives permission
- c ☐ expresses prohibition
- d ☐ expresses absence of necessity

2 Complete the sentences about your country using the appropriate modal.

> In my country ...
> 1 you .... drive on the left.
> 2 you .... smoke in public places.
> 3 drivers .... wear their seatbelts.
> 4 you .... vote when you are 16 years old.
> 5 diners .... leave a tip in restaurants.
> 6 you .... be 18 to obtain a credit card.
> 7 children under 16 .... work.

▶ **Listening**

3 🎧 Listen to someone talking about his job and tick (✓) the correct column. What is his job? Make full sentences.

	MUST/ HAVE TO	CAN'T	DON'T HAVE TO
Be polite and cheerful	✓		
Wear expensive clothes			
Take short breaks			
Eat or drink at work			
Work overtime			

A ... has to be polite and cheerful.

4 Tell your partner three things that you (don't) have to do at work/home/school, etc.

I have to water the plants and take the rubbish out, but I don't have to help with the shopping.

▶ **Reading**

5 a. Where would you see the signs (1-3)? What does each sign mean? Read and choose the best answer (A-C).

> A If you buy two, you can have another one free.
> B If you buy two, you can have one of them free.
> C If you buy two, then another one, you may get them all free.

BUY TWO AND GET ONE FREE

> A You can only try on three items.
> B You mustn't try on more than three items at a time.
> C You cannot buy more than three items.

NO MORE THAN THREE ITEMS ALLOWED IN FITTING ROOMS

> A If you touch these items, they may break.
> B You may hurt yourself if you touch these items.
> C You mustn't touch these items.

DO NOT TOUCH THE DISPLAY

b. Underline the modals in the correct answers. What do they express?

Modals (past forms)
Grammar Reference

6 Read the sentences (1-4) and complete the past forms.

1 She **could** swim when she was 5 years old. *(ability in the past–repeated action)*
2 Jim played well, but in the end Tony **was able to** beat him. *(ability to do sth in one particular situation in the past–single action)*
3 She left her credit card at home so she **couldn't/ wasn't able to** do her shopping. *(inability in the past)*
4 He couldn't come yesterday. He **had to** work late. *(he decided to do so)*

Present	Past
have to / must →	....
can →	....
be able to →	....

58

5c

7 Tell your partner:
- something you had to/didn't have to do yesterday
- something you could/couldn't do when you were six
- something you were able to do in one particular situation

Making assumptions
Grammar Reference

8 Look at the picture and read the sentences. Which one talks about something that:
- is impossible? • is possible?
- we are quite sure about?
- was possible in the past?

They **must be** tourists on holiday.
They **may/might be** sisters.
They **can't be** shopping for winter clothes.
They **may/might have been** shopping all day.

9 Look at the pictures and make assumptions.

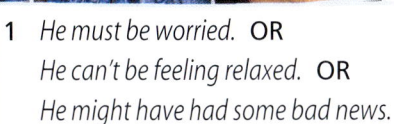

1 *He must be worried.* OR
   He can't be feeling relaxed. OR
   He might have had some bad news.

Making requests

10 Study the examples. In pairs, act out exchanges for each situation (1-5).

- **Can** you call me later? (informal)
- **Could** you call Mr Jones for me, (please)? (formal)
- **May** I have a glass of water, (please)? (very formal)

Positive Responses: Sure / Of course / Certainly.
Negative Responses: I'm sorry, but I can't. / I'm afraid not.

1 You want to borrow your friend's pencil.
   A: *Can I borrow your pencil?*
   B: *Sure.*
2 You call a department store and ask to be connected to the menswear department.
3 You want your mum to make you a sandwich.
4 You want your boss to give you Friday off work.
5 You want your friend to give you a lift to work tomorrow.

Too / Enough
Grammar Reference

11 Fill in the gaps with *too* or *enough*.

- This skirt is .... **long**; you can't wear it without shortening it first!
- I can wear this coat; it's **long** .... to cover my skirt.

12 Answer the questions.

1 A: That sofa over there is great! Why don't we buy it? **(expensive)**
   B: Well, I'm afraid it's *too expensive*.
2 A: What do you think of these shoes for the trip? **(comfortable)**
   B: Yes, they look ....
3 A: Come with me to the flea market. **(crowded)**
   B: Thanks, but it's ....
4 A: I don't understand this instruction manual. **(easy)**
   B: Let me try. It looks .... to me.

Phrasal verbs

13 Explain the phrasal verbs, then complete the sentences.

(look: forward to, out, up, for, after)

1 I'm .... a long black dress.
2 I always .... for pickpockets.
3 My holiday starts next week. I am really .... it.
4 Could you .... my dog while I'm away?

Writing

Portfolio: Make a poster of ten Dos and Don'ts for school/work.

DOs: *I have to be at work at 7:30.*

59

5d Listening & Speaking skills

Losing patience

▶ **Intonation**

1 🎧 Listen and underline the stressed syllables (1-8). Listen again and repeat.

1 Come on!
2 For goodness' sake!
3 Finally, we'll be off soon.
4 Oh no, not again!
5 Don't be long.
6 What is it now?
7 That's it!
8 I've had enough!

▶ **Reading**

2 a. Look at the picture and the first exchange in the dialogue. Where do you think the people might be? Who seems to be rather impatient?

b. Read the dialogue and complete the sentences.

1 Jim doesn't like ....
2 Ann can't make up her mind about ....
3 Ann finally chooses ....
4 Jim decides to take ....
5 The security guard asks to ....

Calming down

3 Underline the phrases Ann uses to calm Jim down. Match them to these explanations.

1 wait a bit (x3)   3 almost finished
2 don't lose your
   temper

4 Listen to the dialogue. Then, take roles and act out a similar dialogue.

5 🎧 In pairs, discuss what you think will happen next. Listen and check.

Describing objects

6 a. Look at the pictures. Use words from the table to describe items 1-5.

b. Bring various objects to class and describe them.

Jim: Come on, Ann! Can't we go now? You know I hate shopping.
Ann: Just a minute, Jim – I can't decide which cardigan to get. I think I'll get the red one. No, wait a minute – maybe the black one suits me better.
Jim: For goodness' sake, make up your mind so we can leave.
Ann: OK, don't get upset. I'll take the black one. Could you put the red one back for me, please?
Jim: Finally, we'll be off soon.
Ann: Hold on a second. Maybe the red one will look better. Could you bring it back?
Jim: Oh no, not again! Here, take it. I'll put the other one away. I'm taking the rest of our shopping and waiting for you in the car. Don't be long!
Ann: Nearly done! Oh, dear. Jim?
Jim: What is it now?
S G: Excuse me, sir, may I check your shopping bags, please?

Opinion:	nice, beautiful, pretty, ugly, terrible, etc
Size/Weight:	large, small, heavy, long, etc
Age:	old, antique, modern, old-fashioned, etc
Shape:	round, triangular, oval, square, rectangular, etc
Pattern:	floral, striped, checked, plain, polka-dot, etc
Colour:	yellow, red, blue, green, white, black, etc
Material:	metal, straw, leather, silk, cotton, plastic, wooden, clay, etc

1 It's a square black plastic suitcase with wheels.

1 — wheels
2 — peak
3 — laces
4 — handle
5 — small buttons

60

5d

▶ **Listening**

StudySkills

Choosing the right picture

Read the questions. Look at the pictures and think of words you expect to hear. This makes it easier for you to identify the correct one while listening.

7 🎧 Look at the pictures and think of words related to each. Listen and tick (✓) the correct picture.

1 Which is the best watch for Peter?
   A ☐   B ☐   C ☐

2 What did the woman order online?
   A ☐   B ☐   C ☐

3 Which bag do they decide to buy for their daughter?
   A ☐   B ☐   C ☐

4 Which ball do they need for the game? 
   A ☐   B ☐   C ☐

5 Which jacket does the man try on? 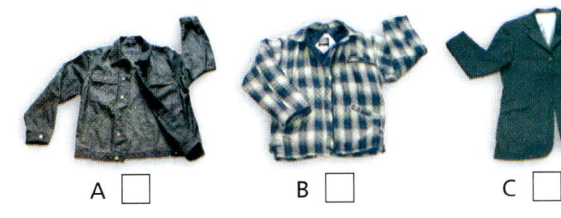
   A ☐   B ☐   C ☐

8 Work in pairs. Imagine you have lost your suitcase on a train. Make a list of what was in it. Describe the suitcase and the items to the clerk at the lost property office.

A: What exactly is your suitcase like, Mrs Turner?
B: Well, it's a large black leather one with wheels. ...

Offering and accepting gifts

9 Match the souvenirs (A-D) to the country (1-4) they come from, then make sentences.

1 ☐ Russia   3 ☐ Mexico
2 [A] Japan   4 ☐ Greece

This is a silk kimono from Japan.

A kimono (silk)
B sombreros (straw)
C Matryoshka doll (wooden)
D pot (clay)

10 Use the language below and the prompts in Ex. 9 to make dialogues as in the example. You can also use your own ideas.

Offering a gift	Accepting a gift
• I bought this for you from ...	• How lovely!
• Here – this is for you!	• Thank you so much!
• I hope you like this ...	• That's very kind/ thoughtful of you.
• I was on holiday in ... and brought you a ...	• That's great! Thank you!
• I know you love ... and so I bought you ...	• Wow! What a fantastic/ wonderful present!
	• You shouldn't have!
	• I've always wanted one of these.

A: Here – this is for you. It's a silk kimono from Japan.
B: Wow! What a wonderful present! Thank you so much!

FUN TIME

Why are you wearing only one glove? Did you lose the other one?

No, I found this one!

61

5e Writing a report assessing good & bad points

Getting started

1 Which of the following are true when we write a report? Look at the report in Ex. 2 and answer.

a The style of writing is informal.
b The person who is going to read it is a person in authority.
c We write our points under subheadings.

Let's look closer

2 a. Underline the key words in the rubric. Who is the report for? What is its purpose?

> A new shopping centre has opened in your town and the editor of the local newspaper you work for has asked you to write a report assessing its good and bad points. Write your report, describing the shopping centre and what it has to offer.

b. Read the report and fill in the subheadings below.

• Shops • Conclusion • Facilities • Introduction

To: Mr B Fox
From: Frank Watts
Subject: Sutton Shopping Centre
Date: 14th March

A ....
The aim of this report is to describe Sutton Shopping Centre and assess its good and bad points.

B ....
Sutton Shopping Centre is centrally located with plenty of parking. **However**, the car park fees are quite expensive. **What is more**, there are escalators and lifts to the upper levels. There are also a lot of fast food restaurants and cafés with seating for 250 people. **Yet**, the area is often dirty and untidy and this is also true of the toilets.

C ....
There are over 200 different shops inside the Sutton Shopping Centre. There is a variety of large well-known chain stores and smaller shops and boutiques. **However**, most of the shops are rather expensive.

D ....
To sum up, Sutton Shopping Centre offers a wide range of facilities and a variety of shops in a good location. **Although** it could be cleaner, cheaper and better organised, I think it is a good place to go shopping.

Linkers

3 a. Look at the linkers in bold. Which add more points to the same topic? Which make contrasting points?

b. Expand the prompts into full sentences.

- staff: friendly – helpful
- coffee shop: spacious – dirty
- restaurant: comfortable – variety of dishes
- products: of high quality – expensive

The staff are very friendly. What is more, they are very helpful.

Your turn

4 Underline the key words in the rubric. Answer the questions in the plan, then write your report.

> The editor of the newspaper you work for has asked you to write a report assessing the good and bad points of a new department store in your area. Write your report describing the store's facilities/services and departments.

Plan

Introduction (Para 1)
Why are you writing the report?

Main Body (Paras 2 & 3)
♦ *What are the facilities/services like?* (restaurant/café, toilets, car park, staff, etc)
♦ *What are the departments like?* (size, variety of products, prices, quality, etc)

Conclusion (Para 4)
Would you recommend it?

AMAZING FACTS!

After the Chinese discovered how to make silk, they kept it secret for 2,000 years.

Culture Clip 5

Styles of Homes in the USA

▶ *Reading & Listening*

1 Look at the pictures. Which house would you buy? Why?

2 In one minute, list as many words as possible related to houses.

3 Look at the pictures. Which show(s):
- small window panes
- wooden shutters
- a steep, uneven roof
- a wide porch
- long rows of windows
- a symmetrical shape
- room(s) in the attic
- a central doorway
- a slate roof

4 Look at the pictures and try to answer the questions (1-3). Read and check.

Which style of house ...
1 is the smallest?
2 is an original American style?
3 is often made of wood?

Explain the words in bold.

▶ *Speaking*

5 Read again and list all the features of the three houses. Work in pairs. Imagine you live in one of them. Use your notes to describe it to your partner.

6 Project Portfolio: What style of house is the most popular in your country? Write a short description of the style. Write about its:
- history
- building materials
- interior/exterior
- features

A Colonial style

The Colonial style started in the early 18th century, when America was still a British **colony**, and **copied** English houses of that time. **Typical** Colonial houses have a simple, **symmetrical** rectangular shape. The living room, dining room and kitchen are on the first floor, and the bedrooms and bathrooms are on the second floor. There is a central doorway with two windows on each **side** of the first floor, and a **row** of five windows on the second floor. Colonial houses are usually built of wood or **brick**, with wooden **shutters** and a large **frame** around the front door.

B Cotswold Cottage style

The Cotswold Cottage style first became popular in the U.S.A. during the 1920s and 30s. It copies **traditional** cottages built in the Cotswold area of England since the 14th century. They are small with **stone** or **brick** walls, low doors and small window panes. The **steep**, **uneven** roof is usually **slate**. There are two or three rooms downstairs and one or two rooms upstairs. These rooms have **sloping** walls because they are in the **attic**.

C Prairie style

The Prairie style was **developed** by America's most famous **architect**, Frank Lloyd Wright, in the early 1900s. These large houses have strong **horizontal** lines, with long rows of windows and quite **flat** roofs that **stick out** from the walls. There is usually a wide **porch** with a flat roof, too. They are often made of stone.

6a Happy Days!

Lead-in

1 Close your eyes and listen to the music. What images come to mind? What can you see, smell and hear? Describe the place and your feelings to your partner.

2 What can you see in the pictures? What is the theme that links them?

Listening

3 a. Listen to this extract from an Irish poem. Which event is it related to? Is it modern or traditional? Give reasons.

*Marry when the year is new,
always loving, kind and true.
When February birds do **mate**,
you may **wed**, nor **dread** your **fate**.
If you wed when March winds blow,
joy and **sorrow** both you'll know.*

b. Read the extract. Which month is suggested but not mentioned? Which is/are the best month(s) to marry in?

c. Match the words in bold to their meanings.

- luck/fortune
- get married
- sadness
- be afraid of
- couple

Reading

4 a. Read the title and subheadings of the article. How might the article be related to the poem you heard?

b. Think of three questions you would like to ask about a traditional Irish wedding. Listen and read to check if the text answers your questions.

5 a. Read the text and mark the statements True *(T)* or False *(F)*.

1 Irish couples don't follow ancient customs. .....
2 The groom couldn't go to the bride's house before the wedding. .....
3 Irish brides don't carry expensive bouquets. .....
4 In the past the wedding cake was homemade. .....
5 It is unlucky for Irish brides to wear green. .....

A Traditional Irish Wedding

"Marry in April if you can, joy for maiden and for man"

So says one Irish wedding tradition which, like many others, has its roots in ancient history, folklore and interesting superstitions! Even in these modern times, many couples try to include ancient customs in their wedding, in the hope that it will bring them luck and happiness. Here are some of the traditions that Irish people follow on their wedding day.

A treat for the groom

In the past, the groom was invited to the bride's house just before the wedding and a goose was cooked in his honour. Many Irish people believe that showing such generosity to the groom will make sure that he won't change his mind about the wedding at the last minute!

Bride, be beautiful!

A traditional Irish bride doesn't spend a fortune on bouquets of exotic flowers. Instead, she usually wears a wreath of wild flowers in her hair, freshly picked on the morning of her wedding. She carries more wild flowers in her hands, as well as a 'magic' handkerchief and a horseshoe for luck. Part of the bride's wedding dress is usually used to make the christening robe for the first-born child.

The icing on the cake

In the old days, an older female member of the family would take great pride in producing a traditional three-tier fruitcake for the reception. Nowadays, however, most Irish couples visit their local baker and order a cake which is decorated with Irish themes such as swans or fairies. According to tradition, the couple save the top layer of the cake. They often store it in a tin and use it as the christening cake for their first baby.

Fairies and luck

Whether you believe in them or not, Ireland is traditionally the home of fairies, who are said to love beautiful things – especially brides! For this reason, Irish wisdom advises brides never to wear green on their wedding day or to dance with both feet off the ground, as both of these things will tempt the fairies to carry them off forever!

StudySkills

Understanding new words

While reading do not use your dictionary each time you come across an unfamiliar word. Read the whole sentence. This will help you guess the meaning from the context.

Speaking

b. Explain the highlighted words. Which meanings can you guess from the context?

6. In pairs, list the wedding traditions in Ireland and in your country under the headings below. How similar are they?

- groom • bride • wedding cake • reception
- other traditions

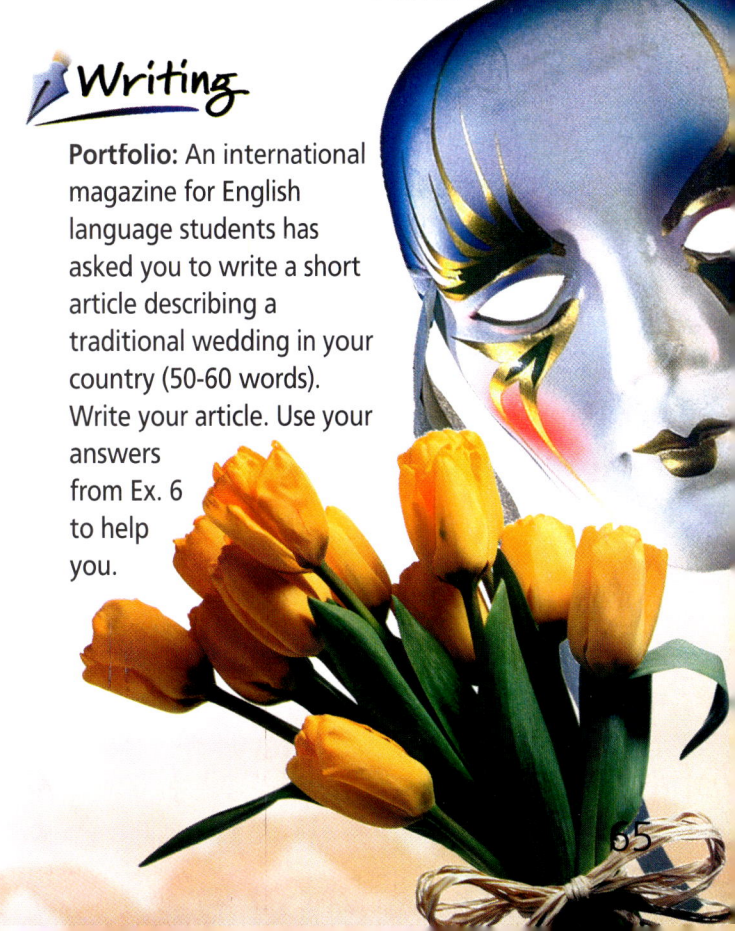

Writing

Portfolio: An international magazine for English language students has asked you to write a short article describing a traditional wedding in your country (50-60 words). Write your article. Use your answers from Ex. 6 to help you.

6b Vocabulary Practice

Celebrations and customs

1 🎧 Listen to the music. Which celebration (A-E) does it match? Which of these events do you celebrate in your country? When?

2 a. Match the lists of customs (1-5) to the festivals (A-E). Can you think of more customs?

- [1] children make pumpkin lanterns ... wear strange costumes ... scare friends ... trick or treat
- [2] buy new clothes ... pray in mosques ... children receive money as gift ... visit friends and neighbours ... have fairs ... eat special cake
- [3] pull crackers ... hang up stockings ... sing carols ... decorate tree ... exchange gifts
- [4] dress up ... watch street parade ... dance ... throw streamers
- [5] watch fireworks ... sing songs ... go to parties ... wait until midnight ... exchange greetings

A Carnival (spring)
B New Year's Eve (December 31st)
C Christmas (December 25th)
D Eid Al-Fitr (after Ramadan)
E Halloween (October 31st)

b. Choose a celebration and describe it to your partner.

Halloween is celebrated on October 31st. Children make pumpkin lanterns and wear strange costumes to scare their friends. They go from house to house and play 'trick or treat'.

Feelings

▶ Listening

3 a. Listen to the descriptions and match them to the events. Which words helped you decide? Listen again. What can you see, hear and feel? How does each person feel? Why?

[A] May Day
[B] Independence Day
[C] Bridal Shower

b. Are there similar events in your country? How do you celebrate them? Talk about:
• time of year • place • reason • activities

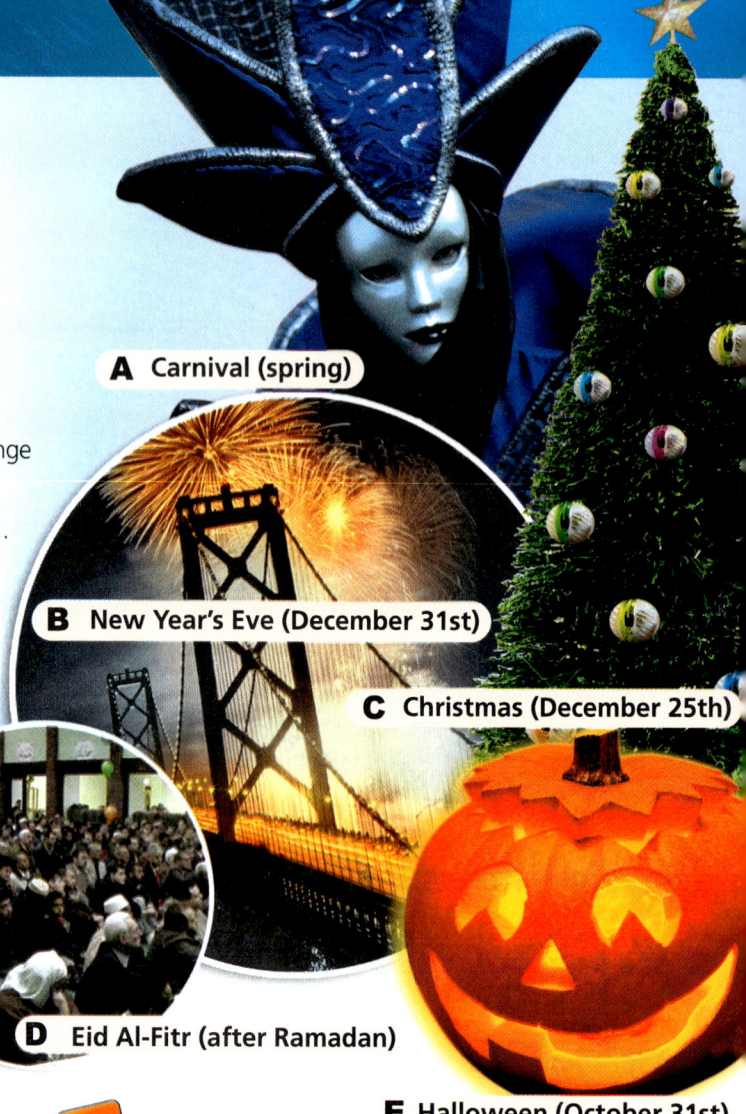

GAME
Play in pairs. One describes a celebration, the other mimes the activities. The best mime wins.

Congratulating & thanking

4 Work in pairs. Use the table and the prompts to act out dialogues as in the example.

Congratulating	Thanking
• Congratulations!	• Thanks (a lot).
• That's great!	• You're too kind.
• Well done!	• Thank you very much.
• That's fantastic!	

A: I got a job!
B: That's great.

A: Thanks. I'm really excited!

• get a job
• win the match
• pass my driving test
• get married
• have a new baby brother
• graduate from college
• get a promotion

excited
pleased
relieved
satisfied
thrilled
fascinated

66

6b

▶ *Speaking*

StudySkills

Recording yourselves

Record yourselves when you do a pairwork activity. This will help you evaluate your performance in terms of grammar, syntax, vocabulary, fluency and intonation.

5 **Portfolio:** Imagine you have attended one of the events listed. In pairs, use the adjectives below to discuss how you liked/disliked it.

an engagement party
a rock festival
a fancy dress party
a dinner party
a play
a retirement party

Positive
- fantastic • exciting • interesting
- thrilling • spectacular • amusing
- fun • entertaining • superb

Negative
- boring • crowded • tiring • dull
- disappointing • terrible • unpleasant

Record yourselves, then evaluate your performance.

A: Tony's engagement party was fantastic. I really enjoyed it.
B: Well, I found it rather tiring. It went on for so long!

Greetings Cards

▶ *Reading*

6 a. Look at the short texts. What are they? Where could you read them?

b. Match the texts to the occasions/events.

- Christmas • New Year • accident
- birthday • wedding • retirement
- graduation • new born baby • anniversary

1. Season's Greetings
2. GOOD LUCK
3. All the best for the future
4. Best wishes for your future together
5. Best wishes for a Happy New Year
6. Congratulations on the birth of your son
7. Many happy returns
8. Happy 21st
9. Well done!
10. Get well soon!
11. Happy silver anniversary
12. Best wishes for a speedy recovery

✎ *Writing*

Portfolio: Write greetings cards for the following situations:

- Your sister has just had a baby.
- Your best friend is in hospital.
- Your brother has graduated from college.
- It's your nephew's birthday next week.
- Your friend has just got engaged.
- Your colleague is about to retire.

67

6c Grammar in use

▶ **Reading & Listening**

LAST MONDAY, JOHN FOUND A PENGUIN IN THE PARK AND TOOK HIM TO THE POLICE STATION.

Officer, I found this penguin in the park. What shall I do with him?

Take him to the zoo.

OK, I will do that.

THE NEXT DAY...

I thought I told you to take the penguin to the zoo.

Yes, I took him to the zoo yesterday ...

tonight I'm taking him to a rock concert ...

and tomorrow I'm going to take him to a fancy dress party

Oh dear!

Future forms

Grammar Reference

1 a. Look at the pictures and guess the story. Why is the police officer surprised? Listen and read to find out.

b. Underline the future forms in the cartoon strip. Find examples of a future intention, a fixed arrangement, an on-the-spot decision.

2 Fill in: *be going to* or *will*.

1 A: We're running out of time.
   B: Don't worry. I .... help you.
2 A: Are you coming home for dinner?
   B: I don't think so. I .... probably be late tonight.
3 A: I'm worried about my exam next week.
   B: Don't worry, Ann. You .... pass.
4 A: Look at the clouds! It .... rain.
   B: Don't worry. I've got my umbrella with me.
5 A: Why are you wearing those old clothes?
   B: I .... paint the fence.

3 Choose the correct verb form. Give reasons.

1 Be good or you **won't go/aren't going** out.
2 Guess what! Ann **gets/is getting** married!
3 The concert **starts/is going to start** at 9 o'clock.
4 That's a lovely dress! **I'm buying/I'll buy** it.
5 Tina **is travelling/travels** to Rome on Monday.
6 She **will have/is going to have** a baby in May.
7 The train **reaches/is reaching** York at 7:15pm.
8 **Are you coming/Do you come** to the party?

▶ *Speaking*

4 What are your plans for this Sunday? Ask and answer in pairs.

A: *What are you going to do this Sunday?*
B: *I'm going to go on a trip.*

How? Where? What? How long? Who/with?

GAME

In teams, try to guess what the leader is going to do. Each team can ask two questions.

Leader: *I'm making a cake.*
Team A S1: *Are you going to have a party?* etc.

Present Simple or will?

5 Complete the sentences.

1 I'll call you when ....
2 After we finish shopping, ...
3 We'll let you know as soon as ....
4 Don't tell anyone before ....
5 We .... while he ....
6 I don't know when he ....

Future continuous

Grammar Reference

6 Match the verb form in bold to the meaning.

a the person will be in the middle of doing sth at a certain time in the future
b the person makes a prediction

This time next week, **I'll be travelling** to Tahiti!

▶ Reading

7 a. Name the types of messages (A-E). Imagine it's Sunday 12th June. What will Frank be doing:

- tomorrow evening? • at 7:15 next Saturday?
- tomorrow afternoon at 3:00pm?
- at 8:00pm next Wednesday evening?
- at 11:00am tomorrow?
- at 9:00pm next Sunday?
- next Friday evening at 8:30?

Use the verbs: *attend, fly, discuss, watch, go, have dinner*.

b. What will you be doing at the same times next week?

Sentence transformations

8 Complete the second sentence so that it means the same as the first. Use up to three words.

1 Why don't you hire a costume?
   You .... a costume.
2 It's too cold to have the party by the pool.
   It isn't .... have the party by the pool.
3 There are still some invitations to send.
   We .... all the invitations yet.
4 She probably won't make it to the party.
   I don't think she .... to the party.

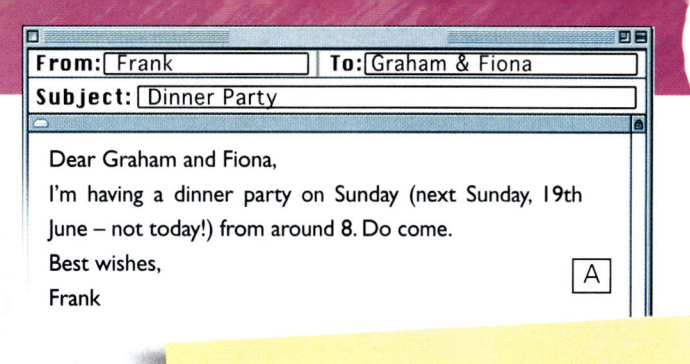

6c

From: Frank   To: Graham & Fiona
Subject: Dinner Party

Dear Graham and Fiona,
I'm having a dinner party on Sunday (next Sunday, 19th June – not today!) from around 8. Do come.
Best wishes,
Frank

A

Hi Frank
John called. He's booked tickets for Wed. 15th 7:30 – Rex Cinema. Call him for details.
Tony

B

Mr Frank Parker
is cordially invited to attend
The Annual Business Awards Ceremony
to be held at
Hatfield Business Centre
8 pm, Friday 17th June
RSVP: Mr S Hill

C

Dear Frank,
I'm having a fancy dress party!
Place: 27, Millford Lane
Time: 7:30, Saturday 18th June
Hope you can make it!
Yours,
Tim

D

AUGUST
MONDAY 13
10:30 plane leaves for Madrid
2:30 – 5:30 meeting with Mr Jones
7:30 – 9:00 business dinner with Mr Jones

E

Phrasal verbs

9 Explain the phrasal verbs, then fill in the correct particles.

into / through / down / off / away / out (of) — **break**

1 John and Lyn broke .... their engagement.
2 Greg broke .... prison a week ago.
3 Thieves broke .... her house and stole all her jewellery.
4 His car broke .... so he had to walk to work.

Writing

Portfolio: Send a short e-mail to your friend inviting him/her to a barbecue. Write:

• date • place • time • what to wear

You can use text A in Ex. 7 as a model.

69

6d Listening & Speaking skills

Making arrangements

1 Read the invitation and answer the questions.

1. Who sent the invitation?
2. What is the invitation for?
3. Where will the party be held?
4. What time does the party start/end?
5. What should you do if you can't go?

▶ Reading

2 Read the first exchanges. What is Mark's and Joyce's relationship to Elizabeth?

Mark: Hi, Joyce! How are things? Found a job yet?
Joyce: Give me a break, Mark – your sister and I have only just graduated! Has she started job hunting?
Mark: Not yet. Speaking of which, you're coming to her graduation party, aren't you?
Joyce: I just got the invitation in the post this morning. Sounds like it's going to be quite posh!
Mark: Well, you know what our mother's like. She always has to do things in style, doesn't she?
Joyce: So Elizabeth says. Who else will be there?
Mark: Some other students from your course ... our neighbours ... a few relatives ... some of our parents' friends.
Joyce: Oh, so there'll be a good mix of ages. How formal will it be, Mark? I mean, there won't be a fancy sit-down meal, will there?
Mark: No, no. The caterers are doing a sort of buffet.
Joyce: OK. I can't wait!
Mark: See you there, then!

3 Listen and read. Underline the phrases which give us the following information:

1. Joyce still hasn't got a job.
2. Joyce is looking forward to Elizabeth's party.
3. There will be young and old people at the party.
4. Elizabeth's mum won't cook the food for the party herself.

Read the dialogue aloud in pairs.

4 **Portfolio:** Work in pairs. Imagine you are having a party. Invite your friend. Give details about it *(place, date, food, etc)*. Record your dialogue.

Hats Off

Mr and Mrs Roderick Green request the pleasure of your company at a

Graduation Party

for their daughter

Elizabeth

on Saturday, 28th June
7 - 11 pm
13 Apple Road, Darleigh

Regrets only by 15th June 824-6951

▶ Intonation (in question tags)

Grammar Reference

5 a. Underline the question tags in Ex. 2. How do we form them?

b. Fill in the appropriate tag. Listen and tick. Listen again and repeat.

	sure ↘	not sure ↗
1 Let's dance, ...?		
2 They had a party, ...?		
3 This is your costume, ...?		
4 Don't forget to tell Sue, ...?		
5 Call her, ...?		
6 He has put on weight, ...?		
7 You'll pick me up, ...?		
8 They've invited you, ...?		
9 We can't do that, ...?		
10 She left early, ...?		

FUN TIME

— You are coming to my party on Saturday, Anne, aren't you?
— Yes, of course. What's the address?
— 42, Apple Street. Just push the bell with your elbow.
— Why with my elbow?
— Well, you won't be empty-handed, will you?

Giving gifts

▶ *Listening*

6 a. You will hear part of a radio programme about giving gifts in other countries. Read questions 1-5 and predict the correct answer, *Yes* or *No*. Listen and check.

		Yes	No
1	In Japan, it's impolite to give money as a gift.	☐	☐
2	The Japanese like to receive gifts which are colourfully wrapped.	☐	☐
3	The Chinese never open a gift as soon as they receive it.	☐	☐
4	People in South America think highly of leather gifts.	☐	☐
5	When visiting a British home, you don't need to take a gift.	☐	☐

b. Are there any special customs about giving gifts in your country? What are they? Tell the class.

Describing a picture

StudySkills

Describing pictures

Avoid describing pictures in too much detail. It makes your description unimaginative and uninteresting. e.g. *Don't say, "There is a spoon on the plate."*

7 a. Work in pairs. Describe the picture to your partner. Think about:

- where the people are
- what they are wearing/doing
- how they feel

Evaluate your partner's description.

b. How do you celebrate this occasion?

Inviting

8 Listen to the exchanges. How formal or informal is each one? Who accepts the invitation?

1 A: *Would you like to come to our party tonight?*
B: *Thanks! I'd love to.*

2 A: *It's our son's wedding next Saturday, and we'd love it if you could be there.*
B: *Oh dear! I'm afraid I'll be away that weekend – but do give my very best wishes to the happy couple.*

9 Look at the expressions in the box. Which are formal / informal? In pairs, act out dialogues for situations 1-4.

INVITING/SUGGESTING	ACCEPTING/REFUSING
• How would you like to …?	• Thanks! I'd love / like to.
• Do you want to …?	• That sounds great.
• I'd / We'd be delighted if you could ….	• I'd love/be delighted to.
• What / How about … ?	• I'd love to but I can't.
• Let's … / Shall we … ?	• I'm (terribly) sorry, but …
• Why don't we … ?	• I'm afraid I can't.

1 Ask a friend from work/school if they want to join you for lunch.
2 Invite your boss to the office staff's Christmas dinner party.
3 Ask your mum to go to a concert with you.
4 Invite your school teacher to your graduation party.

Verbs with prepositions

10 Fill in: *to*, *on*, *in*, *with*, *of*. Use the verbs in bold and the prepositions to make sentences of your own.

1 We **congratulated** them .... the birth of their son.
2 She **succeeded** .... passing her exams.
3 She **agreed** .... help me with the preparations.
4 She **agreed** .... Tony about having a party by the pool.
5 She **insists** .... having the reception at the hotel.
6 I'm **thinking** .... going to the festival next week.

71

6e Writing a postcard

Getting started

1 How often do you send postcards? Who to? When? Why?

Let's look closer

2 Read the rubric, underline the key words and answer the questions.

> Imagine you are on holiday in a city. Write a postcard to a friend. Write about:
> • where you are staying • what there is to see and do there • what you think of the place

1 What will the postcard be about?
2 Which beginnings/endings can you use? Circle.

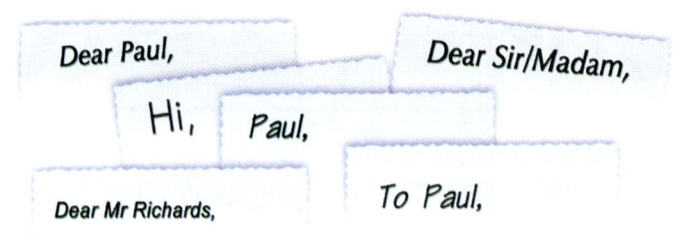

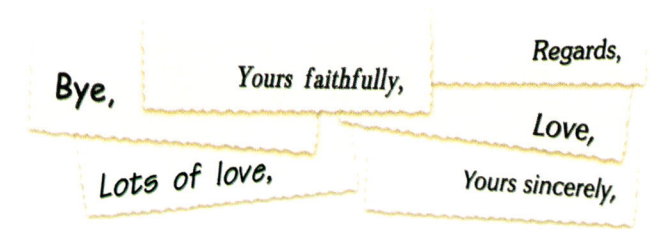

- Dear Paul,
- Dear Sir/Madam,
- Hi, Paul,
- Dear Mr Richards,
- To Paul,

- Bye,
- Yours faithfully,
- Regards,
- Love,
- Lots of love,
- Yours sincerely,

3 Read the postcard and answer the questions.

Dear Lucy,
Greetings from Rio! I'm having a nice time. I'm staying at a good hotel. The food is nice and there's lots to do. The shops are good with nice souvenirs. It's Carnival time here. There are lots of nice parades in the streets. Street bands play nice music with guitars and drums. Everyone is dancing, singing and throwing streamers. It's a pity you aren't here. See you soon!
Take care,
Jane
XOXOX

Lucy Palmer
87 Princess Street
Manchester
M16 2NG
UNITED KINGDOM

1 Where do we write the person's address?
2 What does XOXOX mean?

4 Jane uses the same two adjectives to describe everything. Find and circle them. Replace them with others from the list.

• amazing • lovely • great • fantastic
• delicious • wonderful • attractive

Your turn

Study Skills

Interpreting rubrics

Make sure you include all the points in the rubric. The rubric gives us information about the situation, who we are writing to and what we should write about.

5 a. Read the rubric. What information does it give you about: who you are, who you are writing to, what you should write about?

> You are spending New Year with some friends. Write a postcard to your English pen friend. Write about:
> • where you are staying • what you think of the place • how people celebrate the event

b. Answer the questions in the plan, then write your postcard (40-55 words).

Plan

Dear .... ,

- *Which city are you in?*
- *Where are you staying? (house, flat, etc)*
- *Do you like the place? (shops, food, sights, etc)*
- *How do people celebrate New Year there? (decorations, parties, etc)*

Love,
....

Amazing Facts!

It is estimated that about 90% of American children go out 'trick-or-treating' for Halloween.

Culture Clip 6

▶ Reading & Listening

1 Look at the title. How often and in which country do these events take place?

2 🎧 Look at the photos and the subheadings. Think of one question you would like to ask about each event. Listen and read to see if the texts answer your questions.

3 Read and answer the questions. Then explain the words/phrases in bold.

In which festival(s):

1. can you eat the prize?
2. is money collected to help people?
3. is speed important?
4. do the participants act?
5. do the people wear strange clothes?

▶ Speaking

4 Work in pairs. Imagine you are at one of these events. Phone your friend and give your impressions.

5 Make notes under the headings about a bizarre event in your country, then describe it to your partner.

- name • place • date
- activities

Bizarre Annual Events in the UK

A The Bognor Birdman Competition **takes place** in Bognor Regis in May. **Competitors** build strange homemade flying machines or wear unusual costumes and try to 'fly' off the **pier**. The person who flies the furthest wins a large **cash prize**. Many of the fliers take part to raise money for **charity**. As many as 40,000 **spectators** watch this competition every year.

B The Cooper's Hill Cheese Rolling Competition is held in Gloucester every year in May. **Contestants** stand at the top of a very **steep** hill. A huge cheese is **rolled down**, and the contestants have to **chase** it down the hill. Nobody ever manages to catch the cheese, but the person who gets to the bottom first is the winner, and keeps the cheese as a prize!

C Up-Helly-Aa is held every year on the last Tuesday of January in the Shetland Isles. Up to 1000 people dressed as Vikings and holding **flaming torches** pull a Viking galley through the streets. When they reach a certain place, they throw their torches into the **galley** and burn it. Then, they **put on** short funny plays in local halls. The festival is very popular with locals and tourists **alike**.

D The Peel Dip takes place every New Year's Day on the Isle of Man. About 200 people jump into the **freezing** waters of the Irish Sea to raise money for charity. The **dip attracts** people of all ages. All the swimmers get a medal and a **certificate**.

Self-Assessment Module 3

Vocabulary & Grammar

1 Fill in the missing word.

1. Don't forget to stop at the .... and buy some fresh bread.
2. I prefer plain shoes rather than .... ones.
3. Liz is .... married next Saturday.
4. Would you .... to come to the party?
5. You don't .... to wash the dishes. I washed them earlier.
6. This suit is .... expensive for me to buy.
7. That shirt .... you perfectly.
8. He insists .... having a reception by the pool.
9. You can look .... new words in the dictionary.
10. Could I .... these shoes on?

(10 marks)

2 Circle the correct item.

1. At Christmas we .... crackers.
   A blow   B watch   C pull
2. That bag .... your shoes. You should buy it.
   A suits   B matches   C fits
3. This time tomorrow, I .... to Rome.
   A will fly   B be flying   C will be flying
4. They decided to break .... their engagement.
   A up   B down   C off
5. "I've just passed my driving test." " ...."
   A Well done!   B Get well soon!
   C Good luck!
6. I didn't think much .... the parade.
   A in   B on   C of
7. He is sleeping. He .... be tired.
   A can't   B must   C needs
8. He .... to work late yesterday.
   A had   B needed   C must
9. That dress is on special ....
   A offer   B discount   C sale
10. Ted will look .... the dog while we're away.
    A forward   B after   C up

(10 marks)

Use of English

3 Complete the second sentence so that it means the same as the first. Use up to three words.

1. It is not necessary for you to work overtime today.
   You .... to work overtime today.
2. He probably won't go away this weekend.
   I don't think he .... away this weekend.
3. I can't wait to see Mary next month.
   I am .... seeing Mary next month.
4. Jim is too young to get a driving licence.
   Jim isn't .... get a driving licence.
5. I think you should buy a new pair of trainers.
   Why .... buy a new pair of trainers?

(10 marks)

4 Fill in the correct preposition.

1. He paid for his shopping .... cash.
2. She succeeded .... passing her driving test.
3. He decided to pay .... cheque.
4. Mark buys everything .... credit.
5. They congratulated me .... my success.

(10 marks)

Communication

5 Complete the exchanges.

a. Certainly. One moment, please.
b. I bought this for you.
c. How about going to the cinema tonight?
d. Could I try on this dress, please?
e. Well done!

1. A: ....?
   B: That's very kind of you.
2. A: Could you put me through to Mr Smith, please?
   B: ....?
3. A: Guess what – I passed all my exams!
   B: ....
4. A: ....
   B: Of course. The fitting rooms are here.
5. A: ....
   B: I'm afraid I can't.

(10 marks)

74

Self-Assessment Module 3

Listening

6 🎧 You will hear two people talking about a wedding they have been invited to attend. Fill in the missing information in the numbered spaces (1-6).

Mr & Mrs (1) .... would like the pleasure of your company at the wedding of their daughter, (2) .... , to Mr Paul Smith on Saturday, (3) .... June at St Mary's Church at (4) .... am and afterwards at a reception at the (5) .... Hotel

RSVP no later than 30th (6) ....

(12 marks)

Reading

7 Read the text and mark the statements (1-6) as true *(T)* or false *(F)*.

BUY, BUY, BUY...

Do you go shopping whenever you feel depressed? Do you spend too much money on things you don't really need, lose control and then go into debt? If you answered 'yes' to these questions, you may be a shopaholic!

'Shopaholism' is uncontrolled shopping in order to feel better about yourself. Just like some people go on holidays to sunny countries or eat chocolate to feel better, others simply go on shopping sprees. But shopaholics usually come home with bags and bags of items, most of which will never be used, and an empty bank account.

So, what can you do about the problem?

- Always pay in cash. Never take your credit cards with you when you go shopping – or better still, destroy them altogether.
- Make a shopping list before you leave the house and stick to it.
- Work out a monthly budget, so you know what you can spend.
- Take only enough money with you to pay for the absolute essentials.
- Avoid ordering goods from catalogues, and don't watch shopping channels on TV.
- If you see something you feel you must have, ask the shop to keep it for you and go back again a few days later. If you still want it, buy it.

Just follow these simple steps and you should never lose control of your purse or your budget again!

1 Shopaholics always buy more than they need. .....
2 Shopaholics shop to make themselves feel happy. .....
3 If you shop a lot, it is best to leave your cash at home. .....
4 Buying only what you need helps you control your shopping. .....
5 Shopaholics should not watch TV. .....
6 You should be sure you really need something before you buy it. .....

(18 marks)

Writing

8 You ordered a shirt and a pair of trousers from a catalogue. When your order arrived, you realised that the shirt had no buttons, and when you tried on the trousers, the zip broke. Write a letter of complaint, stating that you are returning the clothing and asking for a full refund.

(20 marks)
(Total = 100 marks)

Now I can...

- talk about
  – clothes & prices
  – shops & products
  – celebrations & customs
- make requests & arrangements
- invite, accept & refuse invitations
- write/make
  – a poster of Dos & Don'ts for your school/workplace
  – a report assessing good & bad points of a department store
  – an article about a traditional wedding in my country
  – greetings cards
  – an e-mail to a friend inviting him/her to a dinner party
  – a postcard

...in English

CURRICULAR CUTS — Maths

Ian
2 kilos of steak
1 bottle of Coke
400g of cheese

Pam
1 jar of coffee
1 kg of sugar
1 tub of margarine
1 packet of biscuits

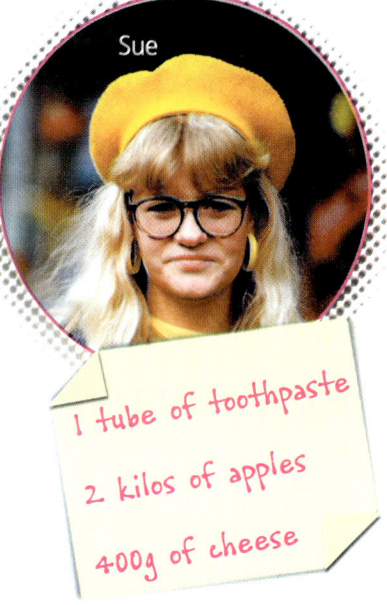

Sue
1 tube of toothpaste
2 kilos of apples
400g of cheese

1. Explain the key in your language.

2. **Problem:** Look at the price list and the three people's shopping lists. How much will each person's shopping cost?

    e.g. Ian
    Answer
    £7.99 X 2 = £15.98
    £15.98 + £1.27 + £1.99 = £19.24

3. Answer the questions.

    1. Whose shopping bill is the highest/lowest?
    2. How much change will Pam get from £10?
    3. Which notes and coins does Sue need in order to give the exact amount?
        A £5, £1, 50p, 2p, 2p
        B £2, £2, £1, 20p, 20p, 10p, 2p, 2p
    4. Which three items on the price list cost exactly £4.50 in total?

Key

+ plus — ADDITION
− minus — SUBTRACTION
× times/multiplied by — MULTIPLICATION
÷ divided by — DIVISION
= equals

Price List

cheddar cheese	£1.99	(400g)
sugar	65p	per kilo
beef steak	£7.99	per kilo
toothpaste	£1.86	
Coke	£1.27	(2 litres)
biscuits	£1.19	
coffee	£3.09	
margarine	£1.29	
apples	£1.69	(2kg bag)

4. A shoe shop has increased its prices by 4%. Look at the old prices and work out the new ones.

    Find 1% of the price. Then multiply by 4 and add this to the price. Give the answer to the nearest whole number.
    e.g. 1% of £30.00 = £0.30
    £0.30 x 4 = £1.20
    £1.20 + £30.00 = £31.20

    1. £30.00
    2. £4.99
    3. £35.99

5. **Project:** Write a shopping list of the things you/your family usually buy each week. Go to the supermarket and write the prices next to each item. Compare your list with your classmates. Say whose is the most expensive weekly bill.

76

Feel Good

Module 4
Units 7-8

▶ **Before you start ...**
- What is your favourite shopping centre? What can you find there?
- What is your favourite celebration? How do you celebrate it?

▶ **Look at Module 4**
- Where are pictures 1-5 taken from?

▶ **Find the unit and page number(s) for**
- restaurant reviews ☐
- a recipe ☐
- a shopping list ☐
- a plan of a sports club ☐
- a memo ☐
- a sports quiz ☐
- a reminder ☐

▶ **Listen, read and talk about ...**
- restaurant etiquette and table manners
- supermarket shopping
- cooking methods and tastes
- cutlery, crockery and appliances
- sports and sports qualities
- sports injuries
- sports places
- the pros and cons of a sport

▶ **Learn how to ...**
- express likes/dislikes related to food
- order a meal
- negotiate
- express opinions about sports

- sympathise and give advice
- describe health problems
- express hesitation

▶ **Practise ...**
- countable/uncountable nouns
- quantifiers (*some, any, much, many, a lot of, a little, a few, no*)
- *some, any, no, every* + *body/thing/where*
- the past perfect
- the passive
- conditionals: Type 0, 1
- linkers (of result, addition, contrast, conclusion)
- intonation (stressed syllables/hesitation)
- phrasal verbs: *give, bring*

▶ **Write / Make ...**
- a short review about an unusual restaurant
- a recipe for a local dish
- a shopping list
- a story
- a postcard
- a message
- a sports quiz
- a pros and cons essay about a sport

Literature Corner: Down the Chocolate River; The Olympic Anthem

Curricular Cuts (Science): A Balanced Diet

7a Eating out!

Lead-in

STUDY SKILLS

Remember new words

Put new words into sentences. This helps you remember them. You can look at the examples in your dictionary to get ideas.

1 How are these words related to restaurants? Make sentences.

- waiter • menu • dessert
- chef • bill • tip • napkin
- soft drinks • linen tablecloth
- side dish • four-course meal
- servings • seafood dishes
- main course • starter

A waiter serves customers in a restaurant.

2 Match the adjectives to the nouns.

a fast, slow, poor, excellent

b high, low, reasonable

c modern, luxurious, simple, unusual

d tasty, spicy, plain, tasteless, traditional

e relaxed, romantic, friendly, formal

decor
food
service
prices
atmosphere

Listening

3 🎧 Listen to some people talking about restaurants they have been to. Who is(n't) satisfied? Why (not)?

LYN   **PAUL**   **JULIE & BILL**

Reading

4 The people (1-4) are trying to decide which restaurant to eat at. Read the descriptions and underline the key words. Read the reviews (A-F) and decide which restaurant would be best for each. Which words helped you decide? Underline them.

1 Dave is a student at university, so he doesn't have much money. He isn't keen on foreign food, and he prefers a variety of plain but tasty dishes. When he eats out, good company is more important than the surroundings.

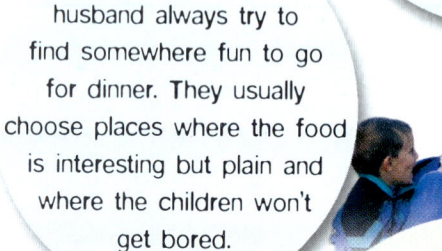

2 Sandra loves French and Italian food. She can't afford to eat out very often, so she likes to go to places that offer good value for money and have interesting decor.

3 Nina and her husband always try to find somewhere fun to go for dinner. They usually choose places where the food is interesting but plain and where the children won't get bored.

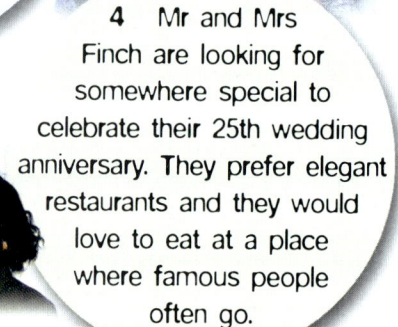

4 Mr and Mrs Finch are looking for somewhere special to celebrate their 25th wedding anniversary. They prefer elegant restaurants and they would love to eat at a place where famous people often go.

5 a. Listen and read. Match the pictures (1-6) to the restaurant reviews (A-F).

b. Explain the words in bold. In pairs, ask and answer comprehension questions.

A: *Where's a good place to go for seafood in Toronto?*
B: *Captain John's Harbour Boat Restaurant.*

Speaking

6 Imagine you are in Toronto. Which restaurant would you like to visit? Tell your partner. Use phrases from Ex. 2.

Writing

Portfolio: Think of an unusual restaurant in your town and write a short review of it (40-50 words). Write about the:

• location • decor • food • prices • atmosphere

A Taste of Toronto

Bob Green reviews a selection of some unusual places to eat in Canada's largest city.

A. Mr Greenjeans
Situated in the Toronto Eaton Centre, a modern shopping mall, Mr Greenjeans offers good food at reasonable prices in a relaxed and friendly atmosphere. Make sure you're really hungry, though, because the **servings** are huge! Salads are served in **flowerpots**, milkshakes come in **jugs** and to finish one of the **'mammoth' appetite**! If you do manage to **save room** for dessert, try A Dish Called Wanda – it includes nine **scoops** of ice cream!

B. Rainforest Café
For those of us who can't get to the real rainforest, Yorkdale shopping centre has the next best thing. The Rainforest Café's tropical menu offers such tasty **dishes** as the Jungle Safari Soup, Planet Earth Pasta and the Rain Forest Burger at very reasonable prices. The unusual decor includes **waterfalls**, huge **aquariums** and live parrots. The sound effects include all sorts of animal calls, and every half an hour there is a huge tropical **thunderstorm**.

C. The Old Spaghetti Factory
Imagine a huge **warehouse** with high ceilings, **gas lamps** and **stained glass** windows. Add an old streetcar and a working **carousel** that's over 100 years old, and you've got the Old Spaghetti Factory on The Esplanade. The service is great and the menu includes traditional pasta dishes such as spaghetti Bolognese and lasagne. Salad or soup, freshly **baked** bread, ice cream and **bottomless** cups of tea, coffee and soft drinks are all **included** in the unbelievably low price of the main courses, which **range** from $8.99 to $14.99.

D. Captain John's Harbour Boat Restaurant
In Toronto harbour there is a beautiful ship, over 300 feet long with five **decks**. This is Captain John's Harbour Boat Restaurant. In this quiet, romantic atmosphere you can enjoy the **gentle rocking** of the boat as you taste some of the best seafood dishes in the city. The prices are a bit expensive but definitely worth it.

E. Sassafraz
One of the most popular but expensive places to eat is Sassafraz in Yorkville. It offers delicious French and Californian **cuisine** in beautiful surroundings. Many **celebrities** choose to eat in the Garden Room, where there are statues, trees **growing** through the floor, a **fountain** and a 40-foot-high glass roof. So, for that once-in-a-lifetime occasion, come to Sassafraz and **dine** in the sun or under the stars while listening to **lively** jazz music.

F. 360: The Restaurant at the Tower
Located in the CN **Tower**, the tallest tower in the world, the restaurant offers the best **view** of Toronto and Lake Ontario. 300 metres above the ground, it slowly **revolves** so that the view outside the windows is **constantly** changing. If you are looking for excellent service, reasonable prices and fine dining in a formal atmosphere, come to 360 – you'll feel on top of the world.

7b Vocabulary Practice

Supermarket shopping

1 a. List two things you usually buy from each supermarket section below.

1. Dairy Products
2. Frozen Food
3. Snacks and Sweets
4. Drinks
5. Fruit and Vegetables
6. Bakery
7. Tinned Food
8. Rice and Pasta
9. Meat and Poultry

b. In pairs, ask and answer questions.

A: *Excuse me, I need to buy some apples. Where can I find them?*
B: *In the Fruit and Vegetables section. That's in aisle 5.*

▶ Reading & Listening

2 a. What type of text can you see below? Where might you find it?

b. Explain the verbs in the list. Use them to complete the gaps. Listen and check.

• pour • sprinkle • cook • put • simmer • add
• fry • chop • drain

c. Read the text. What do the following abbreviations mean?

• 2 tbsps • 2 tsps • 250 g
• 8 mins

GAME

Read the recipe aloud. Your partner mimes the actions. The best mime wins.

Cooking methods

3 How do you like to eat the food in the pictures? Ask and answer.

• fried • baked • boiled
• grilled • roasted • scrambled
• mashed • steamed

eggs — potatoes — vegetables
fish — chicken — rice
lamb — beef

A: *How do you like your eggs – boiled or fried?*
B: *Actually, I prefer them scrambled.*

Pasta with Tomato sauce

Ingredients

For the sauce
2 medium onions
5 small mushrooms
2-3 tbsps of olive oil
3 chopped tomatoes
1/4 litre of water
2 tsps dried basil
2 tsps dried oregano
a pinch of salt and pepper

For the pasta
250 g pasta
2 litres of boiling water
salt

some grated
Parmesan cheese
for topping

• Make the tomato sauce:

1) .... the onions and 2) .... them gently in a little olive oil with the mushrooms. 3) .... the chopped tomatoes, basil, oregano, salt and pepper. 4) .... the sauce for about 20-25 mins.

• Make the spaghetti:

5) .... the pasta into boiling, salted water and 6) .... for about 8 mins. When cooked, 7) .... the water and place the pasta on a warm plate.
8) .... the sauce over the pasta. 9) .... some cheese on top and serve.

serves 4

7b

Tastes
▶ **Speaking**

• spicy • bitter • sour • sweet • creamy
• salty • juicy • hot • strong

4 a. What do the food items in the pictures taste like?

- nuts
- melon
- mayonnaise
- grapefruit
- pickles
- lemons
- cherries
- garlic
- olives
- honey
- grapes
- vinegar
- chilli peppers
- beef sausages
- crisps

Nuts are salty.

b. Use the sentences to discuss in pairs.

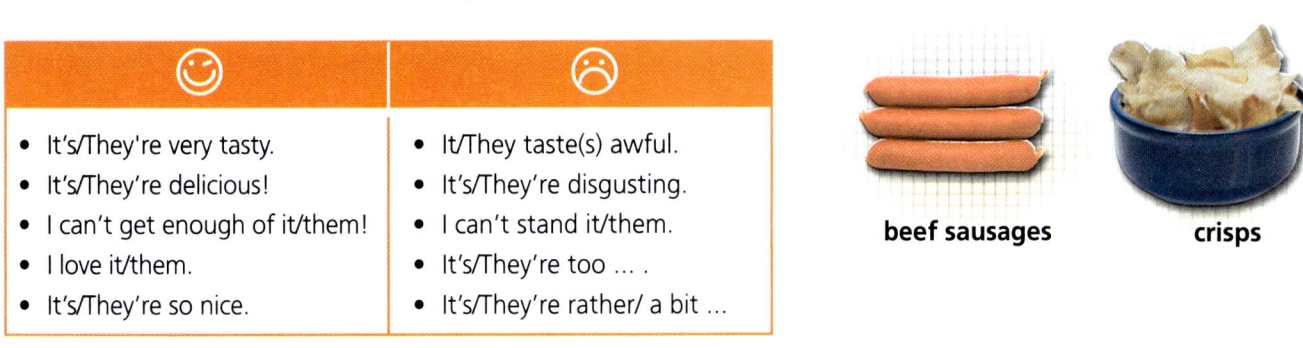

😉	☹
• It's/They're very tasty.	• It/They taste(s) awful.
• It's/They're delicious!	• It's/They're disgusting.
• I can't get enough of it/them!	• I can't stand it/them.
• I love it/them.	• It's/They're too … .
• It's/They're so nice.	• It's/They're rather/ a bit …

A: Do you like nuts?
B: Not really. They're too salty for me. And you?
A: Oh, I can't get enough of them!/I don't like them.

Cutlery, crockery & appliances

5 Mark the items **CU** (for cutlery), **CR** (for crockery) or **A** (for appliance). Make sentences.

1 plate *CR*   2 blender *A*   3 teaspoon *CU*
4 mug .....   5 jug .....   6 saucer .....   7 toaster .....
8 serving dish ....   9 soup bowl .....   10 glass .....
11 tablespoon .....   12 kettle .....
13 dessert fork .....   14 carving knife ......

- We use a plate to serve food on.

Quantities of food

6 Match the words, then ask and answer in pairs.

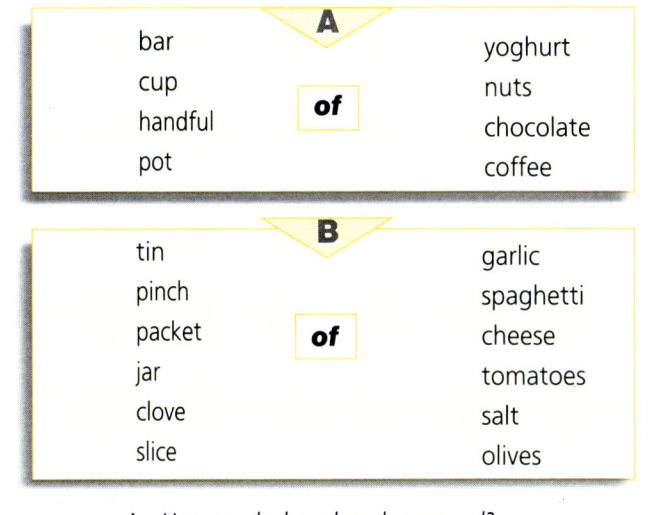

A

bar		yoghurt
cup		nuts
handful	of	chocolate
pot		coffee

B

tin		garlic
pinch		spaghetti
packet	of	cheese
jar		tomatoes
clove		salt
slice		olives

A: How much chocolate do we need?
B: One bar will be enough. / Just one bar.

✍ **Writing**

Portfolio: A cookery magazine has asked you to write the recipe for a typical dish from your country (50-60 words). You can use the recipe in Ex. 2 as a model.

81

7c Grammar in use

Countable and uncountable nouns
Grammar Reference

1 Put the words in the box under the correct heading.

Countable: *pea*, ...
Uncountable: *popcorn*, ...

- popcorn • pea • onion • peach
- lobster • cereal • water • bread
- yoghurt • salmon • meat • salt
- spring onions • cauliflower • wine
- ketchup • lettuce • cheese
- mustard • cabbage • celery

	Countable	Uncountable	Positive Sentences	Negative Sentences	Interrogative Sentences
some	✓	✓	✓		✓
any					
much					
many					
a lot of					
(a) few					
(a) little					
no					

2 Circle the uncountable nouns then make sentences using them.

news, money, furniture, apple, children, information, hair, banana, luggage, house, advice, pear, milk, pasta, time, photo, rice, traffic

Quantifiers
Grammar Reference

3 Fill in: *some, any, much, many, (a) little, (a) few, a lot, no*, then complete the table. Make sentences for each use.

1 How .... pasta do you need?
2 There's .... yoghurt left! We must buy some.
3 We need .... of onions in order to make this dish.
4 How .... pears do we need?
5 Is there .... cheese left? Yes, there's quite ....
6 We have very .... tomatoes left, I'm afraid.
7 There are only .... cherries left. Shall we buy some?
8 There is only .... olive oil left. We must buy ....
9 Don't put too .... salt in the water.
10 Would you like .... tea?

▶ Listening

4 a. Mrs Turner asked her husband to buy some things from the supermarket. Look at the list then listen. What did Mr Turner get wrong?

Shopping List
1 kilo of onions
4 green peppers
5 bananas
2 bottles of mineral water
2 kilos of sugar
3 packets of cereal
1 cauliflower
8 bread rolls
6 eggs
1 litre of milk

b. Read the sentences (1-6). Listen again. Why is Mrs Turner annoyed with her husband? Complete the sentences with: *any, no, too little, too few, too much, too many*.

1 There aren't .... green peppers.
2 He bought .... bananas.
3 There is .... sugar.
4 There is .... cauliflower.
5 He got .... eggs.
6 He bought .... milk.

5 Use *some/any/no/every + body/thing/where* to fill in the gaps.

1 A: Let's go .... quiet and relaxing to eat.
   B: What about that little bistro on the riverside?
2 A: Did you book a table for tomorrow?
   B: I called the restaurant but .... answered. I'll try later.
3 A: Did you enjoy your meal, sir?
   B: .... was fine, thank you.
4 A: Do you know .... who comes from Japan?
   B: I do, actually. There is a Japanese boy in my English class.
5 A: Could you get me some butter from the supermarket?
   B: Sure. Is there .... else you'd like?

7c

▶ *Reading*

6 Look at the title and the picture.

1. Where do you think the story takes place?
2. Who might the main characters be?
3. Why could it be a meal to remember?

Read and check your answers.

Past perfect (continuous)
Grammar Reference

7 Read the text and find examples of an action which happened in the past before another past action.

8 Complete the sentences using the past perfect.

1. We started eating after ....
2. She didn't come with us because ....
3. By the time we reached the restaurant ....
4. There was no more cheese as ....

> The past perfect continuous is the past equivalent of the present perfect continuous.

9 Compare the examples. Which expresses a visible result in the present/past? Which emphasises duration in the present/past?

1. a She's still at the bus stop. She has been waiting for an hour for the bus to come.
   b She had been waiting for an hour before the bus came.
2. a Her eyes are red because she has been crying.
   b Her eyes were red because she had been crying.

10 Make full sentences using the past perfect continuous and the past simple.

1. She/wait/half an hour/before/they/take/order
2. She/be tired/because/she/cook/all morning
3. He/drive/long time/when/realise/he/be lost
4. The boys/be/out of breath/because/they/play football/all afternoon
5. He/be exhausted/because/he type/letters/since morning

Sentence transformations

11 Use the word in bold to complete the second sentence so that it means the same as the first. Use no more than three words.

A meal to remember

Last Friday evening we decided to try out a new restaurant which had recently opened in the centre of town. It was raining quite heavily, but luckily we managed to find a parking space right outside the restaurant. The restaurant was quite busy, but we had made a reservation, so the waitress took us straight to our table. We had a wonderful meal – the service was excellent and the food was delicious. After we had finished our meal, we asked for the bill. It was then that I realised I had left my wallet in the car. My wife stayed in the restaurant and I went outside to get my wallet. Imagine my surprise when I saw that my car was gone!

1. There are only a few apples left. **many**
   There .... apples left.
2. Jane washed the dishes and then went to bed. **after**
   Jane went to bed .... washed the dishes.
3. I was surprised at how good the food was. **expected**
   I .... the food to be so good.
4. We have run out of cheese. **any**
   There .... cheese left.

Phrasal verbs

12 Explain the phrasal verbs, then fill in the correct particle in each of the sentences.

1. The fridge is giving .... a terrible smell.
2. He promised not to give .... my secret.
3. I must give .... chocolate to lose weight.
4. John gave Sam .... the money he owed him.

give: back, out, in, up, away, off

✏ Writing

Portfolio: Write your shopping list for a typical week. Compare your list with your partner.

83

7d Listening & Speaking skills

Eating out

1 Look at the advertisements. How are they related? Where might you see them?

A

Peter's

"Dining in Style"

Twilight Dinner Special
5:00 pm – 7:00 pm
$20.00 + tax + tip

Great food, wonderful service, relaxed atmosphere

Lunch 12 pm – 2:30 pm Monday-Friday
Dinner 7 pm – 10 pm Monday-Sunday

– Live Music every Friday –
Catering available for functions off premises

328 Main St • Eastchester, NY • (914) 961-5577
★ Open 7 days a week   ★ Parking

B

11:00 am to 11:30 pm
(closed Monday)

502 Apple Road
Eastchester, NY 10709

914-961-5656

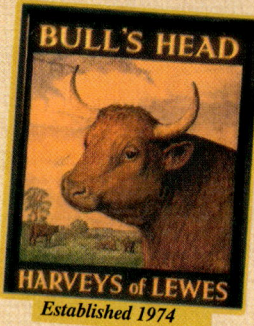

BULL'S HEAD
HARVEYS of LEWES
Established 1974

"The Best Beef in Town"

C

The Blue Moon
70 Park Road, Eastchester, New York
Phone: 914-961-2525   Fax: 914-961-2526

Lunch and Dinner Daily

LIVE Music Every Friday & Saturday Night

KARAOKE Night every Wednesday with DJ Mark
Karaoke Contest – Cash Prizes

PARTY ROOMS AVAILABLE FOR ALL OCCASIONS

2 Which place(s) (A-C) …
1 specialises in one kind of meat?
2 is open six days a week?
3 have performances by singers and musicians?
4 has a weekly competition?
5 will provide food for a party at your home?

3 Work in pairs. Imagine you want to eat out. Choose an advert (A-C) and ask and answer questions about it. Use the prompts:
- which/restaurant?
- where/be?
- what/be/like?
- when/be/open?
- book/table?

Verbs with prepositions

4 Fill in: *with, for, to, of, about* then make sentences related to food.

1 begin ....;   2 complain ....;   3 consist ....;
4 wait ....;   5 apologise .... sb .... sth

How about mushroom soup to begin with?

Table manners

5 a. You will hear someone talking about good table manners in Russian restaurants. Listen and choose the correct answers.

1 Don't eat too much of the first course as
  A there will be many courses to follow.
  B you are expected to eat very little.
  C all the courses will be delicious.

2 In the restaurant, it's not polite to
  A put your hands on the table.
  B sit in the corner of the room.
  C keep your coat on.

3 You should get the waiter's attention by
  A calling.   B waving.   C looking at him.

4 The first toast of the evening should be made by
  A the host.   B the honoured guest.   C a lady.

5 When someone asks you for a knife, you should
  A put it in their hand.   B place it on the table.
  C hold it in your hand.

b. In pairs, compare table manners in your country with table manners in Russia.

▶ *Pronunciation (stressed syllables)*

6 Listen and underline the stressed syllables. Say the sentences in full.

1 Still or sparkling?   2 Ready to order?   3 Help yourself.
4 Rare, medium or well done?   5 Milk and sugar?

84

Ordering a meal

7 a. Read the first few lines of the dialogue. Where are Tony and Julia?

b. Listen and read. Look at the menu and underline what each person orders. How much will they pay in total?

Waiter: Good evening. Are you ready to order, sir?
Tony: I think so. Julia, what would you like?
Julia: I'll have the chef's salad, please, followed by the baked salmon and egg pie.
Waiter: And for you, sir?
Tony: I'd like the mushroom soup, please. And for the main course, I'll have the pasta.
Waiter: Fine. And for dessert?
Julia: Chocolate pudding for me, please. Tony?
Tony: I'll have the fruit salad.
Waiter: And would you like anything to drink?
Tony: Yes – mineral water for Julia and a cola for me, please.
Waiter: Thank you, sir.

Dinner Menu

Starters
* Mushroom soup $4.95
* Chef's salad $4.65
* Seafood cocktail $6.30
* Cream cheese tart $5.45

Main Courses
* Roast lamb with steamed vegetables $11.65
* Pasta with fresh tomato sauce $9.85
* Spicy grilled chicken with fried potatoes .. $11.65
* Baked salmon and egg pie $11.65

Desserts
* Tropical fruit salad $4.85
* Chocolate pudding $4.65
* Strawberry and vanilla ice cream $3.45

* Fresh fruit juice $1.25   * Soft Drinks $1.60
* Mineral water $0.75   * Tea or coffee $1.60

8 **Portfolio:** Imagine you are at the same restaurant. In groups of three, take roles and act out similar dialogues. Use the dinner menu. Record your dialogues.

StudySkills

Describing pictures effectively

When you describe a picture, use adjectives. This makes your description more interesting.

Describing pictures

9 a. Look at Picture A, then read the text and underline the adjectives. What makes the description interesting?

In this picture there are two smartly dressed people sitting at a table in a restaurant. They may be celebrating something, or they may be colleagues having dinner together. They are talking to a waiter. He looks helpful. There are lots of dishes on the table. The food looks delicious. The restaurant has a stylish decor. It looks quite expensive to me. The people seem to be enjoying their meal.

b. Describe Picture B to your partner. Think about:

- people & clothes
- place
- reason for being there
- activities
- people's feelings

Use adjectives.

FUN TIME

Waiter, what's this fly doing in my soup?

Looks as if it's trying to get out, sir.

85

7e Writing a story

Getting started

1 *When setting the scene of a story, we need to decide on the characters, the place, the time and the action.* Look at the picture, read the beginning and answer the questions.

> It was a lovely sunny afternoon. Bill and Ann were having a picnic in the park with their dog, Snowy. They felt very relaxed. "It's so good to get out of the house for a change", said Ann.

1 Who are the main characters in the story?
2 Where are they?
3 What are they doing?
4 When does the story take place?
5 What is the weather like?

2 *We can end a story by referring to the characters' feelings.* Read the ending. How do the characters feel in the end?

> Bill and Ann put their picnic blanket on the living room floor and sat down. They were relieved to be out of the rain and glad that their food was still dry. "Perhaps being in the house isn't so bad after all," said Bill.

Let's look closer

3 Read the title and think of a beginning and an ending. Then, read the story and put the paragraphs into the correct order. How does Martin feel in the end?

An Unexpected Surprise!

A Extremely disappointed, he went into the living room and sat on the sofa. Imagine his surprise when, picking up the TV remote control, he saw a little note stuck to it, saying: "Now that I have your attention … Happy Anniversary! Meet me at Les Quatres Saisons at 8.30pm for a special dinner." He had just enough time to make it!

B Martin opened the front door slowly. All was quiet. "Good, she's not here yet," he thought. He went straight into the kitchen and put down the heavy bags of shopping.

C Busily chopping, slicing and frying, Martin finally got everything ready. He felt proud and excited. However, by 7 o'clock there was still no sign of Fiona. Later, looking at the clock, Martin saw it was almost 8 and finally lost his temper. "At least I can watch the news", he thought.

D He pulled out the recipe he had found on the Internet. It had seemed quite difficult, but the lady at the supermarket had explained everything to him. "Fiona will love the surprise anniversary dinner," he thought. His wife always prepared the meals but tonight was going to be different!

4 Which of the following has the writer used to make the story more interesting? In pairs, find and underline examples of:

- variety of adjectives/adverbs
- present participles (-ing)/past participles (-ed)
- characters' exact words (direct speech)

Your turn

StudySkills

Organising ideas into paragraphs

When you write a story, organise your ideas into paragraphs. This helps you to create a logical structure and guides your reader through your story.

5 Look at the rubric and answer the questions in the plan. Then write your story (100-120 words).

> Your English teacher has asked you to write a story with the title: *A Dinner Party*.

Plan

Introduction (Para 1)
How will you start your story? Who are the main characters? Where are they? When does the story take place?

Main Body (Paras 2-3)
What happens first? What happens next? What's the climax event?

Conclusion (Para 4)
What happens in the end? How do the characters feel?

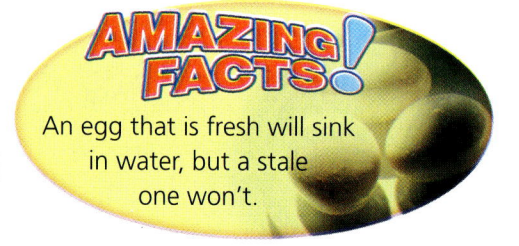

Amazing Facts!

An egg that is fresh will sink in water, but a stale one won't.

Literature Corner 7

▶ Reading & Listening

1 What is strange about the picture? Read the text below and say who the people are.

Roald Dahl (1916-1990) was a popular British author who first became a successful writer of short stories for adults. Then he began writing books for children and one of his best known is **Charlie and the Chocolate Factory**.

Charlie lives next to Mr Wonka's mysterious chocolate factory which nobody has ever been inside. Then five lucky children win a ticket to visit the factory. Charlie is one of them. Each child can take an adult with them, so Charlie goes with his Grandpa Joe.

2 Read the signs on the doors. What is behind each door? Listen and read to find out.

3 Read the extract and explain the highlighted words. The writer plays with the words '*look round*'. How does he use them?

▶ Speaking

4 In pairs, think of another room for Mr Wonka's chocolate factory. What is in the room?

Down the Chocolate River

A steamy mist was rising up from the great warm chocolate river. "Look, Grandpa!" cried Charlie. "There's a door in the wall!" It was set into the wall of the tunnel just above the level of the river. STOREROOM No 54, it said. ALL THE CREAMS – DAIRY CREAM, WHIPPED CREAM, VIOLET CREAM, COFFEE CREAM, PINEAPPLE CREAM, VANILLA CREAM AND HAIR CREAM.

The boat stopped. Mr Wonka stepped out. The children and their parents all scrambled after him. Grandpa Joe and Charlie were half running and half walking to keep up with Mr Wonka, but they were able to read what it said on the doors as they hurried by.

HOT ICE CREAM FOR COLD DAYS, it said on the next door. "Extremely useful in the winter," said Mr Wonka, rushing on. "Hot ice cream warms you up no end in freezing weather. I also make hot ice cubes for putting in hot drinks. Hot ice cubes make hot drinks hotter."

COWS THAT GIVE CHOCOLATE MILK, it said on the next door. "Ah, my pretty little cows!" cried Mr Wonka. "How I love those cows!"

On the next door, it said, SQUARE SWEETS THAT LOOK ROUND. "Wait!" cried Mr Wonka. "I am very proud of my square sweets that look round. Let's take a peek."

The top half of the door was made of glass. Grandpa Joe lifted Charlie up so that he could get a better view, and looking in, Charlie saw a long table, and on the table there were rows and rows of small white square-shaped sweets. Each of them had a funny little pink face painted on one side.

"There you are!" cried Mr Wonka. "Square sweets that look round!"

"They don't look round to me," said Mike Teavee.

"They look square," said Veruca Salt. "They look completely square."

"But they *are* square," said Mr Wonka. "I never said they weren't."

"You said they were round!" said Veruca Salt.

"I never said anything of the sort," said Mr Wonka.

"But they *don't* look round!" said Veruca. "They look square!"

"They look round," insisted Mr Wonka.

"They most certainly don't look round!" cried Veruca Salt.

Mr Wonka took a key from his pocket, and unlocked the door, and flung it open ... and suddenly, at the sound of the door opening, all the rows of little square sweets looked quickly round to see who was coming in. The tiny faces actually turned towards the door and stared at Mr Wonka.

"There you are!" he cried triumphantly. "They're looking round! There's no doubt about it! They are square sweets that look round!"

"By golly, he's right!" said Grandpa Joe.

87

8a Fit for Life

Lead-in

1 Match the races to the countries they are held in. Is there a famous race in your country?

The Monaco Grand Prix is held in Monaco.

A — Monaco Grand Prix
B — Dragon Boat Race
C — London Marathon
D — Iditarod Trail Sled Dog Race
E — Kentucky Derby

1 the USA (2)
2 the UK
3 China
4 Monaco

to be	to have
strong/fit/brave/well-trained/ disciplined/competitive/fast/ organised/careful/patient/ determined	stamina/ a sense of direction/ lots of determination a sense of adventure

A: In my opinion, you probably need to be very fit and strong to take part in this race. What do you think?
B: I agree. You also need to have a sense of adventure.

StudySkills

Reading: Self-assessment

After you read, think about how difficult the text was for you. Think about: unknown words, style, grammar structures, and the reading task.

4 Read the article and mark each statement *(T)* True or *(F)* False. Then, explain the highlighted words. How difficult was the text for you?

1 The Iditarod Trail Sled Dog Race is famous all over the world.
2 Only people from Alaska may enter the race.
3 The rules say how far each sled should run every day.
4 Mushers must have determination and be well-organised.
5 Dog sleds are still more popular than snowmobiles in Alaska.
6 The race has saved a part of the traditional way of life in Alaska.
7 The race follows the same route every year.
8 The race is named after a village in the area.

Listening

2 🎧 Listen to some friends taking part in a sport. Can you guess the sport? How do they feel?

Reading

3 a. Look at the title and the pictures. What do you think the article is about?

b. Read the introduction and conclusion to the article. What qualities do you think you need to take part in this race? Use the prompts to discuss.

Speaking

5 🎧 Listen and read, then list three reasons why the Iditarod is difficult to complete. In pairs, discuss whether or not you would take part in such a race, giving reasons.

Writing

Portfolio: Imagine you are in Iditarod to watch the race. Send a postcard to your friend. Include:

• information about the race (mushers, dogs, route)
• what the weather is like   • how you feel

The Last Great Race

The dogs and drivers (mushers) line up for the start of the race. You can feel the excitement in the air. The dogs paw the ground anxious to be off, while the mushers make last-minute preparations for the long trek ahead. The onlookers cheer and encourage them. This sled race is known internationally to be one of the longest and toughest sled races in the world. It's the Iditarod Trail Sled Dog Race in Alaska, USA. It has become very popular over the years with over 65 teams taking part from Alaska as well as many other countries.

The Mushers
The musher is the person who drives the sled and guides the dogs. Each musher must decide how many miles to run every day, what to eat on the trail and the best places to stop and rest. A good musher has to be disciplined and really want to win this race.

The Dogs
The perfect sled dog is the Alaskan Husky with its thick fur and strong legs. Each dog must be healthy, so vets examine them carefully before the race begins. These dogs were originally used to transport goods and mail all over Alaska. However, when people started using snowmobiles, travelling by sled became less popular. This traditional form of transport seemed to be dying out until the Iditarod Race was started in 1973.

The Route
The race goes from Anchorage to Nome on the west coast. It passes through more than twenty towns on its way there. The route is extremely challenging, crossing icy rivers and lakes, mountains and valleys. It varies slightly, depending on the year. In odd-numbered years the route goes south after Ophir to include the village of Iditarod, while in even-numbered years it goes north through Ruby and Galena.

Do you love a challenge? Can you cope with bad weather conditions? Can you travel over snow and ice for many hours? Do you like dogs? If you answered *yes* to these questions, then this race is for you! Get your snow boots on and head for Alaska!

Try this!

In pairs, prepare and act out an interview with a musher. Record yourselves.

8b Vocabulary Practice

Sports

▶ **Listening**

1 a. Listen to the sounds. Which sports do they match? Number the pictures in the order you hear them.

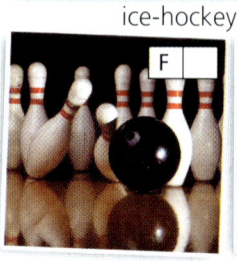

A basketball
B cricket
C baseball
D ice-hockey
E boxing
F bowling
G skateboarding
H rugby

b. Which of these are *team sports (T)* and which are *individual sports (I)*? Which sport(s) do you play?

2 a. Study the tip then complete the dialogue.

> We use: **'play'** with most ball games (*e.g. football*); **'go'** with most sports ending in 'ing' (*e.g. swimming*); **'do'** with other sporting activities and martial arts (*e.g. athletics, gymnastics, aerobics, karate, boxing*).

A: Do you play any sports, Bob?
B: Yes, I .... volleyball. How about you?
A: Well, I've never .... volleyball, but I .... gymnastics and I sometimes .... windsurfing.
B: Windsurfing? That sounds like fun! Have you ever .... skiing?
A: No, I haven't – but I'd like to try.
B: So would I! Why don't we .... skiing this weekend?
A: That's a great idea!

▶ **Speaking**

b. Choose sports from Ex. 1a and act out similar dialogues in pairs.

Sport injuries

3 a. Match the collocations. Have you ever had any of these problems while playing sports?

to pull — an ankle
to break — a muscle
to twist — a leg
to sprain — a wrist

b. Read the dialogue. In pairs, use the prompts in Ex. 3a to act out similar dialogues.

A: What's the matter?
B: I pulled a muscle in my (leg/neck/back, etc).
A: Really? How?
B: While I was playing football.

Adjectives with prepositions

4 Complete the sentences with *of*, *with*, *in* or *to*. Then use these phrases to make sentences related to sports you enjoy.

1 The hockey coach was **dissatisfied** .... his team's performance.

2 I was **proud** .... my team when they won the championship.

3 The rules of American football appear to be **similar** .... the rules of rugby.

4 Be **careful** .... the dog.

5 The captain got **angry** .... the referee for not giving a penalty.

6 Mary never gets nervous before a big match. She is **experienced** .... playing in front of huge crowds.

8b

Sports places

5 a. Complete the map of Astley Sports Club with words from the list.

- ring • pool • hall
- alley • course
- pitch • court

b. In pairs, ask and answer, as in the example.

A: *Can you go skateboarding at the Astley Sports Club?*
B: *Yes. It's got a great/huge skate park.*

Astley Sports Club

- A — football ....
- B — golf ....
- C — skate *park* (roller skating, skateboarding)
- D — snooker .... (snooker, billiards)
- E — boxing ....
- F — bowling ....
- G — swimming .... (swimming, diving, water polo)
- H — ice *rink* (ice skating, ice hockey)
- I — tennis ....
- J — basketball *court*
- K — running *track*
- L — Shopping and Information Centre

Messages

▶ **Reading**

6 a. What type of text (1-3) is each? Where could you see them?

b. Read and choose the correct explanation (A-C).

1

memo
To: All club members
From: The management

There is no hot water after 9:45pm, so don't use the showers after that unless you want a cold one!

A Members cannot use the showers after 9:45pm.
B Members can have a hot shower after 9:45pm.
C Members can only have a cold shower after 9:45pm.

2

THIS POOL IS FOR CHILDREN UNDER 10 ONLY

A Only children up to ten years old can swim here.
B Only ten children at a time can swim here.
C Only children between 6 and 10 years old can swim here.

3

John – your karate class will be on Monday evening this week instead of Tuesday, but back to normal next week.

John's karate class …
A will be on a Tuesday for the next two weeks.
B will be on Mondays from now on.
C will be on a different day this week.

Writing

Portfolio: Use the reminder to write a short message to Carol about the changes in her tennis lessons. Use text 3 in Ex. 6 as a model.

Must remember to tell Carol
TUE 6:30 — lesson **CANCELLED**
FRI 5:30 - 6:30 instead
Just for this week!

91

8c Grammar in use

The passive

▶ **Listening** Grammar Reference

1 a. Do the sports quiz, then listen and check your answers.

Are you a true sports fan?

1 If you hear the umpire call "love-forty", which sport **is being played**?
   A basketball   B football   C tennis

2 Which country **was** the 2002 Football World Cup **won** by?
   A England   B Brazil   C France

3 Which country **has been awarded** the highest number of medals throughout the history of the Olympics?
   A the USA   B Germany   C China

4 In athletics, what do we call the long distance race which **is run** over 26.2 miles (42.1 km)?
   A a marathon   B a decathlon   C a pentathlon

5 In which sport **must** a lifejacket **be worn** at each training session?
   A swimming   B water polo   C canoeing

b. Say what the passive verb forms in bold are.

2 Fill in the missing passive or active forms. How do we form the passive? When do we use it?

Active	Passive
• They **hold** the Olympics every four years.	• The Olympics 1) .... every four years.
• They **are installing** new equipment in the gym.	• New equipment 2) .... in the gym.
• The mayor 3) .... the new gym.	• The new gym **will be opened** by the mayor.
• TV producers 4) .... this sport on TV before.	• This sport **has not been broadcast** on TV before.
• The organisers **cancelled** the competition.	• The competition 5) .... by the organisers.
• A reporter **was interviewing** Ronaldo in his home.	• Ronaldo 6) .... by a reporter in his home.
• You 7) .... those old trainers.	• Those old trainers **should be thrown out**.

▶ Reading

3 Match the texts (1-5) to the places you could read them (A-E). Expand the texts into full sentences using the passive.

1 ☐ KEEP OUT OF REACH OF CHILDREN

2 ☐ TODAY'S MATCH POSTPONED DUE TO BAD WEATHER

3 ☐ NO DOGS ALLOWED ON PITCH

4 ☐ REFRESHMENTS INCLUDED IN TICKET PRICE

5 ☐ ALL FORMS TO BE RECEIVED BEFORE 31st MAY

A on a poster
B on a bottle of medicine
C on a noticeboard
D on a sign
E on an application form

1 *B Medicine must be kept out of reach of children.*

4 Fill in **with** or **by**.

1 His wall was covered .... pictures of basketball stars.
2 The race was won .... a 20-year-old driver.
3 The athlete's wound was cleaned .... some surgical spirit.
4 The plan to build a new stadium was rejected .... the Town Council.
5 The team's uniforms were made .... a local company.

5 Complete these rules of karate, using the passive.

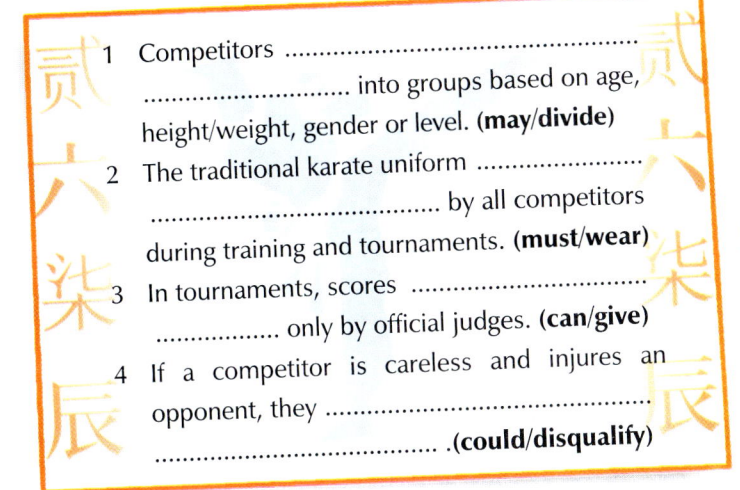

1. Competitors .... into groups based on age, height/weight, gender or level. (**may/divide**)
2. The traditional karate uniform .... by all competitors during training and tournaments. (**must/wear**)
3. In tournaments, scores .... only by official judges. (**can/give**)
4. If a competitor is careless and injures an opponent, they ....(**could/disqualify**)

Conditionals: type 0, 1

Grammar Reference

6 a. Read the sentences. Which refers to: a general truth? a probable situation in the future?

A: If water freezes, it turns into ice.

B: If it stops snowing, we'll go skiing.

b. Complete the rules.

Type	Condition	Main Clause
0	If/When + ...,	present simple
1	If + present simple,	imperative OR can, will, may, etc + bare infinitive

7 Expand the sentences. What type is each?

1 heat ice / melt; **2** not exercise regularly / put on weight; **3** miss the train / take a taxi; **4** buy a sports car/ pay higher insurance; **5** heat metal / expand; **6** rain / not go out; **7** iron get wet / rust

1 *If/When you heat ice, it melts. (Type 0)*

GAME

Choose a leader. Imagine he/she will give a ticket to Hawaii to the person who makes the funniest promise. In teams make a funny promise. The winner is the one who makes the funniest promise.

Team A S1: *If you give me a ticket to Hawaii, I'll juggle three ice cream cones.*

8 Complete the conditional sentences.

1. Don't wait for me if ....
2. If we leave now, ...
3. If you feel sick, ...
4. She won't join us if ....
5. If you study, ...

9 Study the examples. Then, rewrite the sentences using *if* and *unless*.

unless = if not

1. Train regularly or else you won't be ready in May.
   *If you **don't train** regularly, you won't be ready in May.*
   *Unless you **train** regularly, you won't be ready in May.*
2. Listen to the coach or you won't know what to do.
3. You need to be a member to be able to exercise in the gym.
4. We'd better hurry or we'll miss the start of the match.
5. You must register to be able to enter the race.

Sentence transformations

10 Complete the second sentence so that it means the same as the first. Use up to three words.

1. He can't see without his glasses.
   He can't see .... his glasses.
2. Wear your helmet or else you'll get injured.
   You won't get injured .... your helmet.
3. She'll be late if she doesn't leave now.
   She won't get there in time .... now.

Phrasal verbs

11 Explain the phrasal verbs, then fill in the correct particles.

bring — back, out, round, about, up

1. The publisher brought .... a book on football.
2. It took the coach several minutes to bring the unconscious player ....
3. This song brings .... childhood memories.
4. She brought .... her children by herself.

Writing

Portfolio: Use the quiz in Ex. 1 as a model to write your own sports quiz. Use the passive.

8d Listening & Speaking skills

Doing sports

1 a. Look at the picture. Listen to the sounds. What images come to mind?

b. Which of these statements about sailing do you agree with? Give reasons.

> There's nothing more relaxing than being out on the water.

> It's quite dangerous, specially when there's a storm or the weather gets rough.

▶ Listening

2 Listen to the conversation between Jim and Melanie about sailing. Then decide if the statements (1-6) are correct or incorrect. Tick the box *Yes* or *No*.

		Yes	No
1	Melanie paid a lot of money to go sailing.	☐	☐
2	Jim doesn't feel well when he's on boats.	☐	☐
3	Melanie finds sailing relaxing.	☐	☐
4	Jim would be scared of bad weather if he was on a boat.	☐	☐
5	Melanie liked sleeping on the boat.	☐	☐
6	Jim decides to go sailing.	☐	☐

Negotiating

3 You want to go to a sporting event *(e.g. a football match)* this Saturday with your friend.

- invite him/her to come with you
- turn down his/her other suggestion *(e.g. to a tennis match)*
- suggest a compromise *(e.g. go bowling instead)*

Describing pictures

4 a. Describe the picture to your partner. Think about:

- where the people are
- what they are wearing
- what they are doing
- how they feel

STUDY SKILLS

Supporting your opinion

When answering questions always support your opinions with reasons or examples. Use linkers such as *because, since as,* etc.

b. Look at the picture again and answer the questions. Use the phrases in the box.

Expressing opinions
• In my opinion/view ...   • I don't think that ...
• I feel ...   • I strongly believe ...
• I think ...   • I'd say .../I wouldn't say ...

1 How dangerous is this sport? Why (not)?
2 Why do some people choose to do dangerous sports?
3 Would you do a sport like this? Why (not)?

94

At the doctor's

▶ Reading

5 a. Look at the first column of the dialogue. Who might ask these kinds of questions? To whom might they be speaking? Where are the people?

b. Complete the dialogue by matching responses A-D to the spaces (1-4). Listen and check. In pairs, read the dialogue aloud.

D: Hello, Mr Harris. What seems to be the matter?
P: 1) ....
D: How long has it been bothering you?
P: 2) ....
D: Do you have any history of this kind of trouble?
P: 3) ....
D: I see. Are you taking any medication at the moment?
P: 4) ....
D: OK, let's have a look at you. Could you please take off your shirt?

A No – just an aspirin from time to time to kill the pain.
B Good morning. I have a terrible backache.
C No, this is the first time. Actually, it all started after a game of tennis.
D Well ... about a couple of days.

c. What do you think Mr Harris' problem is? What will the doctor ask him to do? Discuss in pairs. Listen and check.

Sympathising – Giving advice

6 a. Read this short dialogue. Which phrases are used to: give advice? express sympathy? ask about health? describe health problems?

A: What's the matter?
B: I've got a really sore throat.
A: Oh dear. Perhaps you should see a doctor.

Asking about health	Describing health problems
• Are you all right? • You don't look well. What's wrong? • Is something wrong? • What's the matter?	• My ... is / are a bit sore. • My ... (really) hurts / aches. • I've got a ... .

Sympathising	Giving advice
• Oh dear. • Oh (no), that's awful. • I'm sorry to hear that. • That's terrible.	• You should ... . • You ought to ... . • Why don't you ... . • If I were you, I'd ... .

b. In pairs, use the prompts below and the table to act out similar dialogues.

• headache • toothache
• back hurts • leg aches

• rest • hot bath • aspirin
• dentist

Hesitating

▶ Intonation

7 a. Listen and repeat.

1 A: Do you have a healthy diet?
   B: **Um ... I guess so.**
2 A: Are you good at tennis?
   B: **You could say that.**
3 A: Do you like water sports?
   B: **Er, sort of.**
4 A: Would you agree that swimming can be dangerous?
   B: **In a way, yes.**

b. **Portfolio:** In pairs, make up similar short exchanges to find out about your partner's preferences on the following: *eating habits*, *sports*, *dangerous sports*. Use the table. Record yourselves.

Hesitation
• Um / Er / Well, ... • I suppose / I guess (so). • You could say that. • Sort of / Kind of. • Not really / exactly. • In a way.

FUN TIME

I'm nervous - this is the first operation I've ever had.

That's OK - this is the first operation I've ever performed.

95

8e Writing a pros & cons essay

Getting started

1 Read the speech bubbles. What topic are they about? Which is a positive/negative comment?

> **A** Horse riding is a great form of exercise.

> **B** There is a danger of falling while horse riding.

Let's look closer

2 Read the rubric and underline the key words. What information do they tell you about the:
– target reader? – type of writing?

- Your teacher has asked you to write an essay discussing the pros and cons of horse riding.

3 Read the essay. What is each paragraph about?

Horse riding is a popular activity with many people. Before taking it up as a hobby, though, there are certain pros and cons to be considered.

There are a number of advantages to taking up horse riding. **To begin with**, it is an enjoyable activity which one can do by oneself or with others. **Also**, it is a good form of exercise which can help you get fit.

On the other hand, there are some disadvantages to horse riding. **To start with**, it is rather expensive **because** lessons and equipment cost a lot. **In addition**, it can be rather dangerous as a rider can suffer serious injuries if they fall off the horse.

On the whole, although horse riding is expensive and quite dangerous, I believe it is great fun and good exercise. It might be dangerous but, if you can afford it, the experience is unique.

Topic/Supporting sentences

A **topic sentence** is the first sentence of a paragraph and contains the main idea or topic of the paragraph. The **supporting sentences** further develop this main idea.

---

4 Read the essay again and underline the topic sentences. What are the supporting sentences?

Linkers

5 Replace the linkers in bold in the text with words below.

Listing: Firstly, To begin/start with
Adding points: What is more, also, In addition, etc
Introducing Results/Examples: As a result, Therefore, Consequently, For this reason, because, As
Showing Contrast: Yet, However, But, Although
Conclude: To sum up, On the whole, All in all

StudySkills

Formulating your opinion

Brainstorm for arguments. Put them into two columns: pros and cons. This will help you explain your arguments and formulate your opinion.

Your turn

6 a. Read the rubric, underline the key words and think of other *for* and *against* points.

- Your teacher has asked you to write an essay discussing the advantages and disadvantages of going sailing. Write your essay.

For	Against
• a fun activity	• need to learn from an expert
• keeps you fit	• need expensive equipment

b. Answer the questions in the plan, then write your essay (100-120 words).

Plan

Introduction (Para 1)
How can you state the topic?
Main Body (Paras 2 & 3)
What pros/cons can you think of? How can you support them?
Conclusion (Para 4)
What is your opinion?

Amazing Facts!

The first Olympic Games (776 BC at Olympia) consisted of only one event, a 210-yard sprint known as the stadion.

Literature Corner 8

The Olympic Anthem

▶ **Reading & Listening**

1 How are the pictures related to the title? What do the rings on the flag stand for?

2 a. Do you know who wrote the Olympic Anthem? Why do you think it was written? Read the text and check.

b. What happened in 1893, 1896, 1958? Read the text again and find out.

3 Read the extract from the Olympic Anthem and match the words to their synonyms.

immortal	come down
antiquity	living forever/everlasting
descend	ancient times
shed	pour

▶ **Speaking**

4 🎧 Listen to the Olympic Anthem. How does it make you feel (*proud/patriotic/cheerful/positive/optimistic/inspired*)?

It makes me feel ...

5 Project Portfolio: Write a short poem about the Olympic Games.

The Olympic Anthem is played at the opening and closing ceremony of the Olympic Games. It has a long and interesting history, just like the Games themselves. It started out as the poem 'Ancient Immortal Spirit', written in 1893 by Kostis Palamas a famous Greek poet. In 1896, it was set to music by the famous Greek composer, Spyros Samaras. It was played at the first modern Olympic Games in Athens in 1896. Since then it has been translated into many languages and for many years different anthems were played at the Olympics. Then in 1958, the International Olympic Committee decided to adopt it as the official Olympic anthem, and it has been played at every Olympic Games ever since.

The Olympic Anthem

Immortal Spirit of antiquity,
Father of the true, beautiful, and good,
Descend, appear, shed over us Thy* light
Upon this ground and under this sky

**Thy = your*

Self-Assessment Module 4

Vocabulary & Grammar

1 Fill in the missing word.

1 I pulled a ……………… in my leg while playing football yesterday.
2 You can find fresh strawberries in the ………… and vegetables section, madam.
3 Can you buy me a ……………… of olives?
4 Let's ………… skateboarding this afternoon, shall we?
5 I'm afraid there are ……………… eggs left.
6 If I were you, I would give ………… smoking.
7 By the time we arrived, most of the food …… been eaten.
8 His book will be brought ………… next month.
9 These vegetables have not ………… cooked properly.
10 The walls are covered ………… nice paintings.

(10 marks)

2 Circle the correct item.

1 The new chef has brought ………… lots of changes at the restaurant.
   A up   B back   C about
2 Who's the player who ………… interviewed over there?
   A is being   B is   C should have
3 Kelly has been ………… aerobics for years.
   A playing   B doing   C going
4 How many ………… of garlic should I use?
   A cubes   B pinches   C cloves
5 At the end of the meal we asked for the ………… .
   A bill   B menu   C tip
6 He doesn't take ………… sugar in his coffee.
   A a lot   B much   C many
7 The milk is giving ………… a terrible smell.
   A out   B away   C off
8 I'm afraid I won't be able to come to football practice because I've ………… my ankle.
   A headed   B pulled   C twisted
9 Kevin isn't fond of ………… dishes; he doesn't even like salt and pepper on his food.
   A creamy   B spicy   C juicy

10 This salad tastes even better when you ………… some fresh herbs on top.
   A chop   B pour   C sprinkle

(10 marks)

Use of English

3 Complete the second sentence so that it means the same as the first. Use up to three words.

1 You cannot play this sport without a ball.
  This sport ……………………… without a ball.
2 Remember to book a table for Saturday.
  Don't ……………………… a table for Saturday.
3 I was surprised at how delicious the meal was.
  I hadn't ……………………… to be so delicious.
4 That fish smells awful.
  That fish is ……………………… an awful smell.
5 Unless you get more rest, you won't feel better.
  If you ……… more rest, you won't feel better.

(10 marks)

Communication

4 Complete the exchanges.

a Would you like still or sparkling?
b Er, I suppose so.
c Of course – help yourself.
d I've got a terrible headache.
e Why don't you see a doctor?
f Sure. Milk and sugar?

1 A: ………………………………………………
  B: Why don't you take an aspirin?
2 A: A bottle of mineral water, please.
  B: ………………………………………………
3 A: Have you been playing golf long?
  B: ………………………………………………
4 A: I've got a sore throat.
  B: ………………………………………………
5 A: May I have a bit more of that cake?
  B: ………………………………………………
6 A: I'd like a cup of coffee, please.
  B: ………………………………………………

(12 marks)

98

Self-Assessment Module 4

Listening

5 You will hear a radio review of a restaurant. For each question, put a tick (✓) in the correct box.

1 The Italian restaurant has
  A ☐ moved to the centre of the city.
  B ☐ only just opened.
  C ☐ changed its decor.

2 The restaurant is different from others because
  A ☐ it is spacious.
  B ☐ the atmosphere is very formal.
  C ☐ it has an unusual name.

3 All the food at Angelo's
  A ☐ looks beautiful.
  B ☐ tastes good.
  C ☐ is served with pasta.

4 What does the presenter says about the starters?
  A ☐ They are all very light.
  B ☐ There is a wide variety.
  C ☐ You can choose between hot or cold soup.

5 What does the presenter say about the desserts?
  A ☐ They are all delicious.
  B ☐ They are all homemade.
  C ☐ They aren't as good as the coffee.

6 The presenter recommends Angelo's
  A ☐ for romantic dinners only.
  B ☐ mainly for its pasta.
  C ☐ for anyone who wants a good meal.

(18 marks)

Reading

6 Read and choose the correct word for each space.

Tai Chi Chuan — A Slow Dance for Health

There are **0)** *few* forms of exercise so popular with **1)** .... the young and old as Tai Chi Chuan, which was developed over 700 years **2)** .... as a method of self-defence for monks. Because **3)** .... its smooth, gentle movements it looks **4)** .... a slow, graceful dance. As Tai Chi requires **5)** .... of concentration, it has also **6)** .... described as 'moving meditation'. It is based **7)** .... the Taoist belief that good health results from a balanced *chi*, **8)** .... life force. All movements of Tai Chi **9)** .... practised to balance the body's *chi*. People around the world consider it an art as **10)** .... as a relaxing form of exercise for people of all ages and fitness levels.

0	A some	B̂ few	C little	D many
1	A and	B either	C both	D neither
2	A before	B back	C past	D ago
3	A in	B to	C of	D that
4	A after	B as	C like	D for
5	A much	B lots	C enough	D bit
6	A be	B being	C is	D been
7	A on	B in	C at	D of
8	A to	B or	C either	D in
9	A will	B are	C had	D was
10	A that	B much	C far	D well

(20 marks)

Writing

7 You are planning a dinner party. Write an e-mail to your friend, Daniel, inviting him to the party (40-60 words). You should include details about:

• the date, time, place of party
• who else will be there • how he should dress

(20 marks)

(Total = 100 marks)

Now I can...

• talk about
  – restaurants & table manners
  – cooking methods & tastes
  – sports & sports qualities
• express my likes/dislikes related to food
• sympathise with someone & give advice
• order a meal
• write
  – a short review of a restaurant
  – a recipe
  – a shopping list
  – a story
  – a postcard/a note
  – a sports quiz
  – a pros & cons essay

...in English

CURRICULAR CUTS: Science

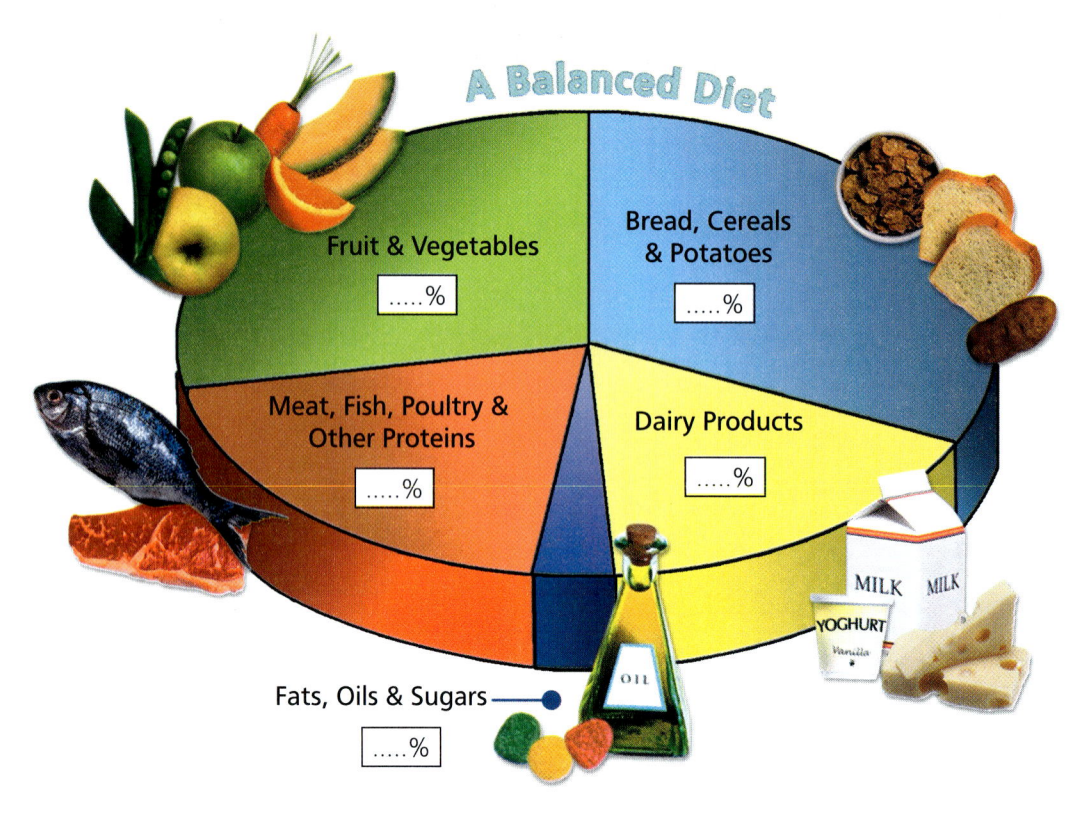

A Balanced Diet

- Fruit & Vegetables .....%
- Bread, Cereals & Potatoes .....%
- Meat, Fish, Poultry & Other Proteins .....%
- Dairy Products .....%
- Fats, Oils & Sugars .....%

1 Look at the diagram and name food/drinks for each group. What percentage of a balanced diet should each food group be? Fill in: *3, 17, 20, 28, 32*.

2 Listen and read, then answer questions 1-5. Explain the words in bold.

> The food we eat should give us what we need to grow, be active and stay healthy. We need **protein** for growth and repair of muscle, skin etc. We need **carbohydrates** and fats for energy. We need **vitamins**, **minerals** and **fatty acids** for the **chemical reactions** that take place in body processes. Each food group gives us something of what we need each day so it is important to make sure we have a balanced diet with the right **amounts** of various foods from all five food groups. The table below shows what each food group provides. The servings **vary** depending on such things as the age, gender and lifestyle of the individual.

FOOD GROUP	PROVIDES MAINLY …	ESTIMATED NUMBER OF SERVINGS DAILY (1 serving = e.g.)	REMARKS
bread, cereals & potatoes	carbohydrates*; calcium, iron B vitamins	6-11 (1 slice bread; 1/2 cup cooked rice/pasta; small baked potato)	eat some of these with every meal
fruit & vegetables	vitamin C* vitamins A, B, C; calcium, iron	2-4 (1 apple/banana/etc; 3/4 cup fruit juice) 3-5 (1 cup salad greens; 1/2 cup other vegetables)	eat a wide variety of different types
meat, fish & other proteins	protein*; iron; B vitamins (esp. B12)	2-3 (70-80 g cooked chicken; 1 egg; 1/2 cup cooked dried beans)	2+ servings of fish a week; no fatty meat
dairy products	protein*; calcium*; vitamins A, B2	2-3 (1 cup low-fat milk/yoghurt; 40 g hard cheese)	eat low-fat products
fats, oils & sugars	fatty acids*; vitamins A, D, E, K* carbohydrates	– [we need some fat in our diet, but we should eat only very small amounts from this group]	olive oil is the healthiest source of fat

* = is a/the main source of this   [Food & Nutrition Board of the National Academy of Sciences]

1 Why is it important to have a balanced diet?
2 How many servings of fruit and vegetables should we eat a day?
3 How much fish should we eat a week?
4 Which group is the main source of calcium?
5 Which group should be part of every meal?

3 **Project:** Write down everything you eat in one day and assess your diet. Do you have a balanced diet?

Modern Living

Module 5
Units 9-10

▶ **Before you start ...**
- How often do you eat out? Where? Describe the place. How would you recommend it?
- What is your favourite sport? How do you play it? Do you think sport is good for young people? Give reasons.

▶ **Look at Module 5**
- Where are pictures 1-5 taken from?

▶ **Find the unit and page number(s) for**
- a magazine review section ☐
- a TV guide ☐
- a cartoon strip ☐
- a classified ad ☐
- text messages ☐
- a science quiz ☐

▶ **Listen, read and talk about ...**
- free time activities
- films, books, newspapers and TV
- TV jobs
- theatre
- paintings
- technology in education
- gadgets, computers and processes
- means of communication

▶ **Learn how to ...**
- make suggestions/agree and disagree
- comment on films and actors
- express regrets

- book tickets
- describe paintings
- discuss the pros and cons of sth
- describe problems and request action

▶ **Practise ...**
- *so/neither-all, most, some, none*
- conditionals: type 2, 3
- wishes
- relatives/relative clauses
- clauses of concession
- reported speech
- indirect questions
- the causative form
- intonation in questions
- phrasal verbs: *turn, take*

▶ **Write ...**
- a review of a school event
- a TV guide
- an interview with a graffiti artist
- a letter to a friend reviewing a film
- a short article about teenagers in your country
- a text message
- a science quiz
- a letter of complaint

Culture Clips: Comic Relief – Red Noses Fight Poverty; The Education System of the UK & the USA

Curricular Cuts (Art & Design): Styles of Painting

101

9a Going out!

Lead-in

1 a. What indoor/outdoor weekend activities do you do?

I usually go to the cinema with my friends.

b. Use the language below to discuss which activities you find *exciting, boring, interesting, entertaining,* etc.

I find (e.g. listening to classical music boring)	✓ So do I.
	✗ Do you? I don't!
I don't find (e.g. going to the cinema exciting)	✓ Neither do I.
	✗ Don't you? I do!

Reading

2 a. Look at the text. Where could you read it? What is its purpose?

b. Look at the posters and the subtitles. What types of entertainment are mentioned?

3 a. The people in pictures 1-4 are all trying to decide what to do this Saturday. Read the short texts about each person and underline the key words.

b. Read the reviews (A-F) and decide which form of entertainment you think each of the people would choose. Then explain the words in bold.

Listening

4 🎧 Listen to two people discussing where to go this weekend. Where do they decide to go? Why?

Elizabeth says, "I go out to have fun. A lot of laughs, a good meal, going dancing – that's my idea of a good time!" ①

Pick of the Week...
By Julia Parker

A **Theme night: Murder Mystery Dinner Theatre**

Dates/Times: *Every week, Thurs–Sun, 7:00 pm*
Location: *Charing Cross Thistle Hotel, The Strand, WC2*
Admission: *£49 (including three-course dinner)*

For an evening of dining and entertainment, **head for** the Charing Cross Thistle Hotel. Enjoy a great dinner while watching a **live** comedy thriller, or play the role of detective and help the actors **solve** the **mystery**. Good food and a good laugh **guaranteed**.

B **Cultural Events: Union Dance**

Dates/Times: *Thurs–Sat 8:00 pm*
Location: *Stratford Circus, Theatre Square, E15*
Admission: *£9 adults, £5 children and seniors*

Experience an evening of **multicultural** music and **movement** at the Stratford Circus. The Union Dance **troupe** is **performing** *Urban Classics II*, a mixture of break-dancing, ballet and **martial arts**, to a **cultural mix** of hip hop, jazz and **traditional** African and Indian music.

C **Cinema: BFi London IMAX**

Dates/Times: *Every week, 12:30 am – 8:30 pm*
Location: *1 Charlie Chaplin Walk, South Bank, SE1*
Admission: *£7.90 adults, £4.95 children*

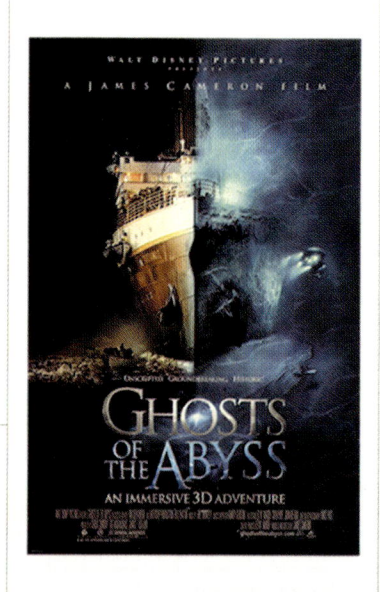

Interested in films? Then don't **miss the chance** to watch the latest 3D **releases** on the UK's largest cinema screen. The BFi London IMAX is a **state-of-the-art** cinema with a 20-metre screen and **digital surround sound**! Now showing: *Bugs, Ghosts of the Abyss* and more!

9a

Melissa loves going to the theatre, and she particularly enjoys comedies. She also likes eating at nice restaurants.

Ann loves music and dance. She is especially fond of shows that combine modern and ethnic sounds. "Nothing too serious, though," she says. "I prefer light, amusing entertainment."

Frank is an art student, and he is interested in images of all kinds and photography. Being a student, he has very little money to spend on entertainment.

D Art Exhibition: Tate Modern

Dates/Times: Mon–Thur, Sun, 10 am – 6 pm. Fri & Sat, 10 am–10 pm
Location: 25 Bankside, Holland Street, SE1
Admission: Free

Don't miss the *Sigmar Polke: History of Everything* exhibition at the Tate Modern. Polke is famous for using a variety of different **materials** and **techniques** to create interesting **images**. His **impressive** works **include** paintings, drawings and photographs. An amazing exhibition – not just for **art lovers**.

E Comedy nights: Jongleurs Comedy Club

Dates/Times: Every Friday & Saturday night, 7 pm
Location: Camden Lock, Chalk Farm Road, NW1
Admission: £15

For **non-stop** laughter and a great night out, Jongleurs Comedy Club is the place to be. Enjoy a meal during the highly entertaining show, then dance the night away at the disco. You're guaranteed a laugh a minute, so come and join in the fun!

F Musical: Anything Goes

Dates/Times: Mon–Sat, 7:30 pm
Location: Theatre Royal, Drury Lane, WC2
Admission: £20 balcony, £35 circle, £45 stalls

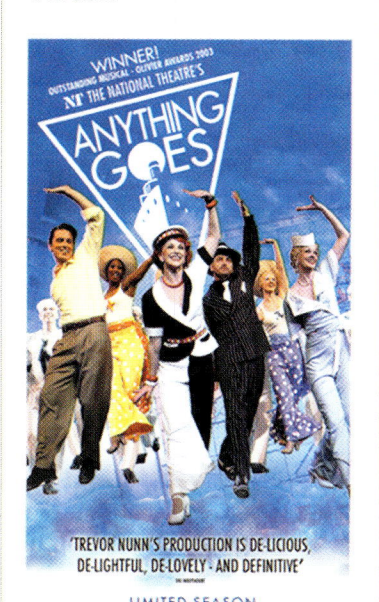

Trevor Nunn's **award-winning production** of the classic Cole Porter musical *Anything Goes* is a singing and dancing **sensation**. John Barrowman and Sally Ann Triplett give brilliant **performances** in this wonderfully entertaining musical comedy.

Speaking

5 Work in pairs. Highlight the special features in each review. Take roles and discuss where to go this Saturday. Use the table below.

Suggesting	Agreeing
• Let's …	• Great idea!
• Shall we …?	• That would be great.
• We could …	• Why not?
• What/How about …?	• (That's a) good idea.
• Why don't we …?	**Disagreeing**
• Do you fancy …?	• I don't really like …
• Would you like to see …?	• I'm not in the mood.
	• I'd love to but …

A: Do you fancy going out to dinner?
B: That would be great! Where should we go?
A: We could go …

Writing

Portfolio: Your school is putting on a special event (play, concert, etc). Write a review. Include:

• dates/times • location
• price of admission
• short description of the event

You can use the reviews in Ex. 3b as models.

103

9b Vocabulary Practice

Films, books & newspapers

1 Look at the pictures. What types of films do you think they are? Choose from the list.

- romance • cartoon • historical drama • horror • science fiction • musical • comedy • action

Monsters, Inc.
SCREENING: 13:30

Bean
SCREENING: 15:45

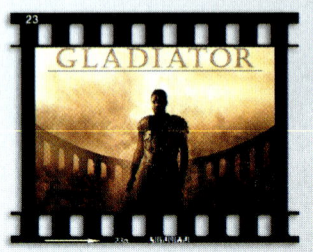

Gladiator
SCREENING: 17:50

The Matrix Reloaded
SCREENING: 20:00

2 In pairs, think of a film you have both seen. Use the expressions and your own ideas to discuss it.

Films	• It was excellent/great/fantastic/superb/ moving/touching/fascinating/hilarious, etc. • I was/wasn't impressed/thrilled by it. • It was disappointing/awful/unoriginal.
Actors	• She's/He's good/amazing/great/brilliant. • I (don't) really like him/her. • She's/He's awful/dreadful.

A: Have you seen *Gladiator*?
B: Yes. It was a superb film.
A: What do you think of Russell Crowe?
B: He's amazing. I really like him.

Prepositional phrases

at the end: in the last part of sth
in the end: finally, at last
at the beginning: in the first part of sth
in the beginning: originally

3 Fill in: *at* or *in*.

1 .... the **end** of the film everyone felt very moved.
2 He wanted to call the police but .... **the end** he decided not to.
3 .... **the beginning** of the story, Harry Potter doesn't know he is a wizard.
4 Harry goes to Hogwart's school. .... **the beginning** things are very strange to him but he soon settles in.

StudySkills

Reading widely

Reading outside class will increase your vocabulary and improve the level of your English. You can read books, newspapers and magazines or browse the Net.

4 What do you like to read? When do you usually read? How much of it is in English?

- thrillers • poetry • science fiction • comics
- newspapers • reviews • world news
- adventure/short/detective/historical stories
- romance/humorous novels • biographies

I like short stories best. I usually read at the weekends. I sometimes read English short stories.

5 Talk about a book you read recently. Think of the:

- title • author's name • type of book
- main characters • plot

Harry Potter by JK Rowling is an adventure story. The main characters are … .

6 Underline the correct word in each sentence.

1 Do you enjoy going to the **movies/films**?
2 Holly Marie Combs **stars/plays** in *Charmed*.
3 This is my favourite radio **channel/station**.
4 The **location/setting** of the book is in 19th century England.
5 The film is so popular there are three **screenings/showings** every night.

104

9b

TV

▶ Listening

7 a. Which of the TV-related professions below can you see in the pictures (A-D)?

reporter *newsreader* *quizmaster* *makeup artist* *cameraman* *weather forecaster*

Who works:
– behind the scenes?
– in front of the camera?

b. Listen and match the speakers (1-5) to the jobs in Ex. 7a. Which words helped you decide?

Speaker 1 .....   Speaker 4 .....
Speaker 2 .....   Speaker 5 .....
Speaker 3 .....

▶ Reading

8 a. Look at the extract. Where is it taken from? Read and say what the types of programmes are. Choose from the list.

- sports • drama series • quiz show • chat show
- reality show • sitcom (situation comedy) • news report
- soap opera • documentary • movie

Thursday 12th May

CHANNEL 4

- **6:00** *Friends* Joey and Chandler leave baby Ben on a bus in this laugh-a-minute episode.
- **6:30** *Big Brother* Watch them sweat as they wait to see who's been voted out of the house.
- **7:00** *Channel Four News*
- **7:30** *Speed Machines* The history of speed and the titanic battle in the 1920s and '30s to break the land speed record.
- **8:30** *Who wants to be a millionaire?* Once again, contestants test their knowledge and compete for the grand prize of £1,000,000.
- **9:00** *ER* In this week's dramatic episode, a fire fills the emergency room at County General and Lewis has to give some bad news to a young cancer patient.
- **10:00** *The Firm* Thriller about corruption in a top law firm, starring Tom Cruise.

b. Which programme(s) can someone watch if they:

1 want to keep up with what is happening around the world?
2 like comedies?
3 enjoy films?

▶ Speaking

9 Use the TV guide in Ex. 8 and the prompts below to talk in pairs.

- Is there a (good) ... *(film / comedy / quiz show, etc)* on TV tonight?
- What's on Channel 4 ... *(at 7:30 / after the news, etc)*?
- When is that ... *(chat show / documentary, etc)* on?

A: *Is there a good comedy on TV tonight?*
B: *Let's see. There's* Friends *on Channel 4 at 6 o'clock – that's a sitcom.*

✏ Writing

Portfolio: Write a TV guide for a few hours' viewing on one or two local channels. Use the TV guide in Ex. 8 as a model.

105

9c Grammar in use

Conditionals: type 2 & 3
Grammar Reference

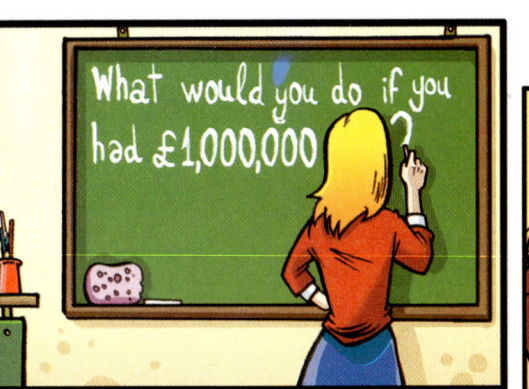

Speech bubbles:
- What would you do if you had £1,000,000?
- Bill, you haven't done anything. Why is that?
- Because that's what I'd do if I had £1,000,000.

1 Which are the conditional sentences in the picture strip? Do they describe:

a an imaginary situation in the present/ future?
b an unreal situation in the past?

Complete the rule.

| Type 2 | If + ... , → would + ... |

2 What would you do if:

1 you had £1 million?
2 you wanted to change your image?
3 you wanted to be a pop star?
4 you wanted to find a job?

If I won £1,000,000, I'd buy a big house.

3 Read the sentence, then complete the rule. What sort of situation do conditionals type 3 describe?

If you had studied, you would have passed the exam. Now you have to resit it.

| Type 3 | If + ... , → would/could/might + ... + ... |

4 Complete the sentences.

1 If I had known it was your birthday, ...
2 If you had called me earlier, ...
3 If Joe hadn't studied for his test, ...
4 If I had seen you, ...
5 If Jane had left on time, ...
6 If I hadn't overslept, ...
7 If you had lent me the money, ...
8 If Ian had caught the bus, ...

5 Correct the mistakes. Justify your corrections.

1 If he got a job, he will move to a bigger house.
2 If I were you, I will tell her the truth.
3 If he had read the book, he might to have understood the play.
4 If she has had enough money on her, she would have bought the jumper.
5 If I hadn't been tired, I would has gone out.

Wishes
Grammar Reference

6 a. Study the examples. Which is a wish for the present? a regret for the past?

- I wish I had some friends.
- If only I had played better.

Complete the table.

| I wish/If only + ... tense. (wish for the present) |
| I wish/If only + ... tense. (regret for the past) |

b. Use the prompts to make sentences.

- I've lost my keys.
- I didn't have any help.
- I didn't bring my camera.
- I don't know how to drive.
- I ate too much chocolate – I feel sick now.
- I didn't start earlier.
- I don't have enough time.
- It's raining again.
- I have to work tomorrow.
- I can't afford to go on holiday.

I wish I hadn't lost my keys.

Relative clauses
Grammar Reference

7 a. Fill in: *which*, *where*, *who* or *whose*. Which of these words can be omitted in the defining relative clauses?

Defining
a I like films .... are about aliens.
b Tom Cruise is the actor .... I admire most.
c The man .... I wanted to see was on holiday.

Non-defining
d Bob, ... father is a pianist, is an actor.
e York, ... she lives, is a quiet city.
f Tom, ... was born in Wales, moved to Lisbon.
g Monaco, ... is visited by a lot of film stars, is very expensive.

b. Which relative clauses can be omitted without changing the meaning of the sentences?

8 Use appropriate relatives to join the sentences.

1 Paul loves swimming. He is 80 years old.
2 *Chicago* is a great film. I saw it last night on TV.
3 Venice is in Italy. It attracts many tourists.
4 Ann is my colleague. We saw her yesterday.
5 The painting is worth £10,000. It was painted in 1875.

9 Match the columns to make complete sentences.

That's ... | Josh, / the film / the Hilton, / my friend | who / whose / which / where | came out last week. / they stayed last year. / lives next door to us. / sister is a lawyer.

That's Josh, who lives next door to us.

Phrasal verbs

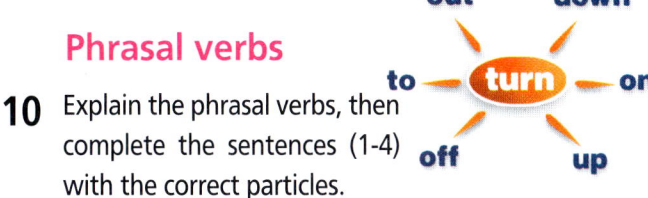

10 Explain the phrasal verbs, then complete the sentences (1-4) with the correct particles.

turn — out / down / to / on / off / up

1 Please turn .... the TV. I want to read.
2 Don't worry – everything will turn .... fine.
3 John turned .... at the very last minute.
4 Please turn .... the music. It's too loud.

GAME

Play in teams. One team makes sentences about objects, people's jobs or places. The other team tries to guess the answer.

Team A S1: *This is a place where we listen to live music.*
Team B S1: *It's a concert hall.*

▶ **Reading & Listening**

11 Read the title. What do you think of graffiti? Read the text and fill in the gaps 1-10 with one word. Listen and check.

Graffiti — Is it Art?

Graffiti began in the 1960s in New York City 0) ...*when*... someone started writing his signature or 'tag' on as many surfaces 1) .... he could. Other young people copied him and soon there were designs and paintings 2) .... walls everywhere. Graffiti also takes the form of slogans 3) .... put across the artists' opinions about certain social and political issues.

Graffiti is something you either love 4) .... hate. Some people feel that graffiti makes a city ugly. On the other hand, there are people 5) .... believe it is a form of artistic expression, and graffiti may even 6) .... found on display in famous art galleries.

Graffiti is actually illegal and some countries try to deal with the problem 7) .... not allowing people under the 8) .... of 18 to buy spray paints. In other countries, the authorities provide special walls 9) .... people can practise graffiti. Whichever way you look 10) .... it, graffiti is a popular form of expression.

Writing

Portfolio: Write an interview with a graffiti artist based on the text above.

107

9d Listening & Speaking skills

Going to the theatre

1 Match the collocations. What topic are they related to? Make sentences using them.

performance — circle
running — performance
upper — times
15-minute — interval
matinee — time

▶ *Listening*

2 You will hear a recorded message. Read and try to guess what the missing words might be. Listen and complete. Were your guesses correct?

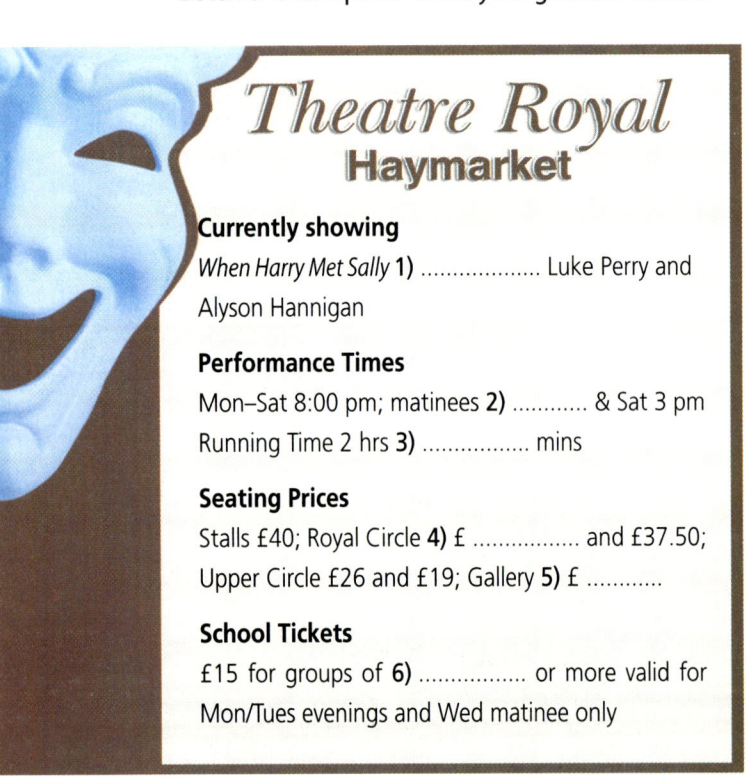

Theatre Royal Haymarket

Currently showing
When Harry Met Sally 1) .... Luke Perry and Alyson Hannigan

Performance Times
Mon–Sat 8:00 pm; matinees 2) .... & Sat 3 pm
Running Time 2 hrs 3) .... mins

Seating Prices
Stalls £40; Royal Circle 4) £ .... and £37.50;
Upper Circle £26 and £19; Gallery 5) £ ....

School Tickets
£15 for groups of 6) .... or more valid for Mon/Tues evenings and Wed matinee only

Booking tickets

▶ *Reading*

3 a. Read the first three lines of the dialogue. What are the speakers talking about?

b. In which context do you expect to find these words in the dialogue? Listen and read to check.

- showing • fully-booked • credit card
- box office • tickets • screenings

A: UCI booking line. Can I help you?
B: Hello ... yes ... I'd like to book two tickets for the new James Bond film, please.
A: Certainly. When for? There are screenings at 5:30 pm, 8 pm and 10:30 pm every day.
B: In that case, I think the 5:30 one on Friday, please.
A: I'll just check. ... Sorry – that showing is fully booked. Would you like me to try the later one?
B: Er ... yes, please. If you could.
A: Yes, there are seats available for the 8 o'clock showing. Can I take your name and credit card number, please?
B: Darren Brown. It's 5747 8259 6398 0102.
A: Thank you. You can collect your tickets from the box office any time from 5 pm today until ten minutes before the start of the film on Friday.
B: Thank you.
A: You're welcome. Goodbye.

4 Read and find phrases/sentences in the dialogue which mean:

1 What can I do for you?
2 What date and time?
3 Let me see.
4 If you don't mind.

5 **Portfolio:** Work in pairs. Imagine that you want to book tickets for a film. Take the roles of customer and cashier and act out the dialogue. Think about the:

- title of the film • performance times
- number of tickets • prices • credit card number

Record your dialogue.

That's the fifth ticket you've bought, sir.

I know, but there's a girl inside who keeps tearing them up!

9d

StudySkills

Describing paintings

When describing paintings you need to give the important details. Talk about the main subject, the setting, the colours and the background. Also, describe your feelings towards the painting. Use present tenses.

Describing paintings

6 a. Look at the painting and complete the text.

In this painting I **1)** .... see a young man sitting **2)** .... a rock by the sea. He is wearing blue-green trousers and a shirt, and he has a green cap **3)** .... his head. He is staring out to sea. I think he is unhappy **4)** .... there is nobody with him. In the background I can see the beach, some houses, a few trees, and mountains. It's hard to see clearly, but it looks as if **5)** .... are some people walking **6)** .... the shore. The artist has used bright, sunny colours but the painting makes me **7)** .... a little sad.

b. Describe the painting. Think about:

- main subject • setting • colours • background
- your feelings

Expressing preferences

7 Look at the magazine extract. What is it advertising? In pairs, ask and answer comprehension questions.

▶ *Intonation (sentence stress)*

8 a. Listen and underline the stressed syllables.

A: *What would you like to do this weekend?*
B: *I'd really like to go to the Rocking Rollers concert.*

b. In pairs, use the phrases in the table to act out similar exchanges.

Asking	Expressing preferences
• What would you like …?	• I'd (really) like/love to ….
• Would you like to …?	• I'd rather …
• What are we going to …?	• That sounds good to me.
• What do you think we should …?	• I think we should …
	• If it were up to me, I'd …

Don't miss out!

The Rocking Rollers Live!
Hanley Stadium
Friday 14th – Sunday 16th, 8 pm

Shakespeare's Hamlet
Hanley Royal Theatre
Thursday 13th – Monday 17th July, 7:30 pm
Starring John Thatcher and Caroline Kingsley

Come to the Circus!
Hanley Arena
Friday 21st July, 2 pm - 7 pm

Annual Hanley Rock Festival
3 nights of great music in Hanley Park
Thursday 13th Saturday 15th July, 7 pm till midnight
The Pinks
Gary Glamour
The Swinging Sisters... and many more!!!

109

9e Writing an informal letter reviewing a film

Getting started

1. Fill in: *acting, cast, plot, action packed, miss, must, effects, highly, computer animated*. What types of texts are these? Where could you read them?

A *Finding Nemo* is a brilliant 1) .... film from Disney and Pixar. Watch Marlin, a clownfish, on an adventure to find his son, Nemo, after he is taken by a diver. A funny and touching film with a great 2) .... Don't 3) .... it!

B *The Return of the King* is the final part in *The Lord of the Rings* trilogy. Frodo and Sam are on their way to Mount Doom to destroy the ring. An incredible film with an all-star 4) .... and great special 5) .... This is a(n) 6) .... see!

C Russell Crowe stars in *Gladiator* as a Roman general who is betrayed and becomes a gladiator to get revenge. A(n) 7) .... film with incredible battle scenes and amazing 8) .... 9) .... recommended.

2. Which phrases does the writer use to recommend these films?

Let's look closer

3. Read the rubric, then read the review. What information does the writer give for points 1-4?

   1. title/type of film
   2. cast/characters
   3. setting
   4. plot summary

   Write a short review of a must see film for a local magazine.

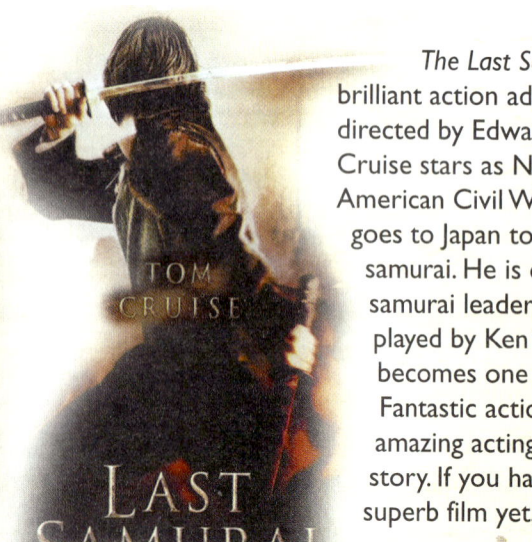

   The Last Samurai is a brilliant action adventure film directed by Edward Zwick. Tom Cruise stars as Nathan Algren, an American Civil War hero who goes to Japan to fight the samurai. He is captured by the samurai leader Katsumoto, played by Ken Watanabe, and becomes one of them. Fantastic action scenes, amazing acting and a great story. If you haven't seen this superb film yet, don't miss it!

4. How does the writer recommend the film? Suggest other phrases to recommend the film.

Your turn

5. a. Underline the key words in the rubric. How does this rubric differ from the rubric in Ex. 3?

   This is part of a letter from your pen friend.

   > In your last letter, you said you like going to the cinema. What was the last film you saw? Was it good? Did you like it? Write and tell me about it.

   Write a letter in reply (80-100 words).

   b. Answer the questions in the plan, then write your letter.

Plan

Dear + *your friend's first name,*
Introduction (Para 1)
How will you greet your friend?
Why are you writing to him/her?
Main Body (Para 2)
- *What details will you give (e.g. title, type of film, actors' names, main characters, plot summary)?*
- *What did you like most? How did you feel? Would you recommend it?*

Conclusion (Para 3)
How can you end your letter?
Yours, + *your first name*

AMAZING FACTS!

Leonardo da Vinci never signed or dated his most famous painting, the Mona Lisa.

Culture Clip 9

COMIC RELIEF

Red Noses Fight Poverty

Take a minute and ask yourself: What do **charity** and comedy have **in common**?

Nothing? Well, *Comic Relief* will certainly **disagree** with you.

Set up by a group of comedians, *Comic Relief* is a charity that uses laughter to **raise** money from the general **public** and help **fight poverty** in the UK and Africa. It began with a few **live** comedy events that were **broadcast** on BBC 1 on Christmas Day 1985, in response to the **famine** in Ethiopia. Since then, they have managed to raise about £300 million!

Comic Relief is best known as the organisation behind Red Nose Day, the biggest **fundraising** event in the UK. On Red Nose Day, held every two years, people **throughout** Britain put on a red plastic nose and do the **craziest** things they can think of – all to raise money for those **in need**. Eating jelly with **chopsticks**, cutting the grass with a pair of **scissors** and eating **grapes** while wearing boxing gloves are just a few of the things people have done. The event includes **moving** documentary films and extraordinary comedy by some of the best British comedians, broadcast on national TV.

Over the years, many **celebrities** have taken part, each in their own special way. 'Mr Bean', Robbie Williams, and Victoria and David Beckham are only some of the famous people who have **offered** their time and **talent** in an event that **unites** the whole nation in trying to help other people and have fun at the same time!

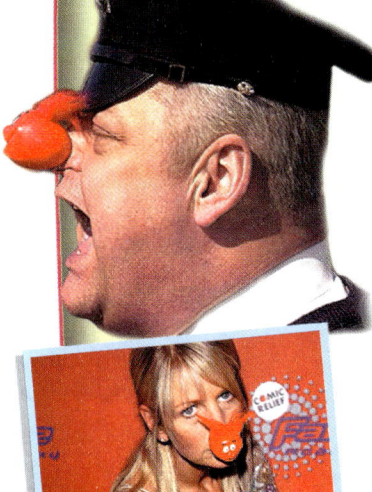

▶ Reading & Listening

1 What are the people in the pictures wearing? Why do you think they are doing this? Listen and read to find out.

2 Read the text and complete the summary, then explain the words in bold.

Comic Relief is a(n) 1) .... It started in the UK on 2) .... So far they have raised 3) .... Every 2 years the British celebrate 4) .... On this day people wear 5) .... and do silly things. The money raised helps people in 6) ....

▶ Speaking

3 Work in pairs. Imagine that one of you is a reporter and the other is involved in Comic Relief. Act out an interview about:

- the aim of the organisation
- how it started
- the special events it involves
- who supports it

4 Project Portfolio: Imagine your school is planning a charity event similar to Red Nose Day. List ten things you could do to raise money (*e.g. run a marathon, climb a mountain, shave your head, etc*). You can make a poster as well.

10a Fast Forward

Lead-in

1 Are these statements true (T) or false (F) about teenagers in your country? Decide in pairs.

1 Most of them have got mobile phones.
2 None of them owns a video camera.
3 Some of them can use a computer.
4 Only a few wear designer clothes.
5 Most of them change their hairstyle frequently.
6 The majority of them listen to hip-hop.
7 Only a few talk in chat rooms.
8 Most of them leave school to work.

2 🎧 Read the list of different kinds of music, then listen and number them in the order you hear them.

reggae ☐	hip hop ☐	garage ☐	rock ☐
nu-metal ☐	jazz ☐	techno ☐	rap ☐
classic ☐	country ☐	pop ☐	disco ☐

Listening

3 🎧 Listen and match the speakers (1-4) to the gadgets (A-D). Which words helped you decide?

A ☐ digital camera   C ☐ computer
B ☐ mobile phone   D ☐ portable stereo

4 Which of the objects in the pictures on p. 113 do you use for: – fun? – work? – study? Tell your partner.

I use my computer for study because I can find lots of information on the Net for school projects.

All About Britain's Teenagers

School
British teenagers can leave school at sixteen after taking their GCSE exams. They study for exams in as many as ten subjects, so they have to work pretty hard! Today's teens spend more time doing their homework than any teenagers in the past, studying for 2½ – 3 hours every evening.

Free Time
It's not all work, of course. What do British teenagers do to have fun? They love watching TV, going out, meeting friends in Internet cafés and listening to music. **Researchers** found that 99% of teenagers **questioned** in a **survey** said their favourite activity was watching TV, while 98% also liked listening to music. Some teens like UK garage music, but others prefer to listen to hip-hop or nu-metal on their portable stereos, personal stereos and CD players. 89% spend most of their free time online, e-mailing their 'mates' or making new friends in their favourite chat rooms.

Technology
As well as the Internet, teenagers in Britain use their computers to play games and do their homework. They also love their mobile phones, and spend hours **texting** their friends and **chatting**. Today, phones are getting smaller and lighter and you can do a lot more with them than just talk. Text messaging has taken over as the coolest and trendiest way to **socialise**. More than 90% of 12- to 16-year-olds have a mobile, and experts say that this trend stops teens from spending their cash on sweets and cigarettes. The latest **craze**, mobile phones with built-in video cameras, is taking the country **by storm**, as are digital cameras with which you can take photos that can be sent over the Internet.

Fashion
At school, almost all British teenagers have to wear a school uniform. However, in their free time they can wear whatever they like, and what they like is **designer labels**. In fact, 40% of British teens say that they think it is important to have the latest **designer gear**. Nike, Diesel and Paul Smith are the top favourites, but looking good doesn't come cheap in Britain, and many teenagers think nothing of spending over £100 on one item of clothing.

computer

personal CD player

personal stereo

TV

mobile video phone

digital camera

10a

StudySkills

Predicting content

The title and the subheadings in an article help you predict what the article is about.

Reading

5 Read the title of the article and the subheadings. What is the article about? How are the objects in the pictures related to the text? Listen and read to check.

6 a. Read the article and choose the correct answer, A, B, C or D, for questions 1-4.

1 What is the writer's main purpose in writing the text?
  A to describe the social life of British teenagers
  B to give statistical facts about British teenagers
  C to describe preferences and trends among British teenagers
  D to complain about teenagers in Britain

2 What would a reader learn about communication between British teenagers?
  A that technology plays an important role in it
  B that they prefer to communicate face to face
  C that it is unimportant to most of them
  D that they have difficulty in communicating

3 What does the writer suggest about British teenagers' attitudes to technology?
  A Mobiles are their favourite items of technology.
  B They only use technology to play games and socialise.
  C They are enthusiastic about new trends in technology.
  D They see technology as cool and fashionable.

4 Which of the following best describes today's British teenagers?

A All they can think about is going out and having fun.

B They spend more time playing with computers than doing their homework.

C They don't meet up with friends any more – they just call, text or e-mail them.

D They seem to have more fun, but in fact they work harder than previous generations of teenagers.

b. Explain the words in bold. In pairs, think of alternative subheadings.

Speaking

7 Make notes about British teenagers under each of the subheadings in the text. In pairs, make similar notes about teenagers in your country. Use your notes to compare teenagers in Britain to teenagers in your country.

British teenagers can leave school at 16, whereas in my country they can leave school ...

Writing

Portfolio: Use your notes from Ex. 7 to write a short article about teenagers in your country.

113

10b Vocabulary Practice

Technology in education

1 a. Which of these objects can be used in a classroom? What for? Choose from the subjects in the list and tell the class.

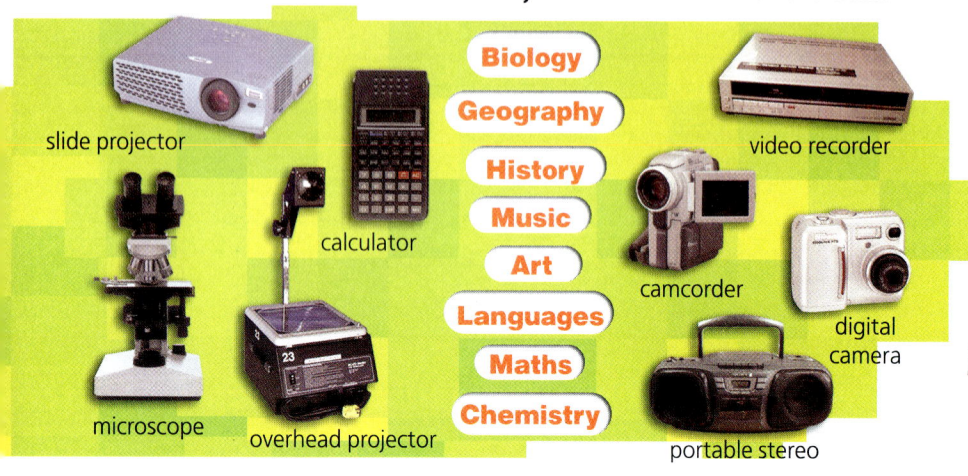

- slide projector
- calculator
- microscope
- overhead projector
- video recorder
- camcorder
- digital camera
- portable stereo

Biology, Geography, History, Music, Art, Languages, Maths, Chemistry

- watch documentaries, foreign language films, etc • do sums
- record & listen • examine cells • film scientific experiments
- listen to music • show drawings & charts • take pictures
- show slides of ancient sites • record performances

A video recorder can be used in Geography lessons to watch documentaries about various countries.

b. Which of these do/did you use at school? Do/Did you enjoy the lessons? Why (not)?

Gadgets

StudySkills

Revising compound nouns

To revise compound nouns, write all the nouns separately on pieces of paper. Mix up the pieces and try to match the halves. This will help you remember them.

2 a. Match the words. Which of these can you see in the pictures?

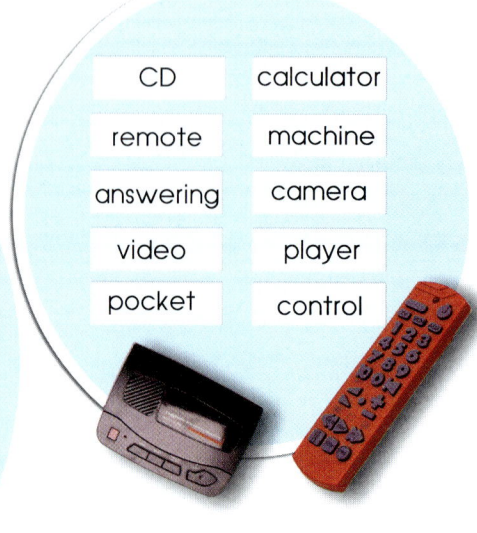

- mobile
- personal
- video
- fax
- walkie
- organiser
- phone
- talkie
- recorder
- machine

- CD
- remote
- answering
- video
- pocket
- calculator
- machine
- camera
- player
- control

b. Conduct a survey of your class and say which items *all, most, some* or *none of you* use *regularly, occasionally, rarely*.

all/most/some + verb in plural
none + verb in singular

All of us **use** mobile phones regularly.
None of us **uses** a walkie talkie.

Means of communication

3 Do you use any of the means of communication below? Use the prompts and the useful language to make sentences about their pros and cons.

- mobile phone
- letter
- fax machine
- e-mail

Pros
• quick • cheap • convenient
• personal • reliable

Cons
• expensive • slow • unreliable
• impersonal • inconvenient

Concession
• Although + clause
• Despite + -ing
• In spite of + -ing
• While + clause, ...
• ... However, ...
• ... On the other hand ...

Although a mobile phone is convenient, it can be quite expensive.

GAME

In teams, think of a device and say one or two sentences about it. The other team(s) try to guess what the device is.

Team A S1: It's possible to send a message with it.
Team B S1: Is it a mobile phone?

10b

Computers
▶ *Reading*

4 In one minute, write down as many words as possible related to computers. Compare with your partner.

floppy disk
CD-ROM
disk drive

5 a. Look at the text. What type of text is it? Where would you find it?

> As new – desktop PC, Pentium 4 processor, 128 MB memory and 60 GB hard drive. Includes modem (56 kbps), mouse, keyboard and 17″ colour monitor. Comes with Windows '98 software and is set up for Internet access. Excellent condition, €599.
>
> Call **0345 234 0044** (leave message)

b. Listen and read to answer the questions.

1 What is the writer's purpose?
2 What is for sale? How much does it cost? What is included?
3 How can the person be contacted?
4 What do *MB*, *GB* and *kpbs* stand for?

6 Fill in the correct verb/noun related to computers. Then complete the sentences.

Action	Opposite	Noun
turn / switch on	....	....
turn up	....	....
plug in	unplug	....
log on	....	....
....	delete	a computer file

1 It's better to .... your computer .... when you are not using it.
2 Oh no! I forgot to .... those new files, and now I've lost the information.
3 .... the volume, please. It's too loud.

4 You need a password to .... to the system.
5 No wonder it's not working. Look, it's not ....

Processes
▶ *Listening*

7 What type is the text below? What verb form is used in such texts? Listen and fill in the gaps (1-4).

> **How to send a text message**
> - Press 'Menu'.
> - Scroll to 'Messages' and 1) .... 'Select'.
> - Scroll to 'Write Messages' and press 'Select'.
> - Use your keypad to 2) .... in your message.
> - Press 'Options'.
> - 3) .... 'Send' and press 'OK'.
> - 4) .... your friend's phone number and press 'OK' to send.

8 Read the text messages (A-D). Use the list of abbreviations to 'translate' them.

A SUP M8? RU OK? Y RNT U AT SCHOOL? CU L8R

B TVM 4 YR TXT. I 12 CU TOM 2. TTYL

C DO U 12 GO 2 CINEMA L8R OR GO 4 COFFEE?

D PLS TELL BOSS IM GNG 2B L8 4 TDYS MEETING

CU = see you	TTYL = Talk to you later
L8(R) = late(r)	TXT = (send a) text message
M8 = mate (i.e. friend)	U = you
PLS = please	Y = why
R(NT)U = are(n't) you ...?	12 = want to
SUP = What's up?	2 = to, too
TDY = today	4 = for
TVM = thanks very much	GNG = going
TOM = tomorrow	2B = to be

Writing

Portfolio: Write a text message to an English friend using abbreviations. Exchange your message with a partner and 'translate' it.

115

10c Grammar in use

Reported speech
Grammar Reference

Statements

1 a. Where could you read this text? Is it formal or informal?

> Parents of pupils at Sandleigh School said yesterday that they **were** very angry and **were planning** a protest march because the Local Education Authority **had not yet kept** its promise to improve computer facilities at the school. "They announced that they **would spend** £1.2m on new equipment last year," said parents' spokesperson, Angela Sullivan. She claimed that, in fact, spending for the previous year **had been** less than £6,000. Mrs Sullivan added that parents **could not accept** the LEA's excuse ... .

b. Use the information from the text in Ex. 1a to complete the table. How have the verb tenses changed?

Direct Speech	Reported Speech
Present Simple "We are very angry."	**Past Simple** Parents said that they 1) .... very angry.
Present Continuous "We are planning a protest march."	**Past Continuous** They said they 2) .... a protest march.
Present Perfect "The LEA has not yet kept its promise."	**Past Perfect** They said the LEA 3) .... its promise.
Past Simple "Spending for last year was less than £6,000."	She claimed that spending for the previous year 4) .... less than £6,000.
will "We will spend £1.2m."	**would** They announced that they 5) .... £1.2m.
can "We cannot accept the LEA's excuse."	**could** They said they 6) .... the LEA's excuse.

2 Fill in: *told/said/asked*. How do we use these verbs in direct/reported speech?

1 "How can I get to the Arts Hall?" he .... me.
2 He .... us he would leave on Monday.
3 He .... to Mary that Ann had left.
4 He .... that he was going to be late.

3 Report what each speaker said.

1 I'm thinking of buying a computer.
2 I haven't heard from him since May.
3 I don't know what John is doing.
4 You can use my computer if you like.
5 He lost all his files.
6 I'll tell Ann I saw you.
7 Where is my mobile phone?

Orders

4 a. Study the examples. How do we form reported orders? Complete the rule.

Switch it on. *Don't touch it!*

He told me **to switch** *it on.*   *He told me* **not to touch** *it.*

positive imperative → to-infinitive
negative imperative → ....

b. Work in groups of three. Give and report orders.

Questions

5 Study the examples and mark the sentences (1-4) as *T* (true) or *F* (false).

Direct	Reported
"What can I do?"	He asked me **what he could do**.
"Are you OK?"	He asked me **if I was OK**.

1 Reported questions can be introduced with 'asked'.
2 Reported questions end with a question mark.
3 We use *if* to introduce a reported *wh-* question.
4 A reported question is never in the interrogative.

6 Report the questions. What object is the speaker asking questions about?

1 Where do the batteries go?
2 Are the headphones included in the price?
3 Does it come with a carrying case?
4 Why is the model so expensive?

10c

Indirect questions
Grammar Reference

▶ **Reading & Listening**

7 a. In pairs, ask and answer the quiz questions (1-5). Use the table below. What do you notice about the subject-verb order?

A: *Do you know/Can you tell me what the normal temperature of human blood is?*
B: *I'm not sure, but I think it's …*

Expressing ignorance	Expressing uncertainty
• I don't know.	• I'm not sure, but I think …
• I haven't a clue.	• I think it might be …
• I haven't the faintest idea.	

b. Listen and check your answers.

Science quiz

1 What is the normal temperature of human blood?
  A 36.7° C   B 42.2° C   C 28.4° C
2 What do we measure using a seismograph?
  A a hurricane   B a tidal wave   C an earthquake
3 What is the force that attracts objects called?
  A density   B gravity   C capacity
4 Which of these inventions was the first to be successfully built and tested?
  A the submarine   B the helicopter   C the parachute
5 How heavy is the average adult human brain?
  A 1 kg   B 1.5 kg   C 2.5 kg

Causative form
Grammar Reference

8 Study the examples and answer the questions.

A — Ted is repairing his car.
B — Ted is having his car repaired.

1 How do the sentences differ in meaning?
2 What changes have been made to the verb forms?

9 Change the following sentences into the causative from.

1 I repaired the TV.
  I had the TV repaired.
2 I'll paint my car red.
3 I am installing air conditioning in my flat.
4 I am going to fix my CD player.
5 I have fixed the microwave oven.

Sentence transformations

10 Complete the second sentence so that it means the same as the first. Use up to three words.

1 "What will happen if I mix them?" he asked.
  He asked ………………………… if he mixed them.
2 Where is the lab exactly?
  Can you tell me where ………………… exactly?
3 Someone stole their test results last night.
  Their test results ………………………… last night.
4 Do you know why they did the experiment?
  Why ………………………… the experiment?

StudySkills

Learning words through pictures

It's easier to learn new words by associating them with pictures. When you learn a new phrasal verb, draw a little sketch beside it in your notebook.

Phrasal verbs

11 Explain the phrasal verbs, then use them to complete the gaps. Choose a phrasal verb and draw a picture of it.

take: after, on, out, up, off

1 The plane ………………… at 9:00 and arrived at Gatwick at 12:45.
2 Her parents ………… Ann ………… to dinner.
3 John decided to ……………… golf as a hobby.
4 He ……………………… his mum. They have the same dark eyes.
5 It was so hot I had to ……………… my shirt.

Writing

Portfolio: Collect information (from the Internet, encyclopaedias, etc), then write your own science quiz. Use the quiz in Ex. 7a as a model.

117

10d Listening & Speaking skills

Pros and cons

1 Which of these points concerning the Internet are pros and which are cons? Can you think of others?

research wide range of subjects	don't know who you are talking to in chatrooms	spend less time face to face with friends
information not always accurate	develop computer skills	find information quickly and easily
keep in touch with friends cheaply	make new friends from other countries	PC can get a virus

▶ *Listening*

2 🎧 You will hear part of a dialogue about the pros and cons of Internet cafés. Read through the sentences and underline the key words. Then, listen and tick (✓) if each sentence is correct (Yes) or incorrect (No).

	A Yes	B No
1 Jean thinks it is better for children to play outside.	☐	☐
2 Kathy thinks that computers damage children's eyesight.	☐	☐
3 Kathy thinks Internet cafés are not healthy.	☐	☐
4 Jean believes that Internet cafés help students research their school subjects.	☐	☐
5 Kathy thinks that children might find unsuitable information on the Internet.	☐	☐
6 Jean thinks Internet cafés are boring.	☐	☐

Describing pictures

STUDY SKILLS

Speaking effectively

If you feel you have made a mistake while speaking, don't worry. What matters is getting the message across.

3 How are the pictures related? Describe them. Talk about:

- the people
- the places
- the activities
- your feelings

Prepositional phrases

4 Fill in: *between, for, with, about, of* or *on*. Use the phrases to make sentences of your own.

1 These days there is a great **demand** .... mobile phones.
2 Simon sometimes has **difficulty** .... his Maths homework.
3 If it is a **choice** .... seeing my friends or surfing the Net, I would rather see my friends.
4 Mr Peters is an **expert** .... computer systems – he can fix any problem.
5 We had a **discussion** .... the Internet in class today.
6 Do you know the **difference** .... a portable stereo and a personal stereo?
7 One **disadvantage** .... mobile phones is that people can call you at inconvenient times.
8 Sam and David set up a **connection** .... their two computers so that they could share files.

▶ *Intonation in questions*

5 🎧 Listen and repeat. In pairs, suggest what another speaker might say in reply.

1 Who is it?
2 Wendy speaking – how may I help you?
3 Can you ring back later?
4 Will you hold?
5 Would you like to leave a message?

118

10d

Requesting action

▶ Reading

6 a. Look at the left hand column of the dialogue. Who do you think is speaking? To whom? Where are they?

b. Complete the dialogue, then listen and check. In pairs, read the dialogue aloud.

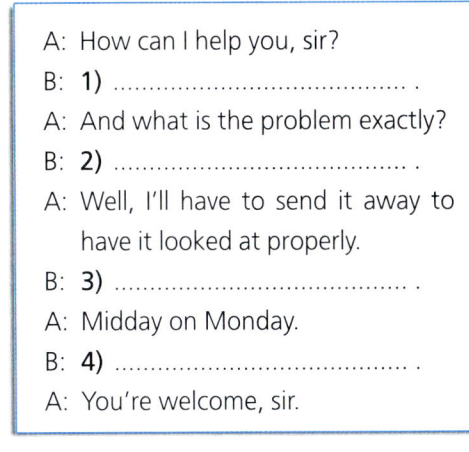

A: How can I help you, sir? B: 1) .... A: And what is the problem exactly? B: 2) .... A: Well, I'll have to send it away to have it looked at properly. B: 3) .... A: Midday on Monday. B: 4) .... A: You're welcome, sir.	a The flash doesn't work at all. Could you have a look at it, please? b That's fine. Thank you very much. c I see. When can I have it back? d I've got a problem with my camera.

7 a. Match the problems (1-6) to the objects (a-f).

a ☐ camera	c ☐ CD player	e ☐ car
b ☐ mobile	d ☐ PC	f ☐1 TV

1 picture – blurred
2 engine – overheating
3 CDs – jumping
4 buttons – not responding
5 lens – broken
6 screen – flickering

b. **Portfolio:** Imagine you have one of the objects (a-f) above but it is not working properly. In pairs, take the roles of a customer and a shop assistant and act out dialogues. Use the table below. You can use Ex. 6b as a model. Record your dialogues.

Describing problems/ requesting action	Responding
• I've got a problem with this … • I think there's something wrong with the … • The … doesn't work / is out of order.	• What's the problem (exactly)? • It needs looking at / checking / repairing. • We'll have to send it away to have it looked at.
Expressing thanks	**Responding to thanks**
• Thank you (very much). • That's (really) very kind of you, thank you.	• My pleasure, sir / madam. • You're welcome (sir / madam). • Don't mention it.

Giving an account of an event

8 Your camera broke on a trip. Now you're back home. Tell your friend:

- how it happened
- where you took it to be fixed
- what happened in the end

FUN TIME

There are all sorts of new gadgets on cars these days but they don't impress me. I'm waiting for someone to invent a windscreen wiper that won't hold parking tickets.

119

10e Writing a letter of complaint

Getting started

1 a. Have you ever bought a faulty item? What was wrong with it? What did you do?

b. Imagine you have bought one of these items. Use the language to complain.

- portable stereo – sound badly distorted
- fax machine – line doesn't receive calls
- pocket calculator – display doesn't work
- DVD player – disc tray gets stuck

Complaining	Responding
• The … I bought is faulty	• Oh, I'm (really) sorry.
• I'd like to return this … because …	• I'm sorry about that.

A: I'd like to return this portable stereo. The sound is badly distorted.
B: Oh, I'm really sorry.

Let's look closer

2 Read the rubric, then read the letter. Which paragraph includes:

1 important facts about your purchase?
2 details about what the problem is?
3 information on how they can contact you?
4 what you want done about the problem?
5 the reason why you are writing?

You bought a camera online. When you received it, you realised that the flash didn't work. Write a letter to the company and:
- state when/how you bought it
- describe the problem
- ask for a replacement

Dear Sir/Madam,
1 ▶ I am writing to complain about a camera which I bought online from your company.
2 ▶ On 20th October, I ordered a Nikon 140 ED camera from your website. Unfortunately, the camera seems to be faulty. When I tried to use it, the automatic flash did not work. As a result, when I had my film developed, the photographs were all too dark.
3 ▶ I would appreciate it if you could exchange it for another camera. I have enclosed copies of my invoice and guarantee. I look forward to your reply. Please contact me on 389 253582, Monday to Friday, 9:00 - 5:00.
Yours faithfully,

Jane Jenkins
Jane Jenkins

Opening/Closing remarks

3 Which sentences are opening/closing remarks? Is the language more / less formal than the language in Ex. 1b?

1 I am writing to express my dissatisfaction with …
2 I hope you will replace …
3 I feel I must complain about …
4 I feel I am entitled to a refund/replacement.

Your turn

4 Read the rubric and answer the questions in the plan. Then write your letter (100-120 words).

● You recently bought a DVD player online which does not recognise your DVD discs. Write a letter to the company. In your letter, you should:
  • state when/where/how you bought it
  • explain what the problem is
  • ask for a refund

Plan

Dear Sir/Madam,
Opening Remarks
(Para 1) *Why are you writing the letter?*
Main Body
(Para 2) *What did you buy? When/How/Where? What is the problem?*
Closing Remarks
(Para 3) *What do you want to be done? What is your contact number/address?*
Yours faithfully,
(your full name)

Study Skills

Checking your writing

Always check your piece of writing before handing it in. Check the grammar, spelling, punctuation. This helps you minimise your mistakes.

Amazing Facts!

The first fax process was patented in 1843 by Alexander Brain but fax machines only went into service in 1964.

Culture Clip 10

The Education System of the UK and the USA

USA

There is no single educational system in the USA – instead, each of the 50 **states** has its own system.

In most states, however, children go to school from about the age of six until at least age sixteen. Each year of school is called a 'grade', and in order to **graduate**, all American students must successfully complete 12th Grade.

In a **typical** case, a student **attends** seven years of primary education, which is often **divided** into four years of Elementary school (Grades 1-4) and three years of Middle school (Grades 5-7). This is followed by secondary school, **split** into Junior High (Grades 8-9) and Senior High (Grades 10-12).

After finishing Senior High, graduating students receive the High School Diploma. If they choose to, they can then go on to higher education at college or university.

UK

In the UK, all children must go to school from age five to age sixteen. They go to primary school for seven years and secondary school for five years.

Primary school may be divided into Infant school (three years) and Junior school (four years). There are different kinds of secondary school, but all pupils follow the same **national curriculum** that **leads to** GCSE (General Certificate of Secondary Education) **qualifications**.

After age 16, British students can choose to leave school, or – if their GCSE **results** are good enough – they can go on to attend Sixth Form for a **further** two years. At the end of this time, they sit 'A' (Advanced) Level exams to qualify for entry to college or university.

▶ Reading & Listening

1 Which of the tables in Ex. 2 do you think represents: a) the British education system, b) the American system? Listen and read to check your answers.

2 Read the text and fill in the missing words/ages in the tables. Then explain the words in bold in the text.

Age	School	Level
6-9	....	PRIMARY
10-12	Middle	
13-....	Junior High	
....-17	Senior High	....
	H.......... S.......... D..............	
17+	college/university	....

Age	School	Level
....-7	Infant	....
8-11	....	
12-16	High	SECONDARY
GENERAL CERTIFICATE OF SECONDARY EDUCATION		
17-18	....	FURTHER
Advanced Level		
18+	....	HIGHER

▶ Speaking

3 Make a similar table about the education system in your country. In what ways is it similar/different to the education systems in the UK and the USA? Discuss in groups.

Self-Assessment Module 5

Vocabulary & Grammar

1 Fill in the missing word.

1 If you .... told me earlier, I could have booked tickets for the play tonight.
2 I think I'll turn .... my mobile phone – I don't feel like talking to anyone right now.
3 Please .... Mary that I'll be late today.
4 .... it was expensive, Sheila bought the mobile phone.
5 BBC 1 is my favourite TV ....
6 I wish I .... passed my exams.
7 I'm not in the .... to go out tonight.
8 Kevin has taken .... a lot of responsibility in his new job as manager.
9 Could you copy that file onto a .... disc and give it to me later?
10 I didn't know you'd .... air conditioning installed.

(10 marks)

2 Circle the correct item.

1 There's an interesting programme on Channel 4 tonight – it's a .... about marine life.
   A thriller   B documentary   C performance
2 Could you please turn .... the volume? I'd like to listen to the news.
   A up   B on   C out
3 Make sure you save all your files before you ....
   A unplug   B log off   C pull out
4 The Corrs, ... new record has just come out, are performing in town tonight.
   A who   B whose   C which
5 EastEnders is my favourite soap ....
   A series   B drama   C opera
6 The teacher asked Joe if he knew what ....
   A the answer was   B was the answer
   C is the answer
7 More and more people use personal .... to store information.
   A agendas   B organisers   C calculators
8 Let's go to the 8 o'clock .... of the film.
   A showing   B booking   C show

9 A lot of teenagers like wearing .... labels.
   A designer   B school   C survey
10 It's a good book, but the ..... is hard to follow.
   A plot   B setting   C cast

(10 marks)

Use of English

3 Complete the second sentence so that it means the same as the first. Use up to three words.

1 You'd better study for the test.
   If I .... would study for the test.
2 "Don't worry about the spotlights", said the cameraman to the actress.
   The cameraman told the actress .... about the spotlights.
3 Rembrandt was a master of art. He lived and worked in Holland.
   Rembrandt, ... a master of art, lived and worked in Holland.
4 Can you tell me how I should use this?
   How .... use this?
5 A famous artist is going to paint Nick's portrait.
   Nick is going .... portrait painted by a famous artist.

(10 marks)

4 Fill in the correct preposition.

1 What's the difference ..... these two cameras?
2 Tom is an expert .... computers.
3 There is a huge demand .... the latest PS2 game.
4 The book was a bit boring .... the beginning but then it got better.
5 I'm having difficulties .... my computer. Can you help me?
6 I like films where everything turns out well .... the end.

(12 marks)

Communication

5 Complete the exchanges.

a I'd love to go to the cinema.
b Fancy going out to dinner?
c Two tickets for the 8 o'clock screening, please.
d I haven't got a clue.
e There's something wrong with this calculator.

122

Self-Assessment Module 5

1 A: Do you know the temperature on Mars?
   B: ....
2 A: ....
   B: What is the problem exactly?
3 A: ....
   B: That would be great!
4 A: What would you like to do tonight?
   B: ....
5 A: ....
   B: Sorry – that one is fully booked.

(10 marks)

Listening

6 You will hear part of a conversation between two boys, Jim and Pete, about forming a rock band. For each question, put a tick (✓) in the correct box.

1 Jim wanted Matthew to join their band because
   A ☐ he is an experienced songwriter.
   B ☐ he works as a part-time musician on Saturdays.
   C ☐ he can play more than one instrument.

2 Choosing a lead singer is difficult because both Grace and Charlie
   A ☐ sing really well.
   B ☐ refuse to sing backing vocals.
   C ☐ are equally experienced as singers.

3 The band will get together this weekend to
   A ☐ arrange a rehearsal.
   B ☐ choose between Grace and Charlie.
   C ☐ practise a new song.

4 Jim's mother will allow the band to practise in the garage if
   A ☐ they stop before 10 o'clock.
   B ☐ the neighbours also agree.
   C ☐ they close the windows after 10 o'clock.

(8 marks)

Writing

7 Your school magazine has asked its readers to write a review of their favourite book. Write your review, briefly describing the plot and saying why you like it.

(20 marks)

Reading

8 Read and choose the correct word for each space.

DAEDALUS AND ICARUS

Who was the first man to fly? **0)** *According* to a Greek myth, it was a craftsman and inventor called Daedalus. The story describes **1)** .... Daedalus and his son, Icarus, flew away from King Minos' prison **2)** .... the island of Crete. Using wax and feathers, Daedalus made wings for **3)** .... and Icarus which looked exactly **4)** .... a bird's. Before they set **5)** .... , Daedalus **6)** .... his son not to fly **7)** .... close to the sun, but Icarus did not **8)** .... his father's advice. The sun melted the wax in his wings **9)** .... Icarus fell into the sea and **10)** ....

0	A Similar	**B** According	C Next	D Related
1	A that	B as	C if	D how
2	A on	B in	C at	D of
3	A him	B he	C himself	D them
4	A as	B at	C after	D like
5	A off	B to	C away	D on
6	A told	B reported	C said	D made
7	A enough	B so	C too	D much
8	A do	B take	C listen	D pay
9	A but	B although	C because	D and
10	A killed	B had killed	C was killed	D did kill

(20 marks)
(Total = 100 marks)

Now I can...

- talk about
  – my free time activities
  – my favourite film, book, TV series
  – gadgets, computers & processes
- make suggestions/agree & disagree
- book tickets
- describe
  – paintings
  – problems & request action
- write
  – a review of a school play
  – a TV guide
  – a letter to a friend reviewing a film
  – a text message
  – a letter of complaint

...in English

123

CURRICULAR CUTS — Art & Design

① **Bedroom at Arles** *Vincent Van Gogh*

② **Persistence of Memory** *Salvador Dali*

③ **Dancer Bowing** *Edgar Degas*

④ **Guernica** *Pablo Picasso*

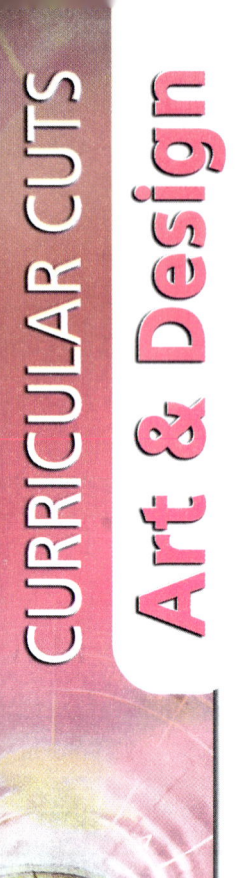

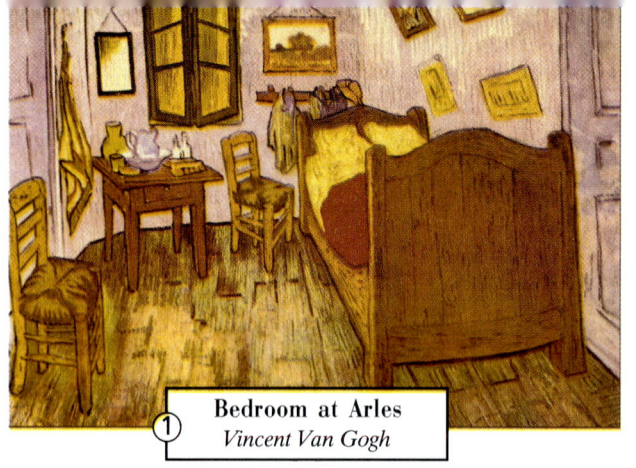

⑤ **Field in Spring** *Claude Monet*

1 Which painting do you like best? Why? Do you find any of them strange or unusual?

2 Read and listen to the texts (A-D). What style is each painting?

STYLES OF PAINTING

Cubism — A
Period: 1907 - 1914
Artists: Pablo Picasso, Georges Braque
Cubism was introduced in the early 1900s. The Cubists tried to create a new way of seeing the world through their art. They chose basic, **geometrical** shapes such as cubes, cones and **cylinders**. They used dull colours such as browns or greys to **represent** the way we see **images** in our **mind's eye** rather than in **reality**.

Impressionism — B
Period: 1867 - 1886
Artists: Pierre Auguste Renoir, Edgar Degas, Claude Monet
Impressionism began in France in the mid 1800s. The Impressionists often painted **outdoors** as they wanted to show **daylight**. Their works are **characterised by** short quick brushstrokes of light colours such as blues, reds and purples. When **viewed up close**, they can look **messy** and unreal. If you step back, the colours are **blended** by the eye and the **subject** becomes clear.

Post-Impressionism — C
Period: Late 1880s - 1900
Artists: Paul Gauguin, Paul Cezanne, Vincent Van Gogh
Post-Impressionism was **inspired** by Impressionism and **emphasises** colour. The artists in this group used thick brushstrokes and lines to express their feelings in their paintings. They preferred bright, bold colours, **especially** yellows and purples.

Surrealism — D
Period: 1920s - 1950
Artists: Salvador Dali, Rene Magritte
Surrealism started in France in the 1920s. Surrealists painted whatever they had dreamt about or **imagined**. Their paintings were very unusual and often showed everyday objects in a strange or **unexpected** way. They preferred bright, primary colours such as blues, reds and greens.

3 Read the texts again and ask and answer comprehension questions. Then, explain the words in bold.

4 **Project:** Find paintings (from the Internet, encyclopaedias, etc) which represent each of the four styles of painting discussed above. Present them to the class.

124

Songsheets

Songsheet 1

1 What do the people below look like? What do you think they are like?

A

B

Character comes from the heart

I once met a beautiful lady
Her hair was as black as the **1)** ....
Her eyes were as blue as the summer sky
She was such a wonderful **2)** ....
But then, as I got to know her
I was unhappy to find
That although she was so **3)** ....
She could also be rude and **4)** ....

*Don't judge a book by its cover
That's not the most important **5)** ....
For beauty is only skin deep, you know
But character comes from the **6)** ....*

I'm glad to say I learned my lesson
And now, when I meet someone **7)** ....
I never judge them by appearances
For that's not the right thing to **8)** ....
If they are friendly and honest
Who cares if they're handsome or tall?
If their heart is fair and good
Their looks shouldn't matter at **9)** ....

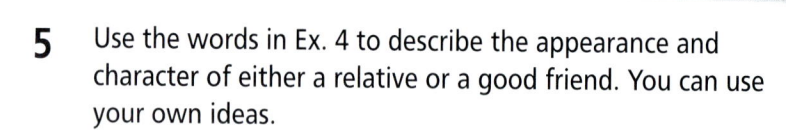

2 Look at the title of the song. How far do you agree with it?

3 🎧 Read the song and try to fill in the missing words. Listen and check. In pairs, think of an alternative title.

4 Read the song. Underline all the words which refer to appearance. Circle all those which refer to character.

5 Use the words in Ex. 4 to describe the appearance and character of either a relative or a good friend. You can use your own ideas.

My best friend has blonde hair, fair skin and blue eyes. She is honest and very friendly but she can be a little selfish sometimes.

6 a. Match the beginnings in column A with the endings in column B to form English sayings, then explain them.

A	B
1 Beauty	is not gold.
2 All that glitters	is only skin deep.
3 Don't judge a book	is in the eye of the beholder.
4 Beauty	by its cover.

b. Are there any similar expressions in your language?

Songsheet 2

1 How are the pictures related to the title of the song? What words do you expect to hear?

2 🎧 Read the song and fill in the words in the list. Listen and check.

• known • sea • return • leave • learn • home

3 Listen and read, then answer the questions.

1. What does the expression "I long to be free" mean?
2. Is the singer leaving his home forever?
3. Why is he going away?
4. Who is he leaving behind?
5. Where do you think he is going?

4 In pairs, discuss the following sayings. What do they mean? Do you agree with them? Are there any similar expressions in your language?

1. Absence makes the heart grow fonder.
2. Out of sight, out of mind.
3. A rolling stone gathers no moss.
4. When in Rome, do as the Romans do.
5. The grass is always greener on the other side.

The Boat Song

Sail, little boat
On the waves of the 1) ....
Carry me far away
I have to 2) ....
I long to be free
But I will be back some day

Take me to lands
Where I've never been
Places so far from 3) ....
Show me a world
I've never seen
A world I have never 4) ....

Tell all my friends
I will 5) ....
They should not cry for me
But there's so much
I need to 6) ....
So much I want to see

Songsheet 3

1 Look at the pictures. What do you think the man is looking forward to? Read the first two lines of the song and check.

I can't wait!

2 In pairs, think of ways to celebrate a birthday.

3 a. Complete the spidergram. Compare with your partner.

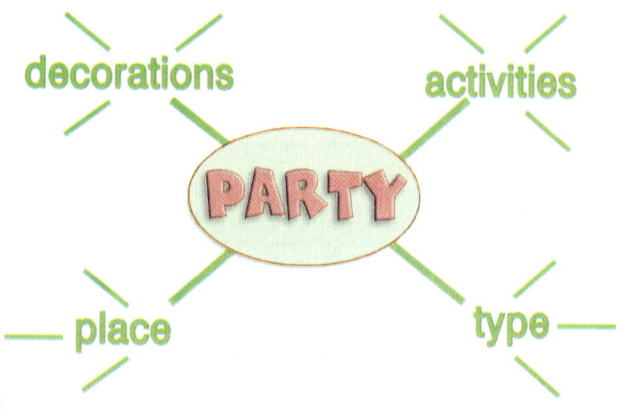

decorations — activities
PARTY
place — type

b. Listen to the song. Which of your spidergram words are heard in the song?

PARTY TIME

It's my birthday very soon
I'm counting off the days
I can't think how to celebrate
There are so many ways
I could go on a picnic
Or go to see a show
But I think I'll throw a party
'Cause they're so much fun to throw

*It's time to have a party
Time to really have fun
It's time to have a party
I'm inviting everyone
There'll be singing, there'll be laughter
We'll be dancing all night long
It's time to have a party
So I'm singing this song*

When you've got something to celebrate
There's just one thing to do
Tell your friends to gather round
And share the fun with you
Play your favourite music –
You're sure to have a ball
Of all the ways of having fun
A party's best of all

4 Read the song. How is the person going to celebrate his birthday?

5 Explain the English sayings. Are there similar ones in your language?

1 All work and no play makes Jack a dull boy.
2 Paint the town red.
3 Have a whale of a time.
4 The company makes the feast.

128

Songsheet 4

1 In pairs, read the phrases and decide which sport (A-D) they refer to. Which words helped you decide?

- the first kick
- to win the match
- to work as a team
- singing fans
- on the pitch
- hear the whistle blow

2 a. Read the first two lines of the song. What sport is being described? Listen and check.

b. Who do you think is narrating the events? Why? Underline the parts of the song that helped you decide.

Score another GO-O-OAL

The teams are on the pitch, the game is just beginning
We're ready for this match, our hearts are set on winning
The first kick of the ball, the crowds have started cheering
We hear the words they call, it's our names that we're hearing

Score another goal, we've got to keep on winning
Hear the whistle blow – all our fans are singing
We're the champions now

With minutes left to go, it looks like we can do it
The fans are going wild, as if they always knew it
This is like a dream, the greatest victory ever
Working as a team, we won the match together

3 a. Read the song and find three verbs related to sound.

b. Read again and find phrases which mean:
1. we want to win
2. be thrilled
3. it can't be true

4 In pairs, take roles and make up a short interview with a famous football player who has just finished playing in the final match of the World Cup. Discuss:

- feelings • reactions • regrets • any self-criticism
- wishes for the future etc.

Songsheet 5

1. Read the letters sent to a magazine problem page. What advice would you give these people?

1

I feel so ugly!

I'm 16 and get bullied at school because I'm fat and have red hair. Only my best friend doesn't hurt my feelings but it must be awful for her having a friend who's so ugly. I just wish I was normal like everyone else.

2

My big bro's driving me MAD!

I'm 16 and my brother is making my life a misery! He comes into my room without asking for permission, listens in on my phone calls and makes fun of my friends. When I complain to my parents they just say he'll grow out of it. What would you do if you were me?

2. Skim through the song. Who is Auntie Susan? What do you think her job is? Think of a title for the song.

3. Read the song and, in pairs, guess what the missing words are. Listen and check. Were your guesses correct?

Auntie Susan's column
Is all I ever 1) ....
She always helps her readers
She knows just what they 2) ....
Susan will advise you
On all life's little pains
She'll soothe away your worries
She'll help you smile again

If you've got a problem
Or something troubling 3) ....
Write to Auntie Susan
She'll tell you what to 4) ....

Auntie Susan's clever
She knows just what to 5) ....
If you need direction
She'll help you find your 6) ....
Susan is an expert
On matters of the 7) ....
She has a lot of wisdom
Which she's willing to 8) ....

4. In pairs, make a list of some typical problems experienced by teenagers. Take roles. One of you explains what the problem is while the other gives advice.

5. Explain the English sayings. Are there similar ones in your language?

1. Where there's a will, there's a way.
2. A problem shared is a problem halved.
3. Every cloud has a silver lining.

Irregular Verbs

Infinitive	Past	Past Participle	Infinitive	Past	Past Participle
be	was	been	lie	lay	lain
bear	bore	born(e)	light	lit	lit
beat	beat	beaten	lose	lost	lost
become	became	become	make	made	made
begin	began	begun	mean	meant	meant
bite	bit	bitten	meet	met	met
blow	blew	blown	pay	paid	paid
break	broke	broken	put	put	put
bring	brought	brought	read	read	read
build	built	built	ride	rode	ridden
burn	burnt (burned)	burnt (burned)	ring	rang	rung
burst	burst	burst	rise	rose	risen
buy	bought	bought	run	ran	run
can	could	(been able to)	say	said	said
catch	caught	caught	see	saw	seen
choose	chose	chosen	seek	sought	sought
come	came	come	sell	sold	sold
cost	cost	cost	send	sent	sent
cut	cut	cut	set	set	set
deal	dealt	dealt	sew	sewed	sewn
dig	dug	dug	shake	shook	shaken
do	did	done	shine	shone	shone
dream	dreamt (dreamed)	dreamt (dreamed)	shoot	shot	shot
drink	drank	drunk	show	showed	shown
drive	drove	driven	shut	shut	shut
eat	ate	eaten	sing	sang	sung
fall	fell	fallen	sit	sat	sat
feed	fed	fed	sleep	slept	slept
feel	felt	felt	smell	smelt (smelled)	smelt (smelled)
fight	fought	fought	speak	spoke	spoken
find	found	found	spell	spelt (spelled)	spelt (spelled)
flee	fled	fled	spend	spent	spent
fly	flew	flown	split	split	split
forbid	forbade	forbidden	spread	spread	spread
forget	forgot	forgotten	spring	sprang	sprung
forgive	forgave	forgiven	stand	stood	stood
freeze	froze	frozen	steal	stole	stolen
get	got	got	stick	stuck	stuck
give	gave	given	sting	stung	stung
go	went	gone	stink	stank	stunk
grow	grew	grown	strike	struck	struck
hang	hung (hanged)	hung (hanged)	swear	swore	sworn
have	had	had	sweep	swept	swept
hear	heard	heard	swim	swam	swum
hide	hid	hidden	take	took	taken
hit	hit	hit	teach	taught	taught
hold	held	held	tear	tore	torn
hurt	hurt	hurt	tell	told	told
keep	kept	kept	think	thought	thought
know	knew	known	throw	threw	thrown
lay	laid	laid	understand	understood	understood
lead	led	led	wake	woke	woken
learn	learnt (learned)	learnt (learned)	wear	wore	worn
leave	left	left	win	won	won
lend	lent	lent	write	wrote	written
let	let	let			

131

Grammar Reference

Unit 1

Present Simple and Present Continuous

We use the present simple for:
- facts and permanent states. *Mark **works** for an advertising company.*
- general truths and laws of nature. *Oil **floats** on water.*
- habits and routines (with **always**, **usually**, etc). *He usually **goes** jogging in the mornings.*
- timetables and programmes (in the future). *The plane to Madrid **takes off** at 6:30 pm.*
- sporting commentaries, reviews and narrations. *Beckham **wins** the ball, then he **crosses** and Owen **scores**.*
- feelings and emotions. *I **love** Paris, because it's a beautiful city.*

The time expressions we use with the present simple are: *Usually, often, always, every day/week/month/year/etc, in the morning/afternoon/evening, at night/the weekend, on Fridays, etc*

- for actions taking place at or around the moment of speaking. *The kids **are playing** video games in the living room.*
- for temporary situations. *They **are painting** the house.*
- for fixed arrangements in the near future. *I **am going** to a party tonight.*
- for currently changing and developing situations. *The rivers **are becoming** more and more polluted.*
- with adverbs such as **always** to express anger or irritation at a repeated action. *She **is always biting** her nails when someone talks to her.*

The time expressions we use with the present continuous are: *Now, at the moment, at present, these days, nowadays, still, today, tonight, etc*

Stative Verbs

Stative verbs are verbs which describe a state rather than an action, and so do not usually have a continuous tense. These verbs are:
- verbs of the senses (**appear, feel, hear, look, see, seem, smell, sound, taste**, etc). *She **seems** really worried.*
- verbs of perception (**believe, forget, know, realise, remember, understand**, etc). *I **believe** what he says.*
- verbs which express feelings and emotions (**desire, detest, enjoy, hate, like, love, prefer, want**, etc). *Jane **hates** eating spicy food.*
- and some other verbs (**be, belong, contain, cost, fit, have, include, keep, matter, need, owe, own, want, weigh, wish**, etc). *This house **belongs** to a very rich man.*

Some of these verbs can be used in continuous tenses, but with a difference in meaning.

Present Simple	Present Continuous
THINK *I **think** he's a very good actor. (= believe)*	*We **are thinking** about moving to a new house. (= are considering)*
HAVE *She **has** hundreds of books. (= own, possess)*	*Everyone **is having** a great time at the party. (= experiencing) He **is having** a bath. (= taking) They **are having** lunch. (= eating)*
SEE *You can **see** my house from up here. (= it is visible) I **see** what he means. (= understand)*	*I'm **seeing** the dentist this evening. (= am meeting)*
TASTE *This pie **tastes** delicious. (= it is, has the flavour of)*	*Ann **is tasting** the soup to see if it's spicy enough. (= is testing)*
SMELL *His perfume **smells** very good. (= has the aroma)*	*He **is smelling** the flowers. (= is sniffing)*
APPEAR *She **appears** to know where she's going. (= seems to)*	*He **is appearing** in a play at the Rex. (= is performing)*
FIT *The skirt **fits** her perfectly. (= it's the right size)*	*John **is fitting** a new lock on the front door. (= is attaching/installing)*

Note:
- The verb **enjoy** can be used in continuous tenses to express a specific preference.
*Bob really **enjoys** going to the cinema.* (general preference)
BUT: *He's **enjoying** the party very much.* (specific preference)
- The verbs **look** (when we refer to somebody's appearance), **feel** (experience a particular emotion), **hurt** and **ache** can be used in simple or continuous tenses with no difference in meaning.
*He **feels** very sad. = He **is feeling** very sad.*

Adverbs of Frequency

These include **always, frequently, often, once, twice, sometimes, never, usually, ever, hardly ever, rarely, occasionally**, etc.
- Adverbs of frequency are normally placed before the main verb.
*I **rarely** drive to work. He **hardly ever** goes to the cinema.*
- However, adverbs of frequency are placed after the verb **to be** and after auxiliary verbs. *Susan **is often** late for work.*
*I **have always** wanted to go on a safari.*

Unit 2

Comparisons

As / Like

We use **like**:
- with nouns/pronouns/-ing form to express similarity.
*She treats him **like a king**. (He isn't a king.)*
- with feel, look, smell, taste. *She **looks like** her mother.*

We use **as**:
- to say what somebody or something really is.
*He works **as a sales manager** for a multinational firm.*

Comparatives and Superlatives

We use the **comparative** to compare one person or thing with another. We use the **superlative** to compare one person or thing with more than one person or thing of the same group. We often use **than** after a comparative and **the** before a superlative. After superlatives we use **in** with places. *She is **younger than** me. She's **the youngest** person **in** the room.* but *This is the happiest day **of** my life.*

Formation of comparatives and superlatives from adjectives and adverbs:
- with one-syllable adjectives, we add **-(e)r** to form the comparative and **-(e)st** to form the superlative. *large – larger – largest*
Note: for one-syllable adjectives ending in **a vowel + a consonant**, we double the consonant. *big – bigger – biggest*
- with two-syllable adjectives ending in **-ly, -y, -w**, we also add **-er/-est**. *narrow – narrower – narrowest*
Note: for adjectives ending in **a consonant + y** we replace the **-y** with an **-i**. *heavy – heavier – heaviest*
- with other two-syllable adjectives or adjectives with more than two syllables, comparatives and superlatives are formed with **more/most**. *intelligent – more intelligent – most intelligent*
Note: **clever, common, cruel, friendly, gentle, pleasant, polite, shallow, simple, stupid, quiet** can form their comparatives and superlatives either with **-er/-est** or with **more/most**. *clever – cleverer/more clever – cleverest/most clever*
- with adverbs that have the same form as their adjectives (**hard, fast, free, early, late, high, low, deep, long, near, right, wrong, straight**) we add **-er/-est**. *fast – faster – fastest*
- two-syllable or compound adverbs take **more/most**. *slowly – more slowly – most slowly*
- Irregular forms:
good – better – best   bad – worse – worst
much – more – most   many/lots – more – most   little – less – least
far – farther/further – farthest/furthest

132

Grammar Reference

Types of comparisons:
- **as + adjective + as** to show that two people or things are similar in some way. In negative sentences we use **not as/so ... as**. *The blue dress is as beautiful as the red one.*
- **less + adjective + than** expresses the difference between two people or things. The opposite is **more ... than**. *I find comedies less interesting than thrillers.*
- **the least + adjective + of/in** compares one person or thing to two or more people or things in the same group. The opposite is **most ... of/in**. *Claire is the least ambitious person in the company.*
- **much / a lot / far / a little / a bit / slightly + comparative** expresses the degree of difference between two people or things. *Brian is slightly taller than Bill.*
- **comparative + and + comparative** to show that something is increasing or decreasing. *The Earth gets warmer and warmer.*
- **the + comparative ... , the + comparative** shows that two things change together, or that one thing depends on another thing. *The harder she studies, the more easily she'll pass the exam.*
- **by far + the + superlative** emphasises the difference between one person or thing and two or more people or things in the same group. *Fred is by far the best student in the class.*

-ing form

The **-ing form** is used:
- as a noun. *Jogging is very good for your health.*
- after certain verbs: admit, appreciate, avoid, consider, continue, deny, fancy, go (for activities), imagine, mind, miss, quit, save, suggest, practise, prevent. *Do you mind my opening the window?*
- after love, like, enjoy, prefer, dislike, hate to express general preference. *Clara enjoys talking to her friends on the phone.* BUT: for a specific preference (would like/would prefer/would love) we use to-infinitive.
- after expressions such as be busy, it's no use, it's no good, it's (not) worth, what's the use of, can't help, there's no point (in), can't stand, have difficulty (in), have trouble, etc. *There is no point in talking to Chris about it – he never listens to you.*
- after spend, waste, or lose (time, money, etc). *He wasted a lot of time doing nothing.*
- after the preposition to with verbs and expressions such as look forward to, be used to, in addition to, object to, prefer (doing sth to sth else). *She prefers swimming to playing tennis.*
- after other prepositions. *He was thinking of getting a new job.*
- after the verbs hear, listen to, notice, see, watch, and feel to describe an incomplete action. *I heard Nick talking to Eva. (I only heard part of the conversation.)*
BUT: we use the infinitive without to with hear, listen to, notice, see, watch, and feel to describe the complete action. *I heard Nick tell the story. (I heard the whole story.)*

Difference in meaning between the to-infinitive and -ing form

Some verbs can take either the **to-infinitive** or the **-ing form** with a change in meaning.
- **forget + to-infinitive** = not remember – *She forgot to lock the door.*
  forget + -ing form = not recall – *We'll never forget travelling around Africa.*
- **remember + to infinitive** = not forget – *Did you remember to turn off the computer?*
  remember + -ing form = recall – *I remember talking to Jenny at the party.*
- **mean + to-infinitive** = intend to – *I'm sorry; I never meant to offend you.*
  mean + -ing form = involve – *If he gets this job, it will mean moving to a new town.*
- **regret + to-infinitive** = be sorry to (normally used in the present simple with verbs such as say, tell, inform) – *We regret to inform passengers that the Air France flight to Paris has been delayed.*
  regret + -ing form = feel sorry about – *I regret losing touch with my old school friend Robert.*
- **try + to-infinitive** = attempt, do one's best – *I tried to call her but I couldn't get through.*
  try + -ing form = do something as an experiment – *Why don't you try changing the batteries?*
- **stop + to-infinitive** = stop temporarily in order to do something else – *After working for five hours they stopped to have a rest.*
  stop + -ing form = finish doing something – *At five o'clock everyone stopped working and went home.*

Infinitive

The **to-infinitive** is used:
- to express purpose. *She went to the clothes shop to buy a new dress for the reception.*
- after certain verbs that refer to the future (agree, appear, decide, expect, hope, plan, promise, refuse, etc). *They plan to buy a new car.*
- after would like, would prefer, would love, etc to express a specific preference. *I would prefer to stay at home tonight.*
- after adjectives which describe feelings/emotions (happy, glad, sad, etc), express willingness/unwillingness (eager, reluctant, willing, etc) or refer to a person's character (clever, kind, etc); and the adjectives lucky and fortunate. *I was very glad to hear that Liz got married.*
Note: With adjectives that refer to character we can also use an impersonal construction. *It was kind of you to help me with my essay.*
- after too/enough. *It isn't warm enough to go out without a coat.*
- to talk about an unexpected event (usually with only). *I finally arrived home only to find that I had left my keys at the office.*
- with it + be + adjective/noun. *It was easy to find the house after all.*
- after be + first/second/next/last/etc. *She was the first person to congratulate me on my promotion.*
- after verbs and expressions such as ask, decide, explain, find out, learn, want, want to know, etc when they are followed by a question word. *Their Maths teacher explained how to solve the problem.*
Note: why is followed by subject + verb, NOT an infinitive. *I wonder why she didn't let us know about it.*
- in the expressions to tell you the truth, to be honest, to sum up, to begin with, etc. *To be honest, I don't trust him anymore.*
Note: If two to-infinitives are linked by and or or, the to of the second infinitive is omitted. *I would like to go and visit Kate at the weekend.*

The **infinitive without to** (also called **bare infinitive**) is used:
- after modal verbs. *Carol can speak Italian and French.*
- after the verbs let, make, see, hear and feel. *They made her fill out a lot of forms.* BUT: we use the to-infinitive after be made, be heard, be seen, etc (passive form). *She was made to fill out a lot of forms.*
Note: When see, hear and watch are followed by an -ing form there is no change in the passive. *I saw him talking to Beth. He was seen talking to Beth.*
- after had better and would rather. *We had better avoid the town centre because the traffic is very heavy at the moment.*
- help can be followed by either the to-infinitive or the infinitive without to. *She helped me (to) paint the kids' bedroom.*

Preference

To express **general preference** we use:
- I prefer + noun/-ing + to + noun/-ing
  I prefer ice cream to chocolate. I prefer swimming to sunbathing.
- I prefer + to-infinitive + rather than + bare infinitive
  I prefer to watch TV rather than read books.

To express **specific preference** we use:
- I'd prefer + to-infinitive (rather than + bare infinitive)
  I'd prefer to stay at home (rather than go out).
- I'd prefer + noun (rather than + noun)
  - Would you like a cup of coffee? - I'd prefer tea, thanks.
- I'd rather + bare infinitive (than + bare infinitive)
  I'd rather watch TV than read books.

Unit 3

Present Perfect

We use the present perfect (have + past participle) for:
- an action that happened at an unstated time in the past. The emphasis is on the action; when it occurred is unimportant or unknown.
  I have washed the dishes. Natalie has been to France twice.
- an action which started in the past and continues up to the present, especially with stative verbs (see Unit 1, above) such as be, have, like, know, etc. *He has known me for six years.*
- a recently completed action. *I have (just/already) finished my essay.*
- personal experiences or changes. *She has put on five kilos.*

133

Grammar Reference

Time expressions used with the present perfect:

already is used in statements and questions (to suggest surprise).
*I have **already** spoken to Ann. Have you finished cooking **already**?*

yet is used with the present perfect in questions and negations.
*Have you paid the bill **yet**? Steven hasn't finished work **yet**.*

Other time expressions we use with the present perfect are: *always, just, ever, never, so far, today, this week/month/etc, how long, lately, recently, still (in negations), etc*

Present Perfect Continuous

We use the present perfect continuous (have + been + verb -ing):
- to put emphasis on the duration of an action which started in the past and continues up to the present. *We **have been working** on this project all morning.*
- for an action which started in the past and lasted for some time. It may still be continuing, or have finished but left a result still visible in the present. *She's tired because she **has been working** very hard lately.*
- to express anger, irritation or annoyance. *She **has been reading** my newspaper without asking me.*
- for repeated actions in the past continuing to the present. *He has lost weight because he **has been going** to the gym every day.*

Time expressions used with the present perfect (simple and continuous):

since (= from a starting point in the past) is used with the present perfect (simple and continuous). *I haven't seen Paul **since** we left school.*

for (= over a period of time) is used with the present perfect (simple and continuous). *They've been working on the project **for** months.*

Note: with the verbs **live, work, teach** and **feel** we can use the present perfect or the present perfect continuous with no difference in meaning. *He has lived/has been living in Manchester for the last six years.*

Clauses of purpose

We use clauses of purpose to explain why somebody does something. They are introduced with the following words/expressions:
- **to + infinitive** – *Helen went to Paris **to study** law.*
- **in order to/so as to + infinitive** (formal) – *They worked overtime **in order to finish** the project on time.*
- **so that + can/will** (present or future reference) – *Give me your number **so that I can call** you if there are any problems.*
- **so that + could/would** (past reference) – *He gave me his number **so that I could call** him if there were any problems.*
- **in case + present tense** (present or future reference) – *Leave your mobile phone on **in case I need** to call you.*
- **in case + past tense** (past reference) – *They had made some sandwiches **in case** they got hungry.*
  Note: **In case** is never used with **will** or **would**.
- **for + noun** (expresses the purpose of an action) – *They went to Pierro's **for a pizza**.*
- **for + -ing form** (expresses the purpose of something or its function) – *Microwaves are used **for heating up** food.*
- **with a view to + -ing form** – *Lucy bought the old house **with a view to renovating** it.*

We can express **negative purpose** by:
- **in order not to/so as not to + infinitive** – *I wrote down the names and phone numbers of all the guests **so as not to forget** to call anyone.*
- **prevent + noun/pronoun + (from) + -ing form** – *The teacher covered up what was written on the board **to prevent the students from reading** it.*

Unit 4

Present/Past Participles

We use **present participles** to describe something. *It was a **boring** film.* (How was the film? Boring.)

We use **past participles** to say how someone felt. *We were **bored**.* (How did we feel? Bored.)

Past Simple

We use the past simple:
- for an action that occurred at a definite time (stated or implied) in the past. *They **spent** their summer holidays in Italy last year.*
- for actions that happened in the past, one immediately after the other. *She **locked** the door behind her and **took off** her shoes.*
- for habits or states which are now finished. *Mr Smith **worked** in a bank when he was younger.*
  Note: **used to** can also be used instead of the past simple for habits/repeated actions in the past (see p. 135).

ago (= back in time from now) is used with the past simple. *I got home about an hour **ago**.*

Time expressions we use with the past simple include: *yesterday, then, when, How long ago?, last night/week/month/year/Sunday/June/etc, in 1980, etc*

Past Continuous

We use the past continuous:
- for an action which was in progress when another action interrupted it. We use the past continuous for the action in progress (the longer action) and the past simple for the action which interrupted it (shorter action). *We **were watching** a horror film on TV when we heard a strange noise.*
- for two or more simultaneous actions in the past. *They **were having** dinner while Michael **was washing** the car.*
- for an action which was in progress at a stated time in the past. We don't mention when the action started or finished. *At 8 o'clock last night I **was walking** home from work.*
- to describe the atmosphere, setting, etc and to give background information to a story. *The birds **were singing** and the sun **was shining**. I **was sitting** outside in the garden when something strange happened …*

Note: When there are two past continuous forms in a sentence with the same subject we can avoid repetition by using just the present participle (-ing form) and leaving out the verb **to be**. *He was walking along, and he was eating an ice cream. = He was walking along, eating an ice cream.*

The time expressions we use with the past continuous include: *while, when, as, all morning/evening/day/week/etc*

Linkers

Linking words show the logical relationship between sentences or parts of sentences.

- **Positive addition:**
  and, both … and, too, besides (this/that), moreover, what is more, in addition (to), also, as well as (this/that), furthermore, etc.
  *Tony is **both** kind **and** helpful.*

- **Negative addition:**
  neither (… nor), nor, neither, either, etc. ***Neither** Sue **nor** I went to the club.*

- **Contrast/Concession:**
  but, however, on the other hand, yet, still, etc
  although (+ clause), in spite of (+ noun/-ing), despite (+ noun/-ing), while (+ clause), whereas (+ clause), even though (+ clause), etc.
  ***Even though** we hurried, we still missed the bus.*

- **Giving examples:**
  such as, like, for example, for instance, especially, in particular, etc.
  *The weather has been bad this week, and Friday **in particular** was very cold.*

- **Cause/Reason:**
  as, because, because of, since, for this reason, due to, so, as a result (of), etc.
  *She had to take a taxi **because** her car had run out of petrol.*

- **Condition:**
  if, whether, only if, in case of, in case, provided (that), providing (that), unless, as/so long as, otherwise, or (else), on condition (that), etc.
  *Joy said she could lend me £50 **as long as** I paid it back by Monday.*

- **Purpose:** (see p. 134)
  to, so that, so as (not) to, in order (not) to, in order that, in case, etc.
  *David went to the bank **to get** a loan.*

- **Effect/Result:**
  such/so … that, so, consequently, as a result, therefore, for this reason, etc.
  *She doesn't really like her job **so** she is looking for a new one.*

134

Grammar Reference

- **Time:**
  when, whenever, as, as soon as, while, before, until/till, after, since, etc.
  *They'll go out **as soon as** I get there.*
- **Exception:**
  except (for), apart from, etc. *He paid all the bills **except for** the electricity.*
- **Relatives:**
  who, whom, whose, which, what, that. *That's the man **who** works in the library.*

Listing words show the sequence of a series of events or the priority of a series of points.

- **To begin:**
  initially, first, at first, firstly, to start/begin with, first of all, etc.
  ***First** the parcel was delivered.*
- **To continue:**
  secondly, after this/that, second, afterwards, then, next, etc.
  ***Next** I unwrapped the box.*
- **To conclude:**
  finally, lastly, in the end, at last, eventually, etc.
  ***Eventually** I read the card in surprise.*
- **Summarising:**
  in conclusion, in summary, to sum up, on the whole, all in all, altogether, in short, etc. ***All in all**, it was one of the best presents I had ever received.*

The indefinite article (*a/an*)

- We use **a/an** with unspecified singular, countable nouns.
  *Jack has bought **a** new car. (There are millions of cars; this is one of them.)*
- We use **a** with words that begin with a consonant sound, and **an** with words that begin with a vowel sound. This depends on how a word is pronounced, not how it is spelt.
  *a banana, a European – **an** apple, **an** honest person*

The definite article (*the*)

We use **the**:
- with nouns when talking about something specific. *Jack owns a car and a motorbike. **The** car is black and **the** motorbike is blue.*
- with nouns that are unique. *(**the** sun, **the** Earth, etc)*
- with names of newspapers (*the Guardian*), cinemas (*the Rex*), theatres (*the Empire*), museums/art galleries (*the Louvre*), ships (*the Titanic*), organisations (*the United Nations*).
- with the names of rivers (*the Thames*), groups of Islands (*the Bahamas*), mountain ranges (*the Alps*), deserts (*the Sahara*), oceans (*the Atlantic*), canals (*the Panama canal*), countries when they include words such as States, Kingdom, Republic (*the USA*), and names or nouns with of (*the Houses of Parliament*), in geographical terms such as *the Antarctic/Arctic/equator*, *the North of Germany*, *the North/East/South/West*.
- with the names of musical instruments and dances (*the guitar, the salsa*).
- with the names of families (*the Jones*) and nationalities ending in -sh, -ch, or -ese (*the Chinese*). Other nationalities can be used with or without **the** (*the Egyptians/Egyptians*).
- with titles (*the ambassador, the President*) but not with titles including a proper name (*Prince Charles*).
- with adjectives/adverbs in the superlative form (*the best film I have ever seen*) but when **most** is followed by a noun it doesn't take **the** (*most people enjoy going to the theatre*).
- with the words **day, morning, afternoon** and **evening**. *It was early in **the** morning and the sun was starting to rise.*
  BUT: at night, at noon, at midnight, by day/night
- with historical periods/events (*the last Ice Age, the Vietnam war*) BUT: World War I
- with **only, last** and **first** (used as adjectives). *He was **the** only one who saw her.*
- with **station, cinema, theatre, library, shop, coast, sea(side), beach, city, country(side), jungle, world, ground, weather**. *They went for a walk along **the** coast.*

We do NOT use **the**:
- with uncountable and plural nouns when talking about something in general. ***Cars** release harmful gases into the atmosphere. **Coffee** is a very popular drink.*
- with proper nouns. ***John** is my cousin.*
- with the names of sports, games, activities, days, months, celebrations, colours, drinks and meals. *They are going to have **dinner** on **Sunday**.*
- with languages unless they are followed by the word **language**. *Andy speaks **Spanish**, **French** and **English** fluently.* BUT: *The French language is spoken in Belgium.*

- with the names of countries which don't include the word **State, Kingdom** or **Republic**. *Germany, India, China*. BUT there are some exceptions: *the Netherlands, the Gambia, the Vatican*.
- with the names of streets (*Bond Street, Penny Lane* BUT: *the M7, the A43*), squares (*Trafalgar Square*), bridges (*London Bridge* BUT: *the Golden Gate Bridge*), parks (*Hyde Park*), railway stations (*Euston, King's Cross*), mountains (*Mount Everest*), individual islands (*Sicily*), lakes (*Lake Baikal*) and continents (*Europe*).
- with possessive adjectives or the possessive case. *That is **my** house.*
- with the names of restaurants, shops, banks, hotels, etc which are named after the people who started them (*Harrods, Tony's Restaurant*).
- with the words **bed, hospital, college, court, prison, school, university** when we refer to the purpose for which they exist. *The injured man had to be taken to **hospital**.* BUT: *He went to **the hospital** to visit Bill.*
- with the word **work** (= place of work). *He needs to be at **work** by 9 o'clock.*
- with the words **home, mother, father**, etc when we talk about our own home/parents.
- with **by** + means of transport *(by bus/ferry/train/car/etc)* We travelled to London **by train**.
- with the names of illnesses. *She's got **pneumonia**.* BUT: *flu/the flu, measles/the measles, mumps/the mumps*.

Used to/Would

We use *used to/would (always/often/etc)* + bare infinitive to refer to past habits or states. *He **used to/would** go jogging every morning when he was younger.*
In such cases **used to/would** can be replaced by the past simple with no change in meaning. *When the children were younger they **woke up/used to wake up** late every day.*
But for an action that happened at a definite time in the past we use the **past simple**, not **used to**. *I drove to work yesterday.* (NOT: ~~I used to drive to work yesterday.~~)

We also use **used to** to talk about past facts or generalizations which are no longer true. *I **used to live** in Rome. Now I live in Madrid.* (NOT: ~~I would~~ live)

Unit 5

Modals

Modals *can/could, may/might, must/[had to], ought to, shall/should, will/would*:
- don't take -*s*, -*ing* or -*ed* suffixes
- are followed by the bare infinitive
- come before the subject in questions and are followed by **not** in negations
- don't have tenses in the normal sense. When followed by a normal bare infinitive, they refer to an uncompleted action or state (i.e. present or future); when followed by the bare perfect infinitive, they refer to a completed action or state.

Obligation/Duty/Necessity

Must: Expresses duty/strong obligation to do sth, shows that sth is essential. We generally use **must** when the speaker has decided that sth is necessary (i.e. subjective). *I **must** remember to send my mother a birthday card.*

Have to: Expresses strong necessity/obligation. We usually use **have to** when somebody other than the speaker has decided that sth is necessary (i.e. objective). *He said we **have to** follow the instructions.*

Had to is the past form of both **must** and **have to**.

Absence of necessity

Don't have to: It isn't necessary to do sth in the present/future. *You **don't have to** do the washing up – I will do it.*
Didn't have to: It wasn't necessary to do sth. We don't know if it was done or not. *He **didn't have to** pay all the bills today. (We don't know if he paid them or not.)*

Permission/Prohibition

Can/May: Used to ask for/give permission. **May** is more formal than **can**. *Can/May I borrow your pen, please? Yes, of course you **can/may**.*

Mustn't/Can't: It is forbidden to do sth; it is against the rules/law; you are not allowed to do sth. *You **mustn't/can't** park your car here.*

Possibility

Can + present infinitive: General/theoretical possibility. Not usually used for a specific situation. *For dessert you **can** have apple-pie or ice-cream.*

135

Grammar Reference

Could/May/Might + present infinitive: Possibility in a specific situation. *He should keep that souvenir – it **may be** valuable one day.*
Note: we can use **can/could/might** in questions BUT NOT **may**. *Do you think that he **can/could/might** fix it?*

Could/Might/Would + perfect infinitive: Refers to sth in the past that was possible but didn't happen. *He **might have** succeeded if he had tried harder.*

Ability/Inability

Can expresses ability in the present/future. *I **can** play the piano.*

Could expresses general, repeated ability in the past. *I **could** talk when I was two.*

Was(n't) able to expresses (in)ability on a specific occasion in the past. *I **wasn't able to** get to the airport in time to catch my flight.*

Couldn't may be used to express any kind of inability in the past, repeated or specific. *I **couldn't** speak French when I was two. I **couldn't/wasn't able to** remember his name when I saw him in the street.*

Logical Assumptions/Deductions

Must, may, can't, etc + bare infinitive: for assumptions about the present.
perfect infinitive: for assumptions about the past.

Must = almost certain that this is/was true.
*She's been working all day, so she **must be** really tired!*
*She was working all day yesterday, so she **must have been** really tired!*

May/Might/Could = possible that this is/was true.
*John isn't at work today – he **may/might be** out of town on business.*
*John wasn't at work yesterday – he **may/might have been** out of town on business.*

Can't/couldn't = almost certain that this is/was impossible.
*That **can't** be Janet over there – she's at her grandparents' at the moment.*
*That **can't have been** Janet you saw – she was at her grandparents' at that time.*

Note how the tenses of the infinitive are formed:
Present simple: (to) cook
Present continuous: (to) be cooking
Present perfect simple: (to) have cooked
Present perfect continuous: (to) have been cooking

Too/Enough

We use **too + adjective/adverb (for sb/sth) + to-infinitive** to show that something is more than is wanted/permitted/etc.
*He is **too young to drive**. (He isn't allowed to drive.)*
*The suitcase is **too heavy (for me) to carry**. (I can't carry it.)*

We use **(not) ... enough ... (for sb/sth) + to-infinitive** to show that something is (not) as much as is wanted/necessary/etc.
*He isn't **old enough to drive**. (He isn't allowed to drive.)*
*The suitcase is **light enough (for me) to carry**. (I can carry it.)*
Enough follows an adjective/adverb, but is placed before a noun.
*I have(n't) got **enough money** to buy a new car.*

Unit 6

Future forms

We use the future simple (will + bare infinitive) for:
- decisions made at the moment of speaking. *It's cold in here – I'**ll close** a window.*
- predictions about the future, based on what we think, believe or imagine, using the verbs **think, believe, expect**, etc, the expressions **be sure, be afraid**, etc, and the adverbs **probably, certainly, perhaps**, etc. *He **will probably come** later.*
- promises, threats, warnings, requests, hopes, and offers. ***Will you help** me wash the dishes?*
- actions, events, situations which will definitely happen in the future and which we can't control. *Tom **will be** three years old in September.*

We use **be going to**:
- for plans, intentions or ambitions for the future. *He's **going to be** a lawyer when he finishes university.*
- actions we have already decided to do in the near future. *Peter **is going to work** with his uncle during the holidays.*
- predictions based on what we can see or what we know, especially when there is evidence now that something will happen later. *It's cloudy; it's **going to rain** tonight.*

We use the present continuous for:
- definite arrangements for the future. *I'**m flying** to Paris tomorrow. (I've bought my ticket.)*

We use the present simple ('timetable future') for:
- fixed routines and arrangements for the future *(timetables, programmes, etc)*, usually decided by someone else. *My flight to Paris **leaves** at 6 o'clock tomorrow.*

The time expressions we use with future forms (future simple, be going to, present continuous, present simple) include: *tomorrow, the day after tomorrow, tonight, soon, next week/month/year/summer, etc, in a week/month, etc*

Future Continuous

We use the future continuous (will be + present participle of the verb):
- for actions which will be in progress at a stated future time. *This time next month I'**ll be flying** to Rome.*
- for actions which will definitely happen in the future as the result of a routine or arrangement. *He **will be visiting** his parents at the weekend.*
- when we ask politely about someone's plans for the near future. ***Will you be finishing** with that book soon?*

Time Clauses about the future

When we use words and expressions such as **while, before, after, until/till, as, when, whenever, once, as soon as, as long as, by the time**, etc to introduce time clauses about the future, they are followed by the **present simple** or **present perfect**, but NOT future forms.
*By the time we **get** to the station the train will have left.*
(NOT: ~~By the time we will get to the station~~ ...)

We also use the **present simple** and **present perfect**, but NOT future forms, after words and expressions such as **unless, if, suppose/supposing, in case**, etc.
*Take an umbrella **in case it rains**. (NOT: ... ~~in case it will rain~~.)*

We DO use **future forms** with:
- **when** - when it is used as a question word. ***When will you be going** shopping next?*
- **if/whether** – after expressions which show uncertainty/ignorance, etc, such as **I don't know, I doubt, I wonder, I'm not sure**, etc. *I doubt **whether he will pass** the exam.*

Unit 7

Countable – Uncountable Nouns

- **Countable** nouns are those that can be counted (*one apple, two apples,* etc). **Uncountable** nouns are those that cannot be counted (*water, bread,* etc). **Uncountable** nouns take a singular verb and are not used with a/an.

Groups of uncountable nouns include:
- mass nouns (*milk, sugar, wine*, etc)
- subjects of study (*Physics, History, Geography*, etc)
- sports (*football, cricket, tennis*)
- languages (*Arabic, French, Chinese*)
- diseases (*chickenpox, malaria, measles*)
- natural phenomena (*rain, snow, mist*)
- collective nouns (*money, furniture, luggage*)
- certain other nouns (*accommodation, anger, luck*)

136

Grammar Reference

Some/Any/No & their compounds

Some, **any** and **no** are used with uncountable nouns and plural countable nouns. *some water, some potatoes.*

- **Some** and its compounds (**somebody, someone, something, somewhere**, etc) are normally used in affirmative sentences. *There is some wine left in the bottle.*
- **Some** and its compounds are also used in interrogative sentences when we expect a positive answer, for example when we make an offer or request. *Would you like something to drink?*
- **Any** and its compounds (**anyone, anything**, etc) are usually used in interrogative sentences. *Has anyone seen Jim today?* **Not any** is used in negative sentences. *There isn't any petrol in the tank.* **Any** and its compounds can also be used with negative words such as **without, never, rarely**. *I have never met anyone like him before.*
- When **any** and its compounds are used in affirmative sentences there is a difference in meaning. *You can do anything you like.* (it doesn't matter what)
  Anyone could have done that. (it doesn't matter who)
- **No** and its compounds can be used instead of **not any** in negative sentences. *Laura didn't say anything.* (= She said **nothing**) *There wasn't anybody in the house.* (= There was **nobody** in the house)
  Note: We use a singular verb with compounds of **some, any** and **no**. *There is nothing they can do.*

A few/Few – A little/Little

A few and **few** are used with plural countable nouns. **A little** and **little** are used with uncountable nouns.

- **A few** means "not many, but enough". *We have a few apples. We can make an apple pie.* **Few** means "hardly any, almost none" and can be used with **very** for emphasis. *There were (very) few people queuing in the bank.*
- **A little** means "not much, but enough". *There is a little coffee left – would you like another cup?*
- **Little** means "hardly any, almost none" and can be used with **very** for emphasis. *There is (very) little sugar left. I'll go and buy some.*

A lot of/lots of – much – many

- **A lot of/lots of** are used with both plural countable and uncountable nouns. They are normally used in affirmative sentences. The **of** is omitted when **a lot/lots** are not followed by a noun. *There are a lot/lots of oranges in the fridge. I can make some juice.*
- **Much** and **many** are usually used in negative or interrogative sentences. **Much** is used with uncountable nouns and **many** is used with plural countable nouns. *There aren't many parks in the centre of the city. Did you spend much money at the supermarket?*
- **How much** and **how many** are used in questions and negations.
  How much + uncountable noun → amount
  How many + countable noun → number
  How much pepper shall I put in the soup?
  How many children do they have?
- **Too much** is used with uncountable nouns. It has a negative meaning and shows that there is more of something than is wanted or needed. *He couldn't sleep because the children were making too much noise.*
- **Too many** is used with plural countable nouns. It has the same negative meaning as too much. *It was very crowded. There were too many people there.*
- We use many/much/some/any/most/(a) few/(a) little/several/one/two, etc + of followed by the/that/this/ these/those and then a noun when talking about a specific group. *Some of the houses in that district are very expensive.* (houses in that district) but: *Some houses are very expensive.* (houses in general)

Past Perfect

We use the past perfect (had + past participle):

- for an action which happened before another past action or before a stated time in the past. *Ann had finished her homework by five o'clock.*
- for an action which finished in the past and whose result was visible at a later point in the past. *She had sprained her ankle a few days earlier and it was still hurting.*
- for a general situation in the past. *Everything had seemed normal at first.*

The time expressions we use with the past perfect are: *before, after, already, just, for, since, till/until, when, by the time, never, etc*

Past Perfect Continuous

We use the past perfect continuous:

- to put emphasis on the duration of an action which started and finished in the past, before another action or stated time in the past, usually with for or since. *He had been driving for an hour when he realised he had forgotten to lock the door.*
- for an action which lasted for some time in the past and whose result was visible in the past. *He had been swimming and his hair was still wet.*

Unit 8

The Passive

We form the passive with the verb **to be** in the appropriate tense and the **past participle** of the main verb. Only transitive verbs (verbs which take an object) can be used in the passive. (*live* does not have a passive form).

We use the passive:

- when the person or people who do the action are unknown, unimportant or obvious from the context. *Linda's purse was stolen.* (We don't know who stole it.) *The car is being repaired.* (It's unimportant who is doing it.) *The robber has been arrested.* (It's obvious that the police arrested him.)
- when the action itself is more important than the person/people who do it, as in news headlines, newspaper articles, formal notices, advertisements, instructions, processes, etc. *The annual meeting was held on March 20th.*
- when we want to avoid taking responsibility for an action or when we refer to an unpleasant event and we do not want to say who or what is to blame. *Four people were injured in the bank robbery.*

Changing from the active to the passive:

- the **object** of the active sentence becomes the **subject** in the passive sentence
- the active verb remains in the same tense but changes into a passive form
- the **subject** of the active sentence becomes the **agent**, and is either introduced with the preposition **by** or is omitted.

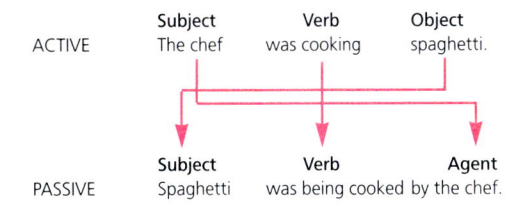

	Subject	Verb	Object
ACTIVE	The chef	was cooking	spaghetti.
	Subject	Verb	Agent
PASSIVE	Spaghetti	was being cooked	by the chef.

- Only transitive verbs (verbs that take an object) can be changed into the passive. **Active:** *Jack lives on the second floor* (intransitive verb) **no passive form:** ~~The second floor is lived on by Jack.~~
  Note: Some transitive verbs (*have, exist, seem, fit, suit, resemble, lack* etc) cannot be changed into the passive. *Mike has a red car.* NOT: ~~A red car is had by Mike.~~
- we can use the verb to get instead of the verb to be in everyday speech when we talk about things that happen by accident or unexpectedly. *Alex got injured when he was playing football.* (Instead of *he was injured...*)
- **By + the agent** is used to say who or what carries out an action. **with + instrument/material/ingredient** is used to say what the agent used. *The sauce was made by Luigi. It was made with fresh tomatoes.*
- The agent can be omitted when the subject is *they, he, someone/ somebody, people, one*, etc. *Somebody has washed the car.* = *The car has been washed.*
- The agent is not omitted when it is a specific or important person, or when it is essential to the meaning of the sentence. *This poem was written by William Blake.*
- With verbs which can take two objects, such as *bring, tell, send, show, teach, promise, buy, sell, read, offer, give, lend, etc*, we can form two different passive sentences.
  Joan gave the parcel to him. (active)
  He was given the parcel by Joan. (passive, more usual)
  The parcel was given to him by Joan. (passive, less usual)
- If in an active sentence a preposition follows a verb, then in the passive it is placed immediately after the verb. *This item hit Maria on the back. Maria was hit on the back by this item.*

137

Grammar Reference

- The verbs **hear, help, see,** and **make** are followed by the bare infinitive in the active but by the to-infinitive in the passive. *Melissa's mum **made** her clean her room. Melissa **was made to clean** her room by her mum.*
- **Let** becomes **be allowed to** in the passive. *The teacher let the children leave early. The children **were allowed** to leave early.*
- To ask questions in the passive we follow the same rules as for statements, keeping in mind that the verb is in the interrogative form. *Have they opened the new fitness centre yet? Has the new fitness centre been opened (by them) yet?*
- When we want to find out who or what performed an action, the passive question form is **Who/What … by?** *Who was the film directed by?*

Conditionals: type 0/1

Type 0 conditionals are used to express a general truth or a scientific fact. In this type of conditional we can use **when** instead of **if**.

If-clause		Main Clause
If/when + present simple	→	present simple
*If/When you **mix** red and yellow paint, you **get** orange.*		

Type 1 conditionals are used to express a **real** or **very probable situation** in the **present or future**.

If-clause		Main Clause
If + present simple	→	future simple, imperative, can/must/may/etc + bare infinitive
*If he **works** hard, he **will/might**/etc **get** a promotion.*		

When the hypothesis comes before the main clause, we separate the two parts with a comma. When the main clause comes before the if-clause, then we do not use a comma to separate them.

Note: With type 1 conditionals we can use **unless + affirmative verb** (= if + negative verb). *He will not be able to finish his homework **unless** Fred **gives** him a hand.* (= if Fred **does not give** him a hand, …)

Unit 9

So/Neither/Nor

- **So** and **neither/nor** are used to express the fact that a statement about one subject (person, thing, action, etc) applies to a second subject in the same way.
- **So** follows a positive statement and **neither/nor** follows a negative statement.
- The word order is **So/Neither/Nor + modal/auxiliary + subject**. The auxiliary is the same as in the statement or, if there is no auxiliary in the statement, we use **do/does** (present simple) or **did** (past simple).
  *Skiing is fun. **So** is skateboarding.*
  *Greta Garbo was a film star. **So** was Marilyn Monroe.*
  *My brother doesn't like chocolate. **Neither/Nor** do I.*

Conditionals: Types 2 and 3

- **Conditionals Type 2 (unreal present)** are used to express imaginary situations which are contrary to facts in the present, and, therefore, are unlikely to happen in the present or the future. We can use either **were** or **was** for 1st and 3rd person singular in the *if*-clause. We can also use the structure *If I were you, …* to give advice.

If-clause		Main Clause
If + past simple/ past continuous	→	would/could/might + bare present infinitive
*If I **spoke** their language, I **would know** what they were talking about.*		
*If Richard **was playing** today, we **would have** a better chance of scoring.*		
*If I **were** you, I **would apologise** to her.* (advice)		

- **Conditionals Type 3 (unreal past)** are used to express imaginary situations which are contrary to facts in the past. They are also used to express regrets or criticism.

If-clause		Main Clause
If + past perfect/ past perfect continuous	→	would/could/might + bare perfect infinitive
*If I **had taken** a taxi, I **would have been** there in time.*		
*If it **hadn't been raining** today, we **would have gone** on an excursion.*		

Wishes

- We can use **wish /if only** to express a wish.

Verb Tense		Use
+ past simple/ past continuous	*I wish I **was** at home now. (but I'm not) If only I **were going** to the wedding. (but I'm not)*	To say that we would like something to be different about a present situation.
+ past perfect	*I wish I **had called** him earlier. (but I didn't) If only they **hadn't broken** up. (but they did)*	To express regret about something which happened or didn't happen in the past.
+ subject + would + bare inf.	*I wish you **wouldn't behave** so rudely. If only it **would stop** snowing.*	to express: • a polite imperative. • a desire for a situation or person's behaviour to change.

- Note: **If only** is used in exactly the same way as **wish** but it is more emphatic or more dramatic.
- We can use **were** instead of **was** after **wish** and **if only**. *I wish I **were/was** on holiday now.*

Relative Clauses

Relative clauses are introduced with either a **relative pronoun** or a **relative adverb**.

Relative Pronouns

We use:
  i. **who(m)/that** to refer to people.
  ii. **which/that** to refer to things.
  iii. **whose** with people, animals and objects to show possession (instead of a possessive adjective).

- **Who, which,** and **that** can be omitted when they are the object of the relative clause. *He's the person (who) I am going to cooperate with.*
- **Whom** can be used instead of **who** when it is the object of the relative clause. **Whom** is always used instead of **who** or **that** after a preposition. *That's the boy to **whom** Stella was talking on the phone yesterday.*
- **Who, which,** or **that** is not omitted when it is the subject of a relative clause. *The man **who** owns that shop is Italian.*
- **Whose** is never omitted. *That's the woman **whose** husband is our new boss.*

Relative adverbs

We use:
  i. **when/that** to refer to a time (and can be omitted) *That was the year (when/that) we graduated from University.*
  ii. **where** to refer to a place. *The restaurant **where** we first met is going to be pulled down.*
  iii. **why** to give a reason, usually after the word reason (why can be omitted). *The reason (why) she left is still unclear.*

Identifying and Non-Identifying Relative Clauses

An identifying relative clause gives necessary information essential to the meaning of the main sentence. It is not put in commas and is introduced with **who, which, that, whose, where, when,** or the **reason (why)**.
*The dress **which** I bought last month doesn't fit me.*

A non-identifying relative clause gives extra information and is not essential to the meaning of the main sentence. It is put in commas and is introduced with **who, whom, which, whose, where,** or **when**.
*Julia Roberts, **who** has starred in a lot of successful films, is my favourite actress.*

Grammar Reference

Unit 10

All/Most/Some/None of

- All/most/some/none refer to more than two people, things, etc
- All/most/some of + plural pronoun is followed by a plural verb.
  Most of us/you/them believe this is wrong.
- None of + plural pronoun is followed by a singular verb.
  None of us/you/them is prepared to make such a sacrifice.

Reported Speech

Reported speech is the exact meaning of what someone said, but not the exact words. We do not use quotation marks. The word **that** can either be used or omitted after the introductory verb *(say, tell, suggest, etc)*.
He said (that) he would come home before 9 o'clock.

Say - Tell

- say + no personal object – She **said** she was very angry.
- say + to + personal object – She **said to us** she was very angry.
- tell + personal object – She **told us** she was very angry.

Expressions used with **say**, **tell** and **ask**.

Say	hello, good morning/afternoon, etc, something/ nothing, so, a prayer, a few words, no more, for certain/sure, etc
Tell	the truth, a lie, a story, a secret, a joke, the time, the difference, one from another, somebody one's name, somebody the way, somebody so, someone's fortune, etc
Ask	a question, a favour, the price, after somebody, the time, around, for something/somebody, etc

Reported Statements

- In reported speech, personal/possessive pronouns and possessive adjectives change according to the meaning of the sentence.
  Peter said, "I'm having my car serviced." (direct statement)
  Peter said (that) he was having his car serviced. (reported statement)
- We can report someone's words either a long time after they were said (out-of-date reporting) or a short time after they were said (up-to-date reporting).

Up-to-date reporting

The tenses can either change or remain the same in reported speech.
Direct speech: Nancy said, "I still **haven't finished** my homework."
Reported speech: Nancy said (that) she still **hasn't/hadn't finished** her homework.

Out-of-date reporting

The introductory verb is in the past simple and the tenses change as follows:

Direct speech	Reported speech
Present Simple → Past Simple	
"My bus **arrives** at 5 o'clock."	She said (that) her bus **arrived** at 5 o'clock.
Present Continuous → Past Continuous	
"I **am playing** tennis this afternoon."	She said (that) she **was playing** tennis that afternoon.
Present Perfect → Past Perfect	
"I **have made** spaghetti."	She said (that) she **had made** spaghetti.
Past Simple → Past Simple or Past Perfect	
"I **paid** six pounds for the CD."	She said (that) she **paid/had paid** six pounds for the CD.
Past Continuous → Past Continuous or Past Perfect Continuous	
"I **was walking** to the bus station."	She said that she **was walking/had been** walking to the station.
Future (will) → Conditional (would)	
"I **will return** the books tomorrow."	She said that she **would return** the books the next day.

- Certain words and time expressions change according to the meaning as follows:
now	→	then, immediately
today	→	that day
yesterday	→	the day before, the previous day
tomorrow	→	the next/following day
this week	→	that week
last week	→	the week before, the previous week
next week	→	the week after, the following week
ago	→	before
here	→	there
come	→	go
bring	→	take

- The verb tenses remain the same in reported speech when the introductory verb is in the present, future or present perfect.
  *Mum **has said**, "Dinner **is** ready."*
  *Mum **has said** (that) dinner **is** ready.*
- The verb tenses can either change or remain the same in reported speech when reporting a general truth or law of nature.
  *The teacher said, "The Thames **is** a river."*
  *The teacher said (that) the Thames **is/was** a river.*

Reported Questions

- Reported questions are usually introduced with the verbs **ask**, **inquire**, **wonder** or the expression **want to know**.
- When the direct question begins with a question word (**who**, **where**, **how**, **when**, **what**, etc), the reported question is introduced with the same question word.
  What time is it, please? (direct question)
  He asked me what the time was. (reported question)
- When the direct question begins with an auxiliary (**be**, **do**, **have**), or a modal verb (**can**, **may**, etc), then the reported question is introduced with **if** or **whether**.
  He asked, "Is there any milk left?" (direct question)
  *He asked me **if/whether** there was any milk left.* (reported question)
- In reported questions, the verb is in the affirmative. The question mark and words/expressions such as **please**, **well**, **oh**, etc are omitted. The verb tenses, pronouns and time expressions change as in statements.
  Can you tell me when the next train to Glasgow is, please? (direct question)
  He asked me when the next train to Glasgow was. (reported question)

Reported Orders

To report orders, we use the introductory verbs **order** or **tell + sb + (not) to - infinitive**.
Cease fire! (direct order)
*He **ordered** them **to cease** fire.* (reported order)
Stop talking! (direct order)
*He **told** us **to stop** talking.* (reported order)

Reported Commands, Requests, Suggestions, etc

To report commands, requests, suggestions, instructions etc. we use a special introductory verb followed by a **to-infinitive**, **-ing form**, or **that-clause**, depending on the introductory verb.

Introductory verb	Direct speech	Reported speech
+ to infinitive agree	"Yes, I'll lend you £25."	He agreed to lend me £25.
*claim	"I'm working on a top secret project."	She claimed to be working on a top secret project.
*demand	"I want to be served immediately."	He demanded to be served immediately.
offer	"Would you like me to help you with your essay?"	She offered to help me with my essay.
*promise	"I promise I'll do this for you."	He promised to do that for me.
refuse	"No, I won't do what they want."	He refused to do what they wanted.
*threaten	"Be quiet or I'll punish you."	He threatened to punish us if we weren't quiet.

* The verbs marked with an asterisk can also be followed by a that-clause in reported speech. *He claimed that he knew nothing about it.* etc

139

Grammar Reference

Introductory verb	Direct speech	Reported speech
+ sb + to-infinitive		
advise	"You should exercise more."	He advised me to exercise more.
allow	"You can watch the film on TV."	He allowed me to watch the film on TV.
ask	"Can you do me a favour?"	He asked me to do him a favour.
beg	"Please, please, help me."	She begged me to help her.
command	"Put the gun down."	He commanded her to put the gun down.
encourage	"You should talk to her about this."	He encouraged me to talk to her about that.
forbid	"You cannot listen to your music at this time of night."	He forbade me to listen to my music at that time of night.
invite	"Will you come to my birthday party?"	She invited me to go to her birthday party.
order	"Do thirty push ups at once!"	He ordered me to do thirty push ups immediately.
*remind	"Don't forget to call me when you get home."	He reminded me to call him when I got home.
*warn	"Be careful, don't believe what she says."	He warned me not to believe what she says.
+ -ing form		
accuse sb of	"He stole my bag."	She accused him of stealing her bag.
*admit (to)	"Yes, I dropped the vase."	He admitted to dropping/having dropped the vase.
apologise for	"I'm sorry I am late."	She apologised for being late.
*boast about/ of	"I'm an excellent actor."	He boasted of being an excellent actor.
*complain (to sb) of/about	"I feel very tired."	She complained (to me) of feeling very tired.
*deny	"I didn't tell her your secret!"	He denied telling/having told her my secret.
*insist on	"I am going to give you a lift home."	He insisted on giving me a lift home.
*suggest	"Why don't we play table tennis tomorrow?"	He suggested playing table tennis the next day.
+ that clause		
explain	"It is quicker to take the train because the traffic is heavy."	He explained that it was quicker to take the train because the traffic was heavy.
inform sb	"The flight has been cancelled due to bad weather conditions."	She informed us that the flight had been cancelled due to bad weather conditions.

- * The verbs marked with an asterisk can also be followed by a that-clause in reported speech. *He claimed that he knew nothing about it.* etc

Note: To report negative commands and requests we usually use **not + to-infinitive**.
  Direct: *Mum said, "Don't touch the oven, it's hot!"*
  Reported: *Mum told us **not to touch** the oven because it was hot.*

- In conversation we use a mixture of statements, commands and questions. When we turn them into reported speech, we use **and, as, adding that and he/she added that, because, but, since**, etc. Words such as **oh!, oh dear, well,** etc are omitted in reported speech.
  Direct: *"Oh! That's a beautiful dress," Jean said to me, "It suits you perfectly."*
  Reported: *Jean said that it was a beautiful dress and added that it suited me perfectly.*

Causative form

- we use **have + object + past participle** to say that we have arranged for someone to do something for us. The past participle has a passive meaning. *Gloria **had her hair dyed** at the hairdresser's.* (She didn't dye it herself.)
- Questions and negations of the verb **have** are formed with **do/does** (present simple) or **did** (past simple). *Did you **have** your coat **cleaned** yesterday?*
- We also use **have something done** to talk about an unpleasant experience that somebody had. *Last night Jeffrey **had his motorbike stolen**.* (= his motorbike was stolen)
- We can use the verb **get** instead of **have** in informal conversation. *He's going to **get** a new lock fitted on the back door.*
  Note: The word order is very important. **Tony had the tyre changed** and **Tony had changed the tyre** have very different meanings. In the first case Tony arranged for someone else to change the tyre whereas in the second case he changed the tyre himself.

	Regular active form	**Causative form**
Present Simple	She **cleans** the house.	She **has** the house **cleaned**.
Present Continuous	She **is cleaning** the house.	She **is having** the house **cleaned**.
Past Simple	She **cleaned** the house.	She **had** the house **cleaned**.
Past Continuous	She **was cleaning** the house.	She **was having** the house **cleaned**.
Future Simple	She **will clean** the house.	She **will have** the house **cleaned**.
Future Continuous	She **will be cleaning** the house.	She **will be having** the house **cleaned**.
Present Perfect	She **has cleaned** the house.	She **has had** the house **cleaned**.
Present Perfect Continuous	She **has been cleaning** the house.	She **has been having** the house **cleaned**.
Past Perfect	She **had cleaned** the house.	She **had had** the house **cleaned**.
Past Perfect Continuous	She **had been cleaning** the house.	She **had been having** the house **cleaned**.
Infinitive	She should **clean** the house.	She should **have** the house **cleaned**.
-ing form	It's worth **cleaning** the house.	It's worth **having** the house **cleaned**.

Rules for Punctuation

Capital Letters

A capital letter is used:
- to begin a sentence. *This is a book.*
- for days of the week, months and public holidays. *Tuesday, February, New Year*
- for names of people and places. *My friend's name is Marco and he's from Milan, Italy.*
- for people's titles. *Mr and Mrs Black; Dr Carpenter; Professor Stevenson; etc*
- for nationalities and languages. *They are Japanese. She's fluent in Spanish and Russian.*

Note: The personal pronoun I is always a capital letter. *Tina and I are going out tonight.*

Full Stop (.)

A full stop is used:
- to end a sentence that is not a question or an exclamation. *I'm having such a wonderful time. I wish you were here.*

Comma (,)

A comma is used:
- to separate words in a list. *We need butter, milk, sugar and flour.*
- to separate a non-identifying relative clause (i.e. a clause giving extra information which is not essential to the meaning of the main clause) from the main clause. *Steve, who is a doctor, lives in Canada.*
- after certain linking words/phrases (e.g. in addition to this, moreover, for example, however, in conclusion, etc). *Moreover, Susan is a very reliable person.*
- when if-clauses begin sentences. *If you have any problem, ask for help.*
  Note: No comma is used, however, when the if-clause follows the main clause.
- to separate question tags from the rest of the sentence. *Mrs Adams is your Maths teacher, isn't she?*

Question Mark (?)

A question mark is used:
- to end a direct question. *Where do you live?*

Exclamation Mark (!)

An exclamation mark is used:
- to end an exclamatory sentence, i.e. a sentence showing admiration, surprise, joy, anger, etc. *That's amazing! What great news!*

Quotation Marks (' ' or " ")

Quotation marks are used:
- in direct speech to report the exact words someone said. *'The meeting is at 5:30 pm,' said Cindy. "What's your name?" she asked him.*

Colon (:)

A colon is used:
- to introduce a list. *There were four of them on the committee: Leo, Jason, Peter and John.*

Brackets ( )

Brackets are used:
- to separate extra information from the rest of the sentence. *The most popular newspapers (i.e. The Times, The Daily Mirror, The Guardian, etc) can be found almost anywhere in this country.*

Apostrophe (')

An apostrophe is used:
- in short forms to show that one or more letters or numbers have been left out. *I'm (= I am) calling you ... She moved to Los Angeles in the summer of '98. (=1998)*
- before or after the possessive -s to show ownership or the relationship between people.
  Nick's dog, my brother's wife (singular noun + 's)
  my parents' friends (plural noun + ')
  men's coats (Irregular plural + 's)

141

Word List

UNIT 1

a little bit (phr)
actual (adj) /ˈæktʃuəl/
address (v) /əˈdres/
admire (v) /ədˈmaɪəʳ/
advert (n) /ˈædvɜːʳt/
advice (n) /ədˈvaɪs/
advise (v) /ədˈvaɪz/
all-time (adj) /ɔːl taɪm/
almond-shaped (adj) /ˈɑːmənd ʃeɪpt/
although (conj) /ɔːlˈðoʊ/
amazing (adj) /əˈmeɪzɪŋ/
ambitious (adj) /æmˈbɪʃəs/
appearance (n) /əˈpɪərəns/
apply (v) /əˈplaɪ/
aristocrat (n) /ˈærɪstəkræt/
audition (n) /ɔːˈdɪʃən/
audition (v) /ɔːˈdɪʃən/
author (n) /ˈɔːθəʳ/
average build (n) /ˈævərɪdʒ bɪld/
average looks (n) /ˈævərɪdʒ lʊks/
bad taste (phr)
band (n) /bænd/
barbaric (adj) /bɑːʳˈbærɪk/
be in a panic (exp)
be in a rush (exp)
beard (n) /bɪəʳd/
beauty (n) /ˈbjuːti/
beholder (n) /bɪˈhoʊldəʳ/
blackmail (v) /ˈblækmeɪl/
Bless you. (exp)
bossy (adj) /ˈbɒsi/
brainstorm (v) /ˈbreɪnstɔːʳm/
brave (adj) /breɪv/
bright (adj) /braɪt/
broad-brimmed (adj) /brɔːd brɪmd/
bump into (phr v) /bʌmp ˈɪntə/
by post (exp)
calm (adj) /kɑːm/
can't help (exp)
caption (n) /ˈkæpʃən/
capture (v) /ˈkæptʃəʳ/
care about (v) /keəʳ əˈbaʊt/
caring (adj) /ˈkeərɪŋ/
carry (v) /ˈkæri/
cartoon (n) /kɑːʳˈtuːn/
casting (v) /ˈkɑːstɪŋ/
central (adj) /ˈsentrəl/
cheek (n) /tʃiːk/
cheerful (adj) /ˈtʃɪəʳfʊl/
chest (n) /tʃest/
chin (n) /tʃɪn/
classmate (n) /ˈklɑːsmeɪt/

cloak (n) /kloʊk/
cold-hearted (adj) /koʊld ˈhɑːʳtɪd/
collar (n) /ˈkɒləʳ/
commercial (n) /kəˈmɜːʳʃəl/
complete (v) /kəmˈpliːt/
complexion (n) /kəmˈplekʃən/
confident (adj) /ˈkɒnfɪdənt/
confused (adj) /kənˈfjuːzd/
consider (v) /kənˈsɪdəʳ/
considerate (adj) /kənˈsɪdərət/
contact (n) /ˈkɒntækt/
corridor (n) /ˈkɒrɪdɔːʳ/
Count (n) /kaʊnt/
cover (n) /ˈkʌvəʳ/
crash diet (n) /kræʃ ˈdaɪət/
create (v) /kriˈeɪt/
creator (n) /kriˈeɪtəʳ/
crooked (adj) /ˈkrʊkɪd/
cruel (adj) /ˈkruːəl/
cuff (n) /kʌf/
cunning (adj) /ˈkʌnɪŋ/
curly (adj) /ˈkɜːʳli/
daring (adj) /ˈdeərɪŋ/
defeat (v) /dɪˈfiːt/
definitely (adv) /ˈdefɪnɪtli/
delivery guy (n) /dɪˈlɪvəri gaɪ/
depressed (adj) /dɪˈprest/
detective (n) /dɪˈtektɪv/
determination (n) /dɪˌtɜːʳmɪˈneɪʃən/
determined (adj) /dɪˈtɜːʳmɪnd/
dishonest (adj) /dɪsˈɒnɪst/
double (v) /ˈdʌbəl/
double-breasted (adj) /ˈdʌbəl ˈbrestɪd/
dress up (phr v) /dres ʌp/
drop (v) /drɒp/
easily (adv) /ˈiːzɪli/
easy-going (adj) /ˈiːzi ˈgoʊɪŋ/
effective (adj) /ɪˈfektɪv/
employer (n) /ɪmˈplɔɪəʳ/
essay (n) /ˈeseɪ/
eventually (adv) /ɪˈventʃuəli/
evil (adj) /ˈiːvəl/
exchange (n) /ɪksˈtʃeɪndʒ/
face (v) /feɪs/
facial (adj) /ˈfeɪʃəl/
fact (n) /fækt/
fair (n) /feəʳ/
fairest (adj) /ˈfeərɪst/
fairy tale (n) /ˈfeəri teɪl/
fearless (adj) /ˈfɪəʳləs/
feature (n) /ˈfiːtʃəʳ/
fed up (adj) /fed ʌp/
feel for (phr v) /fiːl fəʳ/
female (adj) /ˈfiːmeɪl/
fictional (adj) /ˈfɪkʃənəl/

fight (v) /faɪt/
fit (v) /fɪt/
flame-coloured (adj) /fleɪm ˈkʌləʳd/
flatmate (n) /ˈflætmeɪt/
focus on (v) /ˈfoʊkəs ɒn/
follow (v) /ˈfɒloʊ/
forgetful (adj) /fəʳˈgetfʊl/
friendly (adj) /ˈfrendli/
fur-trimmed (adj) /fɜːʳ trɪmd/
gap (n) /gæp/
get back (phr v) /get bæk/
get off (phr v) /get ɒf/
get on (phr v) /get ɒn/
get over (phr v) /get ˈoʊvəʳ/
get up (phr v) /get ʌp/
good looking (n) /gʊd ˈlʊkɪŋ/
good wins over evil (phr)
Grand Duke (n) /grænd djuːk/
greedy (adj) /ˈgriːdi/
greet (v) /griːt/
hairy (adj) /ˈheəri/
halfway (adv) /ˈhɑːfweɪ/
handsome (adj) /ˈhænsəm/
hero (n) /ˈhɪəroʊ/
hide (v) /haɪd/
highlighted (adj) /ˈhaɪlaɪtɪd/
honest (adj) /ˈɒnɪst/
honour (n) /ˈɒnəʳ/
hook (n) /hʊk/
humorous (adj) /ˈhjuːmərəs/
hurt (v) /hɜːʳt/
identity (n) /aɪˈdentɪti/
impatient (adj) /ɪmˈpeɪʃənt/
important (adj) /ɪmˈpɔːʳtənt/
in person (exp)
in the eye of the beholder (exp)
including (prep) /ɪnˈkluːdɪŋ/
indeed (adv) /ɪnˈdiːd/
influence (v) /ˈɪnfluəns/
insecure (adj) /ɪnsɪˈkjʊəʳ/
insensitive (adj) /ɪnˈsensɪtɪv/
instead of (prep) /ɪnˈsted əv/
intonation (n) /ɪntəˈneɪʃən/
issue (n) /ˈɪsjuː/
kidnap (v) /ˈkɪdnæp/
kind-hearted (adj) /kaɪnd ˈhɑːʳtɪd/
larger than life (idm)
leader (n) /ˈliːdəʳ/
lecture (n) /ˈlektʃəʳ/
limb (n) /lɪm/
line (v) /laɪn/
Literature (n) /ˈlɪtrətʃəʳ/
location (n) /loʊˈkeɪʃən/
lonely (adj) /ˈloʊnli/
lose (v) /luːz/

loyal (adj) /ˈlɔɪəl/
magazine (n) /mægəˈziːn/
main (adj) /meɪn/
majesty (n) /ˈmædʒɪsti/
male (adj) /meɪl/
manner (n) /ˈmænəʳ/
medium build (n) /ˈmiːdiəm bɪld/
medium height (n) /ˈmiːdiəm haɪt/
miss (v) /mɪs/
mission (n) /ˈmɪʃən/
mystery (n) /ˈmɪstəri/
neighbour (n) /ˈneɪbəʳ/
neighbourhood (n) /ˈneɪbəʳhʊd/
nod (v) /nɒd/
odd (adj) /ɒd/
on time (exp)
optimistic (adj) /ɒptɪˈmɪstɪk/
option (n) /ˈɒpʃən/
oval (adj) /ˈoʊvəl/
pace (v) /peɪs/
pale (adj) /peɪl/
partner (n) /ˈpɑːʳtnəʳ/
patient (adj) /ˈpeɪʃənt/
pause (v) /pɔːz/
perform (v) /pəʳˈfɔːʳm/
pessimistic (adj) /pesɪˈmɪstɪk/
physical (adj) /ˈfɪzɪkəl/
play (n) /pleɪ/
please (v) /pliːz/
pleasure (n) /ˈpleʒəʳ/
pointed (adj) /ˈpɔɪntɪd/
poisoned (adj) /ˈpɔɪzənd/
polite (adj) /pəˈlaɪt/
popular (adj) /ˈpɒpjʊləʳ/
portfolio (n) /pɔːʳtˈfoʊlioʊ/
power (n) /ˈpaʊəʳ/
proud (adj) /praʊd/
purpose (n) /ˈpɜːʳpəs/
quality (n) /ˈkwɒlɪti/
quick-thinking (adj) /kwɪk ˈθɪŋkɪŋ/
raise (v) /reɪz/
rather (adv) /ˈrɑːðəʳ/
react (v) /riˈækt/
realise (v) /ˈriːəlaɪz/
record (v) /rɪˈkɔːʳd/
recording (n) /rɪˈkɔːʳdɪŋ/
refer to (v) /rɪˈfɜːʳ tə/
relationship (n) /rɪˈleɪʃənʃɪp/
reliable (adj) /rɪˈlaɪəbəl/
remain (v) /rɪˈmeɪn/
remark (v) /rɪˈmɑːʳk/
rephrase (v) /riːˈfreɪz/
reply (v) /rɪˈplaɪ/
reputation (n) /repjʊˈteɪʃən/
respected (adj) /rɪˈspektɪd/

142

Word List

richness (n) /rɪtʃnəs/
ring bearer (n) /rɪŋ beərəʳ/
robe (n) /roʊb/
rosy (adj) /roʊzi/
rubric (n) /ruːbrɪk/
ruin (v) /ruːɪn/
rule (v) /ruːl/
save (v) /seɪv/
scandal (n) /skændəl/
seeking (n) /siːkɪŋ/
selfish (adj) /selfɪʃ/
sensible (adj) /sensəbəl/
sensitive (adj) /sensɪtɪv/
shape (n) /ʃeɪp/
sharp (adj) /ʃɑːʳp/
shooting (n) /ʃuːtɪŋ/
shoulder-length (adj) /ʃoʊldəʳ leŋθ/
shy (adj) /ʃaɪ/
shyness (n) /ʃaɪnəs/
size (n) /saɪz/
slim (adj) /slɪm/
spiky (adj) /spaɪki/
spring (v) /sprɪŋ/
staff (n) /stɑːf/
statement (n) /steɪtmənt/
step (n) /step/
straight (adj) /streɪt/
straighten (v) /streɪtən/
stubborn (adj) /stʌbəʳn/
superhero (n) /suːpəʳhɪəroʊ/
take after (phr v) /teɪk ɑːftəʳ/
take care of (exp)
take off (phr v) /teɪk ɒf/
take off (phr v) /teɪk ɒf/
takeaway (n) /teɪkəweɪ/
team spirit (n) /tiːm spɪrɪt/
teen (adj) /tiːn/
thick (adj) /θɪk/
timeless (adj) /taɪmləs/
trust (v) /trʌst/
trusted (adj) /trʌstɪd/
turn (v) /tɜːʳn/
turn down (phr v) /tɜːʳn daʊn/
uncaring (adj) /ʌnkeərɪŋ/
understanding (n) /ʌndəʳstændɪŋ/
unfriendly (adj) /ʌnfrendli/
unselfish (adj) /ʌnselfɪʃ/
unsure (adj) /ʌnʃʊəʳ/
upper (adj) /ʌpəʳ/
upset (v) /ʌpset/
vain (adj) /veɪn/
valuable (adj) /væljuəbəl/
villain (n) /vɪlən/
waitressing (n) /weɪtrəsɪŋ/
wavy (adj) /weɪvi/
weakness (n) /wiːknəs/

weakness (v) /wiːknəs/
weigh (v) /weɪ/
weight (v) /weɪt/
well-built (adj) /wel bɪlt/
well-known (adj) /wel noʊn/
What's up? (exp)
whether (conj) /ʰweðəʳ/
wicked (adj) /wɪkɪd/
win (v) /wɪn/
wise (adj) /waɪz/
wizard (n) /wɪzəʳd/
You're joking! (phr)

UNIT 2

actual (adj) /æktʃuəl/
aim (n) /eɪm/
area (n) /eəriə/
arrange (v) /əreɪndʒ/
aspect (n) /æspekt/
attraction (n) /ətrækʃən/
availability (n) /əveɪləbɪlɪti/
backyard (n) /bækjɑːʳd/
bank teller (n) /bæŋk teləʳ/
beware of (v) /bɪweəʳ əv/
block of flats (phr)
booked (adj) /bʊkt/
bored (adj) /bɔːʳd/
bull (n) /bʊl/
can't stand (exp)
chat (v) /tʃæt/
city slicker (n) /sɪti slɪkəʳ/
clerk (n) /klɑːʳk/
close at hand (exp)
close by (phr)
comfortable (adj) /kʌmftəbəl/
community (n) /kəmjuːnɪti/
community spirit (n) /kəmjuːnɪti spɪrɪt/
comparative (n) /kəmpærətɪv/
congested (adj) /kəndʒestɪd/
congestion (n) /kəndʒestʃən/
connect (v) /kənekt/
constant (adj) /kɒnstənt/
cool (adj) /kuːl/
corner (adj) /kɔːʳnəʳ/
cosy (adj) /koʊzi/
countryside (n) /kʌntrɪsaɪd/
crop (n) /krɒp/
crowded (adj) /kraʊdɪd/
curriculum vitae (n) /kərɪkjʊləm viːtaɪ/
degree (n) /dɪgriː/
direction (n) /daɪrekʃən/
district (n) /dɪstrɪkt/
down under (exp)
dream town (n) /driːm taʊn/

drought (n) /draʊt/
dull (adj) /dʌl/
elegant (adj) /elɪgənt/
employee (n) /ɪmplɔɪiː/
employer (n) /ɪmplɔɪəʳ/
entertainment (n) /entəʳteɪnmənt/
equal (adj) /iːkwəl/
escalator (n) /eskəleɪtəʳ/
escape (v) /ɪskeɪp/
experienced (adj) /ɪkspɪərɪənst/
extinguish (v) /ɪkstɪŋgwɪʃ/
facility (n) /fəsɪlɪti/
familiar (adj) /fəmɪliəʳ/
fancy (v) /fænsi/
fence (n) /fens/
fitness centre (n) /fɪtnəs sentəʳ/
fluent (adj) /fluːənt/
flying doctor (n) /flaɪɪŋ dɒktəʳ/
fresh (adj) /freʃ/
furious (adj) /fjʊərɪəs/
gain (v) /geɪn/
go off (phr v) /goʊ ɒf/
guide (v) /gaɪd/
head chef (n) /hed ʃef/
head for (v) /hed fəʳ/
healthy (adj) /helθi/
hectare (n) /hekteəʳ/
huge (adj) /hjuːdʒ/
hustle and bustle (exp)
in my element (exp)
in the heart of (exp)
industrial (adj) /ɪndʌstrɪəl/
inspiration (n) /ɪnspɪreɪʃən/
interview (n) /ɪntəʳvjuː/
isolated (adj) /aɪsəleɪtɪd/
journalist (n) /dʒɜːʳnəlɪst/
landmark (n) /lændmɑːʳk/
lane (n) /leɪn/
librarian (n) /laɪbreərɪən/
lifestyle (n) /laɪfstaɪl/
local (adj) /loʊkəl/
look into (phr v) /lʊk ɪntə/
low (adj) /loʊ/
medical centre (n) /medɪkəl sentəʳ/
narrow (adj) /næroʊ/
negative (adj) /negətɪv/
neighbour (n) /neɪbəʳ/
on lead (exp)
organised (adj) /ɔːʳgənaɪzd/
outdoors (adv) /aʊtdɔːʳz/
pace (n) /peɪs/
patient (adj) /peɪʃənt/
pay a visit (exp)
petrol station (n) /petrəl steɪʃən/

plant (n) /plɑːnt/
playground (n) /pleɪgraʊnd/
population (n) /pɒpjʊleɪʃən/
postpone (v) /poʊspoʊn/
practical (adj) /præktɪkəl/
preference (n) /prefərəns/
produce (v) /prədjuːs/
professional (adj) /prəfeʃənəl/
prospective (adj) /prəspektɪv/
provincial (adj) /prəvɪnʃəl/
public transport (n) /pʌblɪk trænspɔːʳt/
put (sb) up (phr v) /pʊt ʌp/
put away (phr v) /pʊt əweɪ/
put off (phr v) /pʊt ɒf/
put on (phr v) /pʊt ɒn/
put out (phr v) /pʊt aʊt/
put through (phr v) /pʊt θruː/
put up with (phr v) /pʊt ʌp wɪð/
qualification (n) /kwɒlɪfɪkeɪʃən/
ranch (n) /rɑːntʃ/
reality (n) /riælɪti/
remote (adj) /rɪmoʊt/
reserve (v) /rɪzɜːʳv/
route (n) /ruːt/
run (v) /rʌn/
rush-hour (n) /rʌʃ aʊəʳ/
sales assistant (n) /seɪlz əsɪstənt/
scenery (n) /siːnəri/
seaside (adj) /siːsaɪd/
security guard (n) /sɪkjʊərɪti gɑːʳd/
semi-detached (adj) /semi dɪtætʃt/
shave (v) /ʃeɪv/
shopper (n) /ʃɒpəʳ/
side (n) /saɪd/
sincere (adj) /sɪnsɪəʳ/
size (n) /saɪz/
skyscraper (n) /skaɪskreɪpəʳ/
sleepy (adj) /sliːpi/
spacious (adj) /speɪʃəs/
spirit (n) /spɪrɪt/
square (v) /skweəʳ/
subheading (n) /sʌbhedɪŋ/
suit (v) /suːt/
suitable (adj) /suːtəbəl/
superlative (n) /suːpɜːʳlətɪv/
surround (v) /səraʊnd/
take a break (exp)
terraced (adj) /terɪst/
tiny (adj) /taɪni/
tour guide (n) /tʊəʳ gaɪd/
Town Hall (n) /taʊn hɔːl/
traditional (adj) /trədɪʃənəl/
traffic (n) /træfɪk/

143

Word List

traffic congestion (n) /ˈtræfɪk kənˈdʒestʃən/
traffic warden (n) /ˈtræfɪk ˈwɔːʳdən/
tree-lined (adj) /triː laɪnd/
turning (n) /ˈtɜːʳnɪŋ/
urge (v) /ɜːʳdʒ/
visa (n) /ˈviːzə/
well-dressed (adj) /wel drest/
well-known (adj) /wel noʊn/
wide (adj) /waɪd/
wood (n) /wʊd/
Yours faithfully (phr)
Yours sincerely (phr)

CURRICULAR CUTS 1: History (p. 28)

ambitious (adj) /æmˈbɪʃəs/
armada (n) /ɑːʳˈmɑːdə/
authority (n) /ɔːˈθɒrɪti/
colony (n) /ˈkɒləni/
coronation (n) /ˌkɒrəˈneɪʃən/
crown (n) /kraʊn/
defeat (v) /dɪˈfiːt/
demanding (adj) /dɪˈmɑːndɪŋ/
determined (adj) /dɪˈtɜːʳmɪnd/
encyclopaedia (n) /ɪnˌsaɪkləˈpiːdiə/
equal (to) (adj) /ˈiːkwəl/
global (adj) /ˈgloʊbəl/
globe (n) /gloʊb/
gown (n) /gaʊn/
image (n) /ˈɪmɪdʒ/
impression (n) /ɪmˈpreʃən/
innocence (n) /ˈɪnəsəns/
innocent (adj) /ˈɪnəsənt/
official (adj) /əˈfɪʃəl/
opposition (n) /ˌɒpəˈzɪʃən/
orb (n) /ɔːʳb/
portrait (n) /ˈpɔːʳtreɪt/
powerful (adj) /ˈpaʊəʳfʊl/
reign (n) /reɪn/
reminder (n) /rɪˈmaɪndəʳ/
rightful (adj) /ˈraɪtfʊl/
rule (v) /ruːl/
sceptre (n) /ˈseptəʳ/
school textbook (n) /skuːl ˈtekstbʊk/
strong (adj) /strɒŋ/
victory (n) /ˈvɪktəri/
wealth (n) /welθ/

UNIT 3

access (n) /ˈækses/
adopt (v) /əˈdɒpt/
adoption (n) /əˈdɒpʃən/
adult (n) /ˈædʌlt/
against (prep) /əˈgenst/
albatross (n) /ˈælbətrɒs/
alert (adj) /əˈlɜːʳt/
amount (n) /əˈmaʊnt/
annual (adj) /ˈænjuəl/
Antarctic (n) /ænˈtɑːʳktɪk/
apologise (v) /əˈpɒlədʒaɪz/
applicant (n) /ˈæplɪkənt/
assistance (n) /əˈsɪstəns/
attend (v) /əˈtend/
average (adj) /ˈævərɪdʒ/
bald eagle (n) /bɔːld ˈiːgəl/
base (n) /beɪs/
belief (n) /bɪˈliːf/
Best regards (phr)
bin (n) /bɪn/
biologist (n) /baɪˈɒlədʒɪst/
bottle bank (n) /ˈbɒtəl bæŋk/
bottom (n) /ˈbɒtəm/
break open (phr)
break through (phr v) /breɪk θruː/
brick wall (n) /brɪk wɔːl/
bulb (n) /bʌlb/
bush (n) /bʊʃ/
calf (n) /kɑːf/
capture (n) /ˈkæptʃəʳ/
carry out (phr v) /ˈkæri aʊt/
certificate (n) /səʳˈtɪfɪkət/
chess set (n) /tʃes set/
chick (n) /tʃɪk/
Christmas carol (n) /ˈkrɪsməs ˈkærəl/
clap (v) /klæp/
clean-up campaign (n) /kliːn ʌp kæmˈpeɪn/
cobra (n) /ˈkoʊbrə/
colony (n) /ˈkɒləni/
come up (phr v) /kʌm ʌp/
competition (n) /ˌkɒmpɪˈtɪʃən/
cover (v) /ˈkʌvəʳ/
crew (n) /kruː/
cross (v) /krɒs/
daily care (n) /ˈdeɪli keəʳ/
decide (v) /dɪˈsaɪd/
deck (n) /dek/
declare (v) /dɪˈkleəʳ/
deforestation (n) /diːˌfɒrɪˈsteɪʃən/
delay (v) /dɪˈleɪ/
directory (n) /daɪˈrektəri/
disappointed (adj) /ˌdɪsəˈpɔɪntɪd/
domestic (adj) /dəˈmestɪk/
electronic (adj) /ɪlekˈtrɒnɪk/
endangered (adj) /ɪnˈdeɪndʒəʳd/
environmental group (n) /ɪnˌvaɪərənˈmentəl gruːp/
environmentalist (n) /ɪnˌvaɪərənˈmentəlɪst/
equipment (n) /ɪˈkwɪpmənt/
event (n) /ɪˈvent/
except (prep) /ɪkˈsept/
excited (adj) /ɪkˈsaɪtɪd/
exchange (v) /ɪksˈtʃeɪndʒ/
expedition (n) /ˌekspɪˈdɪʃən/
experiment (n) /ɪkˈsperɪmənt/
explore (v) /ɪkˈsplɔːʳ/
extinction (n) /ɪkˈstɪŋkʃən/
fee (n) /fiː/
feeding behaviour (n) /ˈfiːdɪŋ bɪˈheɪvjəʳ/
fill out (phr v) /fɪl aʊt/
fine (n) /faɪn/
flipper (n) /ˈflɪpəʳ/
food supply (n) /fuːd səˈplaɪ/
found (v) /faʊnd/
fragile (adj) /ˈfrædʒaɪl/
freezing (adj) /ˈfriːzɪŋ/
global warming (n) /ˈgloʊbəl ˈwɔːʳmɪŋ/
goat (n) /goʊt/
goverment (n) /ˈgʌvəʳnmənt/
grow (v) /groʊ/
grown (adj) /groʊn/
hand out (phr v) /hænd aʊt/
heal (v) /hiːl/
hen (n) /hen/
homeless (adj) /ˈhoʊmləs/
huge (adj) /hjuːdʒ/
humanitarian (n) /hjuːˌmænɪˈteəriən/
hunt (v) /hʌnt/
ice cliff (n) /aɪs klɪf/
iceberg (n) /ˈaɪsbɜːʳg/
illegal (adj) /ɪˈliːgəl/
import (n) /ˈɪmpɔːrt/
imprisonment (n) /ɪmˈprɪzənmənt/
in brief (exp)
in favour (of) (exp)
individual (n) /ˌɪndɪˈvɪdʒuəl/
indoor (adj) /ˈɪndɔːʳ/
inspire (v) /ɪnˈspaɪəʳ/
institute (n) /ˈɪnstɪtjuːt/
international (adj) /ˌɪntəʳˈnæʃənəl/
issue (n) /ˈɪsjuː/
ivory (adj) /ˈaɪvəri/
join (v) /dʒɔɪn/
layout (n) /ˈleɪaʊt/
leader (n) /ˈliːdəʳ/
leaflet (n) /ˈliːflət/
leopard (n) /ˈlepəʳd/
lift (n) /lɪft/
living proof (n) /ˈlɪvɪŋ pruːf/
mammal (n) /ˈmæməl/
medical attention (n) /ˈmedɪkəl əˈtenʃən/
member (n) /ˈmembəʳ/
membership (n) /ˈmembəʳʃɪp/
memorable (adj) /ˈmemərəbəl/
natural habitat (n) /ˈnætʃərəl ˈhæbɪtæt/
ocean (n) /ˈoʊʃən/
orangutan (n) /ɔːˈræŋuːtæn/
ordinary (adj) /ˈɔːʳdɪnri/
over-fishing (n) /ˈoʊvəʳ ˈfɪʃɪŋ/
ozone layer (n) /ˈoʊzoʊn leɪəʳ/
participate (v) /pɑːʳˈtɪsɪpeɪt/
peacock (n) /ˈpiːkɒk/
petrol (n) /ˈpetrəl/
plant (v) /plɑːnt/
polar bear (n) /ˈpoʊləʳ beəʳ/
preschool (n) /priːˈskuːl/
preservation (n) /ˌprezɜːʳˈveɪʃən/
preserve (v) /prɪˈzɜːʳv/
prevent (v) /prɪˈvent/
product (n) /ˈprɒdʌkt/
prohibited (adj) /prəˈhɪbɪtɪd/
proper (adj) /ˈprɒpəʳ/
pudding (n) /ˈpʊdɪŋ/
python (n) /ˈpaɪθən/
reasonable (adj) /ˈriːzənəbəl/
recommendation (n) /ˌrekəmenˈdeɪʃən/
recycle (v) /riːˈsaɪkəl/
recycling centre (n) /riːˈsaɪklɪŋ ˈsentəʳ/
registration (n) /ˌredʒɪˈstreɪʃən/
renew (v) /rɪˈnjuː/
reptile (n) /ˈreptaɪl/
research (n) /rɪˈsɜːʳtʃ/
research station (n) /rɪˈsɜːʳtʃ ˈsteɪʃən/
reuse (v) /riːˈjuːz/
roast (adj) /roʊst/
root (n) /ruːt/
rope bridge (n) /roʊp brɪdʒ/
rubbish tip (n) /ˈrʌbɪʃ tɪp/
rubric (n) /ˈruːbrɪk/
run away (phr v) /rʌn əˈweɪ/
run into (phr v) /rʌn ˈɪntə/
run on (phr v) /rʌn ɒn/
run out of (phr v) /rʌn aʊt əv/
run over (phr v) /rʌn ˈoʊvəʳ/
sanctuary (n) /ˈsæŋktʃuəri/
scheme (n) /skiːm/
scientific (adj) /ˌsaɪənˈtɪfɪk/
sensibly (adv) /ˈsensɪbli/
shoot (n) /ʃuːt/
shrub (n) /ʃrʌb/
sight (n) /saɪt/

144

Word List

similar (adj) /ˈsɪmɪləʳ/
simply (adv) /ˈsɪmpli/
slide (v) /slaɪd/
snakeskin (adj) /ˈsneɪkskɪn/
stick (v) /stɪk/
stray (adj) /streɪ/
strength (n) /streŋθ/
sum up (phr v) /sʌm ʌp/
survive (v) /səˈvaɪv/
tag (n) /tæg/
take part in (exp)
take place (exp)
tank (n) /tæŋk/
task (n) /tɑːsk/
thrilled (adj) /θrɪld/
touching (adj) /ˈtʌtʃɪŋ/
traditionally (adv) /trəˈdɪʃənəli/
underground (adv) /ˌʌndəˈgraʊnd/
underneath (prep) /ˌʌndəˈniːθ/
unleaded (adj) /ʌnˈledɪd/
upset (adj) /ʌpˈset/
vaccination (n) /væksɪˈneɪʃən/
vet (n) /vet/
visible (adj) /ˈvɪzɪbəl/
voluntary (adj) /ˈvɒləntri/
waste (v) /weɪst/
waterfall (n) /ˈwɔːtəfɔːl/
watt (n) /wɒt/
whale (n) /ʰweɪl/
wildlife (n) /ˈwaɪldlaɪf/
wildlife park (n) /ˈwaɪldlaɪf pɑːrk/
worldwide (adv) /ˈwɜːldwaɪd/
wrap (v) /ræp/
zookeeper (n) /ˈzuːkiːpəʳ/

UNIT 4

aboard (prep) /əˈbɔːd/
abroad (adv) /əˈbrɔːd/
absolutely (adv) /ˈæbsəluːtli/
accommodation (n) /əkɒməˈdeɪʃən/
action (n) /ˈækʃən/
action-packed (adj) /ˈækʃən pækt/
active (adj) /ˈæktɪv/
adult (n) /ˈædʌlt/
adventure (n) /ədˈventʃəʳ/
adventurous (adj) /ədˈventʃərəs/
airline (n) /ˈeəlaɪn/
alive (adj) /əˈlaɪv/
all inclusive (phr)
ancient (adj) /ˈeɪnʃənt/
annoyance (n) /əˈnɔɪəns/
apologise (v) /əˈpɒlədʒaɪz/

apology (n) /əˈpɒlədʒi/
approval (n) /əˈpruːvəl/
architecture (n) /ˈɑːkɪtektʃəʳ/
arrow (n) /ˈæroʊ/
awake (v) /əˈweɪk/
backpack (n) /ˈbækpæk/
beachfront (n) /ˈbiːtʃfrʌnt/
beat (v) /biːt/
beef (n) /biːf/
binoculars (n) /bɪˈnɒkjʊləʳz/
bird-watching (n) /ˈbɜːd wɒtʃɪŋ/
block (v) /blɒk/
book (v) /bʊk/
booking (n) /ˈbʊkɪŋ/
border (v) /ˈbɔːdəʳ/
bow (n) /boʊ/
break (n) /breɪk/
breakable (adj) /ˈbreɪkəbəl/
breathe (v) /briːð/
catch a glimpse (exp)
celebrate (v) /ˈselɪbreɪt/
chance (n) /tʃɑːns/
change (n) /tʃeɪndʒ/
check in (phr v) /tʃek ɪn/
chest (n) /tʃest/
climax event (n) /ˈklaɪmæks ɪvent/
coach (n) /koʊtʃ/
come across (phr v) /kʌm əˈkrɒs/
come into (phr v) /kʌm ɪntə/
come out (phr v) /kʌm aʊt/
come round (phr v) /kʌm raʊnd/
come up (phr v) /kʌm ʌp/
complain (v) /kəmˈpleɪn/
completely (adv) /kəmˈpliːtli/
continent (n) /ˈkɒntɪnənt/
corn (n) /kɔːn/
court (n) /kɔːt/
crew (n) /kruː/
culture (n) /ˈkʌltʃəʳ/
daylight (n) /ˈdeɪlaɪt/
dean (n) /diːn/
definitely (adv) /ˈdefɪnɪtli/
disappointing (adj) /dɪsəˈpɔɪntɪŋ/
disapproval (n) /dɪsəˈpruːvəl/
double room (n) /ˈdʌbəl ruːm/
downwards (adv) /ˈdaʊnwədz/
dramatic (adj) /drəˈmætɪk/
drop (v) /drɒp/
dry land (n) /draɪ lænd/
early riser (n) /ˈɜːli raɪzəʳ/
emergency service (n) /ɪˈmɜːdʒənsi sɜːʳvɪs/
engaged (adj) /ɪnˈgeɪdʒd/

entertainment (n) /entəˈteɪnmənt/
enthusiast (n) /ɪnˈθjuːziæst/
escape (v) /ɪˈskeɪp/
excitement (n) /ɪkˈsaɪtmənt/
exhausted (adj) /ɪgˈzɔːstɪd/
exotic (adj) /ɪgˈzɒtɪk/
experience (v) /ɪkˈspɪəriəns/
fabulous (adj) /ˈfæbjʊləs/
factual (adj) /ˈfæktʃuəl/
fallen (adj) /ˈfɔːlən/
fascinated (adj) /ˈfæsɪneɪtɪd/
fascinating (adj) /ˈfæsɪneɪtɪŋ/
fasten (v) /ˈfɑːsən/
fed up (adj) /fed ʌp/
first-aid kit (n) /ˈfɜːst eɪd kɪt/
flash of lightning (phr)
flat tyre (n) /flæt taɪəʳ/
foggy (adj) /ˈfɒgi/
fortune (n) /ˈfɔːtʃuːn/
gently (adv) /ˈdʒentli/
getaway (n) /ˈgetəweɪ/
glamorous (adj) /ˈglæmərəs/
grab (v) /græb/
guided tour (n) /ˈgaɪdɪd tʊəʳ/
heat (n) /hiːt/
hike (v) /haɪk/
hiking boots (n) /ˈhaɪkɪŋ buːts/
hire (v) /haɪəʳ/
hold up (phr v) /hoʊld ʌp/
holiday rep (representative) (n) /ˈhɒlɪdeɪ rep/
How dare you? (phr)
human creature (n) /ˈhjuːmən kriːtʃəʳ/
hurt (v) /hɜːt/
ideal (adj) /aɪˈdɪəl/
in style (exp)
inch (n) /ɪntʃ/
incl. (including) (prep) /ɪnˈkluːdɪŋ/
incredible (adj) /ɪnˈkredɪbəl/
indeed (adv) /ɪnˈdiːd/
independent (adj) /ɪndɪˈpendənt/
insect repellent (n) /ˈɪnsekt rɪˈpelənt/
insist (v) /ɪnˈsɪst/
join (v) /dʒɔɪn/
landmark (n) /ˈlændmɑːk/
laundry (n) /ˈlɔːndri/
length (n) /leŋθ/
let (v) /let/
lie (v) /laɪ/
location (n) /loʊˈkeɪʃən/
lorry (n) /ˈlɒri/
luxurious (adj) /lʌgˈʒʊəriəs/
make fun of (exp)

masterpiece (n) /ˈmɑːstəpiːs/
meal (n) /miːl/
Mediterranean (adj) /medɪtəˈreɪniən/
midnight (n) /ˈmɪdnaɪt/
mild (adj) /maɪld/
mile (n) /maɪl/
mime (v) /maɪm/
missing (adj) /ˈmɪsɪŋ/
nailfile (n) /ˈneɪlfaɪl/
narrate (v) /nəˈreɪt/
narrow (adj) /ˈnæroʊ/
nearly (adv) /ˈnɪəli/
nightlife (n) /ˈnaɪtlaɪf/
north (n) /nɔːθ/
official (adj) /əˈfɪʃəl/
once-in-a-lifetime (exp)
outrageous (adj) /aʊˈtreɪdʒəs/
overcharge (v) /oʊvəˈtʃɑːdʒ/
overturn (v) /oʊvəˈtɜːn/
pack (v) /pæk/
package holiday (n) /ˈpækɪdʒ hɒlɪdeɪ/
packed lunch (n) /pækt lʌntʃ/
pantomime (n) /ˈpæntəmaɪm/
penknife (n) /ˈpennaɪf/
personal (adj) /ˈpɜːsənəl/
playground (n) /ˈpleɪgraʊnd/
pleasant (adj) /ˈplezənt/
pleased (adj) /pliːzd/
plenty (pron) /ˈplenti/
politics (n) /ˈpɒlɪtɪks/
pretend (v) /prɪˈtend/
professionally (adv) /prəˈfeʃənəli/
puzzled (adj) /ˈpʌzəld/
rare (adj) /reəʳ/
reach (v) /riːtʃ/
realise (n) /ˈriːəlaɪz/
receptionist (n) /rɪˈsepʃənɪst/
reservation (n) /rezəˈveɪʃən/
reserve (v) /rɪˈzɜːv/
resort (n) /rɪˈzɔːt/
rock (n) /rɒk/
row (v) /roʊ/
running water (n) /ˈrʌnɪŋ wɔːtəʳ/
sailing (n) /ˈseɪlɪŋ/
sandcastle (n) /ˈsændkɑːsəl/
satire (n) /ˈsætaɪəʳ/
satirist (n) /ˈsætɪrɪst/
seaman (n) /ˈsiːmən/
sequence (n) /ˈsiːkwəns/
set off (phr v) /set ɒf/
setting (n) /ˈsetɪŋ/
severe (adj) /sɪˈvɪəʳ/
shallow (adj) /ˈʃæloʊ/
shape (v) /ʃeɪp/

145

Word List

shipwrecked (adj) /ʃɪprekt/
shut (adj) /ʃʌt/
sigh of relief (phr)
sightseeing (n) /saɪtsiːɪŋ/
slip (v) /slɪp/
snack (n) /snæk/
spectacular (adj) /spektækjʊləʳ/
speed (v) /spiːd/
storm (n) /stɔːʳm/
straight (adv) /streɪt/
strike (v) /straɪk/
struggle (v) /strʌgəl/
stunning (adj) /stʌnɪŋ/
sunbed (n) /sʌnbed/
sunscreen (n) /sʌnskriːn/
sunset (n) /sʌnset/
take off (phr v) /teɪk ɒf/
tale (n) /teɪl/
terrified (adj) /terɪfaɪd/
the line is dead (exp)
the outdoors (n) /ði aʊtdɔːʳz/
thrill (n) /θrɪl/
thrilled (adj) /θrɪld/
thrilling (adj) /θrɪlɪŋ/
throw into (v) /θroʊ ɪntə/
tide (n) /taɪd/
tightly (adv) /taɪtli/
tiny (adj) /taɪni/
tissue (n) /tɪsuː/
to my surprise (exp)
toiletries (n) /tɔɪlətriz/
toothpaste (n) /tuːθpeɪst/
travel agent (n) /trævəl eɪdʒənt/
trek (v) /trek/
triangle (n) /traɪæŋgəl/
underwear (n) /ʌndəʳweəʳ/
unforgettable (adj) /ʌnfəʳgetəbəl/
unlock (v) /ʌnlɒk/
unusual (adj) /ʌnjuːʒuəl/
upwards (adv) /ʌpwəʳdz/
vacancy (n) /veɪkənsi/
vote (v) /voʊt/
voyage (n) /vɔɪɪdʒ/
weather forecast (n) /weðəʳ fɔːʳkɑːst/
wet (adj) /wet/
wheat (n) /ʰwiːt/
white-water rafting (n) /ʰwaɪt wɔːtəʳ rɑːftɪŋ/
wide (adj) /waɪd/
windy (adj) /wɪndi/
wish (v) /wɪʃ/
You're kidding! (phr)
You've got to be joking! (phr)

CURRICULAR CUTS 2: Geography (p. 52)

bitterly (adv) /bɪtəʳli/
climate (n) /klaɪmət/
climate zone (n) /klaɪmət zoʊn/
cloudy (adj) /klaʊdi/
cold (adj) /koʊld/
common (adj) /kɒmən/
cool (adj) /kuːl/
desert (adj) /dezəʳt/
drop (v) /drɒp/
equator (n) /ɪkweɪtəʳ/
equatorial (adj) /ekwətɔːriəl/
foggy (adj) /fɒgi/
form (n) /fɔːʳm/
freezing (adj) /friːzɪŋ/
frozen (adj) /froʊzən/
ground (n) /graʊnd/
map (n) /mæp/
Mediterranean (adj) /medɪtəreɪniən/
mild (adj) /maɪld/
rainfall (n) /reɪnfɔːl/
remain (v) /rɪmeɪn/
rise (v) /raɪz/
subarctic (adj) /sʌbɑːʳktɪk/
temperate (adj) /tempərɪt/
temperature (n) /temprətʃəʳ/
thunderstorm (n) /θʌndəʳstɔːʳm/
tropical (adj) /trɒpɪkəl/
tundra (adj) /tʌndrə/

UNIT 5

absence (n) /æbsəns/
accessory (n) /æksesəri/
acrylic (n) /ækrɪlɪk/
alternative (n) /ɔːltɜːʳnətɪv/
ample (adj) /æmpəl/
anorak (n) /ænəræk/
antique (n) /æntiːk/
architect (n) /ɑːʳkɪtekt/
assess (v) /əses/
assumption (n) /əsʌmpʃən/
attic (n) /ætɪk/
baggy-style (adj) /bægi staɪl/
Bank Holiday (n) /bæŋk hɒlɪdeɪ/
bargain (n) /bɑːʳgɪn/
baseball cap (n) /beɪsbɔːl kæp/
bazaar (n) /bəzɑːʳ/
be held (v) /bɪ held/
be worth (v) /bi wɜːʳθ/
car boot sale (n) /kɑːʳ buːt seɪl/
cardigan (n) /kɑːʳdɪgən/
casual (adj) /kæʒuəl/
cause (n) /kɔːz/
charity (n) /tʃærɪti/
check out (phr v) /tʃek aʊt/
checked (adj) /tʃekt/
chemist (n) /kemɪst/
clay (adj) /kleɪ/
colonial (adj) /kəloʊniəl/
colony (n) /kɒləni/
come up with (phr v) /kʌm ʌp wɪð/
condition (n) /kəndɪʃən/
confectioner (n) /kənfekʃənəʳ/
confusing (adj) /kənfjuːzɪŋ/
consider (v) /kənsɪdəʳ/
copy (v) /kɒpi/
cottage (n) /kɒtɪdʒ/
cotton (adj) /kɒtən/
customer (n) /kʌstəməʳ/
decoration (n) /dekəreɪʃən/
deluxe (adj) /dɪlʌks/
denim (adj) /denɪm/
developing (adj) /dɪveləpɪŋ/
dig out (phr v) /dɪg aʊt/
diner (n) /daɪnəʳ/
display (n) /dɪspleɪ/
donate (v) /doʊneɪt/
dry cleaner (n) /draɪ kliːnəʳ/
elegant (adj) /elɪgənt/
exchange (v) /ɪkstʃeɪndʒ/
fan (n) /fæn/
fancy (adj) /fænsi/
fishmonger (n) /fɪʃmʌŋgəʳ/
fitting room (n) /fɪtɪŋ ruːm/
flea market (n) /fliː mɑːʳkɪt/
floral (adj) /flɔːrəl/
For goodness sake! (exp)
formal (adj) /fɔːʳməl/
frame (n) /freɪm/
full-length (adj) /fʊl leŋθ/
give sb a lift (phr)
half price (n) /hɑːf praɪs/
handle (n) /hændəl/
handmade (adj) /hændmeɪd/
hard-earned cash (phr)
head for (v) /hed fəʳ/
high-heeled (adj) /haɪ hiːld/
hold on (phr v) /hoʊld ɒn/
homeless (adj) /hoʊmləs/
horizontal (adj) /hɒrɪzɒntəl/
hunt (v) /hʌnt/
I've had enough! (exp)
in authority (exp)
in need (exp)
in the mood (exp)
instruction manual (n) /ɪnstrʌkʃən mænjuəl/
item (n) /aɪtəm/
jeweller (n) /dʒuːələʳ/
kimono (n) /kɪmoʊnoʊ/
lace (n) /leɪs/
lace-up shoe (n) /leɪs ʌp ʃuː/
landscape (n) /lændskeɪp/
last (v) /lɑːst/
layout (n) /leɪaʊt/
leather (adj) /leðəʳ/
lighter on sb's pocket (exp)
look after (phr v) /lʊk ɑːftəʳ/
look for (phr v) /lʊk fəʳ/
look forward to (phr v) /lʊk fɔːʳwəʳd tə/
look out (phr v) /lʊk aʊt/
look up (phr v) /lʊk ʌp/
machine washable (adj) /məʃiːn wɒʃəbəl/
major (adj) /meɪdʒəʳ/
material (n) /mətɪəriəl/
menswear (n) /menzweəʳ/
miscellaneous (adj) /mɪsəleɪniəs/
neccessity (n) /nɪsesɪti/
neighbourhood (n) /neɪbəʳhʊd/
newsagent (n) /njuːzeɪdʒənt/
nylon (adj) /naɪlɒn/
obligation (n) /ɒblɪgeɪʃən/
obtain (v) /obteɪn/
old-fashioned (adj) /oʊld fæʃənd/
on offer (exp)
on sale (exp)
online (adj) /ɒnlaɪn/
option (n) /ɒpʃən/
original (adj) /ərɪdʒɪnəl/
oval (adj) /oʊvəl/
overcharge (v) /oʊvəʳtʃɑːʳdʒ/
overtime (n) /oʊvəʳtaɪm/
pane (n) /peɪn/
patience (n) /peɪʃəns/
pattern (n) /pætəʳn/
peak (n) /piːk/
permission (n) /pəʳmɪʃən/
pick up (phr v) /pɪk ʌp/
pickpocket (n) /pɪkpɒkɪt/
plain (adj) /pleɪn/
polka-dot (adj) /pɒlkə dɒt/
polyester mix (n) /pɒliestəʳ mɪks/
porch (n) /pɔːrtʃ/
pot (n) /pɒt/
prairie (n) /preəri/
prohibition (n) /proʊbɪʃən/
pure (adj) /pjʊəʳ/

Word List

quality (n) /ˈkwɒliti/
raise (v) /reɪz/
range (n) /reɪndʒ/
receipt (n) /rɪˈsiːt/
rectangular (adj) /rekˈtæŋɡjʊlər/
reduction (n) /rɪˈdʌkʃən/
refund (n) /ˈriːfʌnd/
refuse (v) /rɪˈfjuːz/
salesperson (n) /ˈseɪlzpɜːrsən/
saving (n) /ˈseɪvɪŋ/
second-hand (adj) /ˈsekənd hænd/
selection (n) /sɪˈlekʃən/
shape (n) /ʃeɪp/
shop till you drop (exp)
shutter (n) /ˈʃʌtər/
silk (adj) /sɪlk/
slate (adj) /sleɪt/
sloping (adj) /ˈsloʊpɪŋ/
sombrero (n) /sɒmˈbreəroʊ/
specialise (v) /ˈspeʃəlaɪz/
square (adj) /skweər/
stationer (n) /ˈsteɪʃənər/
steep (adj) /stiːp/
stick out (phr v) /stɪk aʊt/
stock (n) /stɒk/
straw (adj) /strɔː/
striped (adj) /straɪpt/
subheading (n) /ˈsʌbhedɪŋ/
surprisingly (adv) /səˈpraɪzɪŋli/
swap (v) /swɒp/
swimming trunks (n) /ˈswɪmɪŋ trʌŋks/
symmetrical (adj) /sɪˈmetrɪkəl/
thatch (n) /θætʃ/
tip (n) /tɪp/
trader (n) /ˈtreɪdər/
trendy (adj) /ˈtrendi/
triangular (adj) /traɪˈæŋɡjʊlər/
turn up (phr v) /tɜːrn ʌp/
two-seater (adj) /tuː ˈsiːtər/
unbeatable (adj) /ʌnˈbiːtəbəl/
uneven (adj) /ʌnˈiːvən/
unfortunately (adv) /ʌnˈfɔːrtʃʊnətli/
unisex (adj) /ˈjuːnɪseks/
unwanted (adj) /ʌnˈwɒntɪd/
value (n) /ˈvæljuː/
waterproof (adj) /ˈwɔːtərpruːf/
weekend (n) /ˈwiːkend/
wheel (n) /ʰwiːl/
wooden (adj) /ˈwʊdən/
wool (n) /wʊl/

UNIT 6

according to (prep) /əˈkɔːrdɪŋ tə/
alike (adv) /əˈlaɪk/
amusing (adj) /əˈmjuːzɪŋ/
ancient custom (n) /ˈeɪnʃənt ˈkʌstəm/
annual (adj) /ˈænjuəl/
arrival (n) /əˈraɪvəl/
attract (v) /əˈtrækt/
attractive (adj) /əˈtræktɪv/
barbeque (n) /ˈbɑːrbɪkjuː/
bizarre (adj) /bɪˈzɑːr/
bouquet (n) /ˈboʊkeɪ/
break away (phr v) /breɪk əˈweɪ/
break down (phr v) /breɪk daʊn/
break into (phr v) /breɪk ˈɪntə/
break off (phr v) /breɪk ɒf/
break out of (phr v) /breɪk aʊt ɒf/
break through (phr v) /breɪk θruː/
Bridal Shower (n) /ˈbraɪdəl ʃaʊər/
bride (n) /braɪd/
buffet (n) /ˈbʌfeɪ/
can't wait (phr)
carol (n) /ˈkærəl/
carry off (phr v) /ˈkæri ɒf/
cash prize (n) /kæʃ praɪz/
caterer (n) /ˈkeɪtərər/
celebrate (v) /ˈselɪbreɪt/
certificate (n) /səˈtɪfɪkət/
change one's mind (exp)
charity (n) /ˈtʃærɪti/
chase (v) /tʃeɪs/
christening robe (n) /ˈkrɪsənɪŋ roʊb/
colleague (n) /ˈkɒliːɡ/
collourfully (adv) /ˈkʌlərfʊli/
company (n) /ˈkʌmpəni/
competition (n) /kɒmpɪˈtɪʃən/
competitor (n) /kəmˈpetɪtər/
congratulate (v) /kənˈɡrætʃʊleɪt/
congratulations (n) /kənɡrætʃʊˈleɪʃənz/
contestant (n) /kənˈtestənt/
cordially (adv) /ˈkɔːrdiəli/
cracker (n) /ˈkrækər/
degree (n) /dɪˈɡriː/
delighted (adj) /dɪˈlaɪtɪd/
dip (n) /dɪp/
dread (v) /dred/
dress up (phr v) /dres ʌp/
dull (adj) /dʌl/
elbow (n) /ˈelboʊ/

empty-handed (adj) /ˈempti ˈhændɪd/
engagement (n) /ɪnˈɡeɪdʒmənt/
entertaining (adj) /entərˈteɪnɪŋ/
estimate (v) /ˈestɪmeɪt/
evaluate (v) /ɪˈvæljueɪt/
exchange (n) /ɪksˈtʃeɪndʒ/
fair (n) /feər/
fairy (n) /ˈfeəri/
fancy dress (n) /ˈfænsi dres/
fascinated (adj) /ˈfæsɪneɪtɪd/
fate (n) /feɪt/
fireworks (n) /ˈfaɪərwɜːrks/
fixed arrangement (n) /fɪkst əˈreɪndʒmənt/
flaming torch (n) /ˈfleɪmɪŋ tɔːrtʃ/
flying machine (n) /ˈflaɪɪŋ məˈʃiːn/
folklore (n) /ˈfoʊklɔːr/
forever (adv) /fərˈevər/
fortune (n) /ˈfɔːtʃuːn/
freezing (adj) /ˈfriːzɪŋ/
fruitcake (n) /ˈfruːtkeɪk/
furthest (adv) /ˈfɜːrðɪst/
future intention (n) /ˈfjuːtʃər ɪnˈtenʃən/
galley (n) /ˈɡæli/
generosity (n) /dʒenəˈrɒsiti/
goose (n) /ɡuːs/
graduate (v) /ˈɡrædʒueɪt/
graduation (n) /ɡrædʒuˈeɪʃən/
greeting (n) /ˈɡriːtɪŋ/
greetings card (n) /ˈɡriːtɪŋz kɑːrd/
groom (n) /ɡruːm/
Halloween (n) /hæloʊˈwiːn/
handkerchief (n) /ˈhæŋkərtʃɪf/
hats off (exp)
hire (v) /haɪər/
homemade (adj) /hoʊmˈmeɪd/
horsehoe (n) /ˈhɔːrsʃuː/
hung up (phr v) /hʌŋ ʌp/
icing (n) /ˈaɪsɪŋ/
image (n) /ˈɪmɪdʒ/
in one's honour (exp)
in style (exp)
in the hope (exp)
in the old days (phr)
in the post (phr)
Independence Day (n) /ˈɪndɪpendəns deɪ/
insist (v) /ɪnˈsɪst/
isle (n) /aɪl/
job hunting (n) /dʒɒb ˈhʌntɪŋ/
Jordan (n) /ˈdʒɔːrdən/
joy (n) /dʒɔɪ/
layer (n) /ˈleɪər/
link (v) /lɪŋk/

luck (n) /lʌk/
mate (v) /meɪt/
May Day (n) /meɪ deɪ/
mosque (n) /mɒsk/
occasion (n) /əˈkeɪʒən/
on the spot decision (phr)
parade (n) /pəˈreɪd/
participant (n) /pɑːrˈtɪsɪpənt/
pick (v) /pɪk/
pick sb up (phr v) /pɪk ʌp/
pier (n) /pɪər/
pleasure (n) /ˈpleʒər/
posh (adj) /pɒʃ/
pray (v) /preɪ/
promotion (n) /prəˈmoʊʃən/
pumpkin lantern (n) /ˈpʌmpkɪn ˈlæntərn/
put on (phr v) /pʌt ɒn/
reception (n) /rɪˈsepʃən/
recovery (n) /rɪˈkʌvəri/
regret (n) /rɪˈɡret/
relieved (adj) /rɪˈliːvd/
request (v) /rɪˈkwest/
retire (v) /rɪˈtaɪər/
retirement (n) /rɪˈtaɪərmənt/
roll down (phr v) /roʊl daʊn/
root (n) /ruːt/
run out of (phr v) /rʌn aʊt əv/
satisfied (adj) /ˈsætɪsfaɪd/
sb can make it (exp)
scare (v) /skeər/
Season's greetings! (phr)
sit an examination (exp)
sit-down (adj) /sɪt daʊn/
sorrow (n) /ˈsɒroʊ/
spectacular (adj) /spekˈtækjʊlər/
spectator (n) /spekˈteɪtər/
speed (n) /spiːd/
speedy (adj) /ˈspiːdi/
steep (adj) /stiːp/
stocking (n) /ˈstɒkɪŋ/
store (v) /stɔːr/
strange (adj) /streɪndʒ/
streamer (n) /ˈstriːmər/
succeed (v) /səkˈsiːd/
superb (adj) /suːˈpɜːrb/
superstition (n) /suːpərˈstɪʃən/
swan (n) /swɒn/
take place (phr)
take pride in (exp)
tempt (v) /tempt/
theme (n) /θiːm/
think highly of (exp)
three-tier (adj) /θriː tɪər/
thrilling (adj) /ˈθrɪlɪŋ/
top (adj) /tɒp/
treat (n) /triːt/

147

Word List

trick or treat (phr)
Viking (adj) /ˈvaɪkɪŋ/
wed (v) /wed/
Well done! (exp)
wild flower (n) /waɪld flaʊəʳ/
wisdom (n) /ˈwɪzdəm/
wrap (v) /ræp/
wreath (n) /riːθ/

CURRICULAR CUTS 3: Maths (p. 76)

addition (n) /əˈdɪʃən/
amount (n) /əˈmaʊnt/
change (n) /tʃeɪndʒ/
coin (n) /kɔɪn/
division (n) /dɪˈvɪʒən/
multiplication (n) /ˌmʌltɪplɪˈkeɪʃən/
nearest (adj) /ˈnɪərəst/
note (n) /noʊt/
price list (n) /praɪs lɪst/
shopping bill (n) /ˈʃɒpɪŋ bɪl/
subtraction (n) /səbˈtrækʃən/

UNIT 7

add (v) /æd/
adult (n) /ˈædʌlt/
advice (n) /ædˈvaɪs/
aisle (n) /aɪl/
anniversary (n) /ˌænɪˈvɜːʳsəri/
annoyed (adj) /əˈnɔɪd/
appetite (n) /ˈæpɪtaɪt/
appliance (n) /əˈplaɪəns/
aquarium (n) /əˈkweəriəm/
author (n) /ˈɔːθəʳ/
awful (adj) /ˈɔːfʊl/
baked (adj) /beɪkt/
bakery (n) /ˈbeɪkəri/
bar (n) /bɑːʳ/
basil (n) /ˈbæzəl/
bistro (n) /ˈbiːstroʊ/
bitter (adj) /ˈbɪtəʳ/
boiled (adj) /bɔɪld/
bottomless (adj) /ˈbɒtəmləs/
By golly! (exp)
cabbage (n) /ˈkæbɪdʒ/
carousel (n) /ˈkærəsel/
carving knife (n) /ˈkɑːʳvɪŋ naɪf/
catering (n) /ˈkeɪtərɪŋ/
celebrity (n) /sɪˈlebriti/
celery (n) /ˈseləri/
cereal (n) /ˈsɪəriəl/
chilli pepper (n) /ˈtʃɪli pepəʳ/
chop (v) /tʃɒp/

chopped (adj) /tʃɒpt/
clove (n) /kloʊv/
cocktail (n) /ˈkɒkteɪl/
comfortably (adv) /ˈkʌmftəbli/
competition (n) /ˌkɒmpɪˈtɪʃən/
constantly (adv) /ˈkɒnstəntli/
contest (n) /ˈkɒntest/
cream (n) /kriːm/
creamy (adj) /ˈkriːmi/
crockery (n) /ˈkrɒkəri/
crunchy (adj) /ˈkrʌntʃi/
cuisine (n) /kwɪˈziːn/
cut off (phr v) /kʌt ɒf/
cutlery (n) /ˈkʌtləri/
dairy (adj) /ˈðeəri/
deck (n) /dek/
decor (n) /ˈdeɪkɔːʳ/
dessert (n) /dɪˈzɜːʳt/
dine (adj) /daɪn/
diner (n) /ˈdaɪnəʳ/
disgusting (adj) /dɪsˈɡʌstɪŋ/
doubt (n) /daʊt/
drain (v) /dreɪn/
dressed (adj) /drest/
dried (adj) /draɪd/
elegant (adj) /ˈelɪgənt/
exact (adj) /ɪgˈzækt/
fling (v) /flɪŋ/
flop (adv) /flɒp/
flowerpot (n) /ˈflaʊəʳpɒt/
formal (adj) /ˈfɔːʳməl/
fountain (n) /ˈfaʊntɪn/
four-course meal (n) /fɔːʳ kɔːʳs miːl/
fried (adj) /fraɪd/
frozen (adj) /ˈfroʊzən/
fry (v) /fraɪ/
function (n) /ˈfʌŋkʃən/
garlic (n) /ˈɡɑːʳlɪk/
gas lamp (n) /ɡæs læmp/
gentle (adj) /ˈdʒentəl/
give away (phr v) /ɡɪv əˈweɪ/
give back (phr v) /ɡɪv bæk/
give in (phr v) /ɡɪv ɪn/
give off (phr v) /ɡɪv ɒf/
give out (phr v) /ɡɪv aʊt/
give up (phr v) /ɡɪv ʌp/
grated (adj) /ˈgreɪtɪd/
grilled (adj) /ɡrɪld/
grow (n) /ɡroʊ/
handful (n) /ˈhændfʊl/
Help yourself! (exp)
helpful (adj) /ˈhelpfʊl/
honoured guest (n) /ˈɒnəʳd gest/
host (n) /hoʊst/
ice cube (n) /aɪs kjuːb/
in total (exp)

included (adj) /ɪnˈkluːdɪd/
information (n) /ˌɪnfəʳˈmeɪʃən/
ingredient (n) /ɪnˈɡriːdiənt/
jug (n) /dʒʌg/
juicy (adj) /ˈdʒuːsi/
karaoke (n) /ˌkæriˈoʊki/
keen (adj) /kiːn/
keep up with (phr v) /kiːp ʌp wɪð/
ketchup (n) /ˈketʃʌp/
kettle (adj) /ˈketəl/
knowledge (n) /ˈnɒlɪdʒ/
lettuce (n) /ˈletɪs/
lift up (phr v) /lɪft ʌp/
linen (adj) /ˈlɪnɪn/
live (adj) /laɪv/
lively (adj) /ˈlaɪvli/
located (adj) /loʊˈkeɪtɪd/
lose my temper (exp)
luggage (n) /ˈlʌɡɪdʒ/
luxurious (adj) /lʌɡˈʒʊəriəs/
mall (n) /mɔːl/
mammoth (adj) /ˈmæməθ/
manner (n) /ˈmænəʳ/
mashed (adj) /mæʃt/
mayonnaise (n) /ˌmeɪəˈneɪz/
mineral water (n) /ˈmɪnərəl wɔːtəʳ/
mist (n) /mɪst/
mug (n) /mʌg/
mushroom (n) /ˈmʌʃruːm/
mustard (n) /ˈmʌstəʳd/
mutter (v) /ˈmʌtəʳ/
napkin (n) /ˈnæpkɪn/
no end (phr)
nut (n) /nʌt/
occasion (n) /əˈkeɪʒən/
on top of the world (exp)
oregano (n) /ɒrɪˈɡɑːnoʊ/
pasta (n) /ˈpæstə/
peach (n) /piːtʃ/
pear (n) /peəʳ/
performance (n) /pəʳˈfɔːʳməns/
pickle (n) /ˈpɪkəl/
pinch (n) /pɪntʃ/
pineapple (n) /ˈpaɪnæpəl/
place (v) /pleɪs/
plain (adj) /pleɪn/
pot (n) /pɒt/
poultry (n) /ˈpoʊltri/
pour (v) /pɔːʳ/
premises (n) /ˈpremɪsɪz/
pudding (n) /ˈpʊdɪŋ/
range (v) /reɪndʒ/
reasonable (adj) /ˈriːzənəbəl/
relaxed (adj) /rɪˈlækst/
report (n) /rɪˈpɔːʳt/
reservation (n) /ˌrezəʳˈveɪʃən/

review (v) /rɪˈvjuː/
revolve (v) /rɪˈvɒlv/
rise up (phr v) /raɪz ʌp/
riverside (n) /ˈrɪvəʳsaɪd/
roasted (adj) /ˈroʊstɪd/
rocking (n) /ˈrɒkɪŋ/
row (n) /roʊ/
rush on (v) /rʌʃ ɒn/
salmon (n) /ˈsæmən/
salty (adj) /ˈsɔːlti/
saucer (n) /ˈsɔːsəʳ/
sausage (n) /ˈsɒsɪdʒ/
save room (phr)
sb makes it (exp)
scoop (n) /skuːp/
scramble (v) /ˈskræmbəl/
scrambled (adj) /ˈskræmbəld/
seafood (n) /ˈsiːfuːd/
section (n) /ˈsekʃən/
selection (n) /sɪˈlekʃən/
serving (n) /ˈsɜːʳvɪŋ/
side dish (n) /saɪd dɪʃ/
simmer (v) /ˈsɪməʳ/
situated (adj) /ˈsɪtʃueɪtɪd/
smartly (adv) /ˈsmɑːʳtli/
snack (n) /snæk/
sour (adj) /saʊəʳ/
sparkling (adj) /ˈspɑːʳklɪŋ/
specialise (v) /ˈspeʃəlaɪz/
spicy (adj) /ˈspaɪsi/
sprinkle (v) /ˈsprɪŋkəl/
stained glass (n) /steɪnd glɑːs/
stare (v) /steəʳ/
statue (n) /ˈstætʃuː/
steamed (adj) /stiːmd/
steamy (adj) /ˈstiːmi/
step out (phr v) /step aʊt/
still (adj) /stɪl/
stylish (adj) /ˈstaɪlɪʃ/
surroundings (n) /səˈraʊndɪŋz/
sweet (adj) /swiːt/
tablecloth (n) /ˈteɪbəlklɒθ/
take a peek (exp)
tape (v) /teɪp/
tax (n) /tæks/
tblsp (tablespoonful) (n) /ˈteɪbəlspuːnfʊl/
there is no sign of sb (exp)
thunderstorm (n) /ˈθʌndəʳstɔːʳm/
tin (n) /tɪn/
tinned (adj) /tɪnd/
tiny (adj) /ˈtaɪni/
tip (n) /tɪp/
toaster (n) /ˈtoʊstəʳ/
topping (n) /ˈtɒpɪŋ/
tower (n) /taʊəʳ/

Word List

triumphantly (adv) /traɪˈʌmfəntli/
try out (phr v) /traɪ aʊt/
tsp (teaspoonful) (n) /ˈtiːspuːnfʊl/
tunnel (n) /ˈtʌnəl/
twilight (n) /ˈtwaɪlaɪt/
unusual (adj) /ʌnˈjuːʒuəl/
value (n) /ˈvæljuː/
vanilla (n) /vəˈnɪlə/
view (n) /vjuː/
vinegar (n) /ˈvɪnɪgəʳ/
waitress (n) /ˈweɪtrəs/
warehouse (n) /ˈweəʳhaʊs/
waterfall (n) /ˈwɔːtəʳfɔːl/
wave (v) /weɪv/
weekly (adj) /ˈwiːkli/
well done (adj) /wel dʌn/
whipped (adj) /ˈwɪpt/
yoghurt (n) /ˈjɒgəʳt/

UNIT 8

aerobics (n) /eəˈroʊbɪks/
aggressive (adj) /əˈgresɪv/
alley (n) /ˈæli/
although (conj) /ɔːlˈðoʊ/
ancient (adj) /ˈeɪnʃənt/
antiquity (n) /ænˈtɪkwɪti/
application form (n) /æplɪˈkeɪʃən fɔːʳm/
As a result (exp)
athletics (n) /æθˈletɪks/
attitude (n) /ˈætɪtjuːd/
award (v) /əˈwɔːʳd/
back trouble (n) /bæk ˈtrʌbəl/
backache (n) /ˈbækeɪk/
baseball (n) /ˈbeɪsbɔːl/
based on (adj) /beɪst ən/
be off (phr v) /bi ɒf/
billiards (n) /ˈbɪliəʳdz/
bother (v) /ˈbɒðəʳ/
bowling (n) /ˈboʊlɪŋ/
brave (adj) /breɪv/
bring about (phr v) /brɪŋ əˈbaʊt/
bring back (phr v) /brɪŋ bæk/
bring out (phr v) /brɪŋ aʊt/
bring round (phr v) /brɪŋ raʊnd/
bring up (phr v) /brɪŋ ʌp/
broadcast (v) /ˈbrɔːdkɑːst/
calcium (n) /ˈkælsiəm/
cancel (v) /ˈkænsəl/
careless (adj) /ˈkeəʳləs/
ceremony (n) /ˈserɪməni/
challenge (n) /ˈtʃælɪndʒ/
challenging (adj) /ˈtʃælɪndʒɪŋ/
champion (n) /ˈtʃæmpiən/
cheer (v) /tʃɪəʳ/
cheerful (adj) /ˈtʃɪəʳfʊl/
childhood (n) /ˈtʃaɪldhʊd/
coach (n) /koʊtʃ/
come down (phr v) /kʌm daʊn/
committee (n) /kəˈmɪti/
competitive (adj) /kəmˈpetɪtɪv/
competitor (n) /kəmˈpetɪtəʳ/
compromise (n) /ˈkɒmprəmaɪz/
conclude (v) /kənˈkluːd/
consequently (adv) /ˈkɒnsɪkwentli/
consist of (v) /kənˈsɪst əv/
contrast (n) /ˈkɒntrɑːst/
cope with (v) /koʊp wɪð/
course (n) /kɔːʳs/
court (n) /kɔːt/
cricket (n) /ˈkrɪkɪt/
cross (v) /krɒs/
decathlon (n) /dɪˈkæθlɒn/
descend (v) /dɪˈsend/
determined (adj) /dɪˈtɜːʳmɪnd/
die out (phr v) /daɪ aʊt/
disciplined (adj) /ˈdɪsɪplɪnd/
disqualify (v) /dɪsˈkwɒlɪfaɪ/
dissatisfied (adj) /dɪsˈsætɪsfaɪd/
divide (v) /dɪˈvaɪd/
drop (v) /drɒp/
effect (n) /ɪˈfekt/
encourage (v) /ɪnˈkʌrɪdʒ/
even-numbered (adj) /ˈiːvən ˈnʌmbəʳd/
expand (v) /ɪkˈspænd/
experienced (adj) /ɪkˈspɪəriənst/
express (v) /ɪkˈspres/
fall behind with (phr v) /fɔːl bɪˈhaɪnd wɪð/
finishing line (n) /ˈfɪnɪʃɪŋ laɪn/
fit (adj) /fɪt/
furthermore (adv) /fɜːʳðəʳˈmɔːʳ/
gender (n) /ˈdʒendəʳ/
guide (v) /gaɪd/
gymnastics (n) /dʒɪmˈnæstɪks/
hall (n) /hɔːl/
head for (v) /hed fəʳ/
however (adv) /haʊˈevəʳ/
ice-hockey (n) /aɪs ˈhɒki/
icy (adj) /ˈaɪsi/
immortal (n) /ɪˈmɔːʳtəl/
in a way (exp)
in addition (phr)
In conclusion (exp)
in the air (phr)
in the open (phr)
individual (adj) /ˌɪndɪˈvɪdʒuəl/
inspired (adj) /ɪnˈspaɪəʳd/
install (v) /ɪnˈstɔːl/
insurance (n) /ɪnˈʃʊərəns/
judge (n) /dʒʌdʒ/
keep out of (phr v) /kiːp aʊt əv/
kill pain (phr)
leader (n) /ˈliːdəʳ/
level (n) /ˈlevəl/
line up (phr v) /laɪn ʌp/
mail (n) /meɪl/
management (n) /ˈmænɪdʒmənt/
marathon (n) /ˈmærəθən/
martial art (n) /ˈmɑːʳʃəl ɑːʳt/
medication (n) /medɪˈkeɪʃən/
melt (v) /melt/
memory (n) /ˈmeməri/
moreover (adv) /mɔːʳˈroʊvəʳ/
musher (n) /ˈmʌʃəʳ/
negotiate (v) /nɪˈgoʊʃieɪt/
noticeboard (n) /ˈnoʊtɪsbɔːʳd/
obviously (adv) /ˈɒbviəsli/
odd-numbered (adj) /ɒd ˈnʌmbəʳd/
official (adj) /əˈfɪʃəl/
oil (n) /ɔɪl/
Olympic Anthem (n) /əˈlɪmpɪk ˈænθəm/
on the other hand (exp)
on the trail (exp)
onlooker (n) /ˈɒnlʊkəʳ/
operation (n) /ɒpəˈreɪʃən/
opponent (n) /əˈpoʊnənt/
originally (adv) /əˈrɪdʒɪnəli/
patient (adj) /ˈpeɪʃənt/
patriotic (adj) /pætriˈɒtɪk/
paw (v) /pɔː/
pentathlon (n) /penˈtæθlən/
perform (v) /pəʳˈfɔːʳm/
pitch (n) /pɪtʃ/
pool (n) /puːl/
poster (n) /ˈpoʊstəʳ/
postpone (v) /poʊsˈpoʊn/
proud (adj) /praʊd/
pulled muscle (n) /pʊld ˈmʌsəl/
race (n) /reɪs/
reach (n) /riːtʃ/
refreshment (n) /rɪˈfreʃmənt/
regularly (adv) /ˈregjʊləʳli/
reject (v) /rɪˈdʒekt/
ring (n) /rɪŋ/
rink (n) /rɪŋk/
rough (adj) /rʌf/
route (n) /ruːt/
rugby (n) /ˈrʌgbi/
sb has a history of (exp)
selfish (adj) /ˈselfɪʃ/
sense of direction (phr)
shed (v) /ʃed/
shower (n) /ˈʃaʊəʳ/
skateboarding (n) /ˈskeɪtbɔːʳdɪŋ/
sled (n) /sled/
slightly (adv) /ˈslaɪtli/
snooker (n) /ˈsnuːkəʳ/
snowmobile (n) /ˈsnoʊməbiːl/
sore throat (n) /sɔːʳ θroʊt/
sort of (phr)
sprained wrist (n) /spreɪnd rɪst/
stamina (n) /ˈstæmɪnə/
stand for (phr v) /stænd fəʳ/
surgical spirit (n) /ˈsɜːʳdʒɪkəl ˈspɪrɪt/
sympathy (n) /ˈsɪmpəθi/
take off (phr v) /teɪk ɒf/
target reader (n) /ˈtɑːʳgɪt ˈriːdəʳ/
therefore (adv) /ˈðeəʳfɔːʳ/
thick fur (n) /θɪk fɜːr/
to build sb's confidence (phr)
To sum up (exp)
tough (-tougher -toughest) (adj) /tʌf/
tournament (n) /ˈtʊəʳnəmənt/
Town Council (n) /taʊn ˈkaʊnsəl/
track (n) /træk/
training session (n) /ˈtreɪnɪŋ ˈseʃən/
transport (v) /trænˈspɔːʳt/
trek (n) /trek/
turn down (phr v) /tɜːʳn daʊn/
turn off (phr v) /tɜːʳn ɒf/
twisted ankle (n) /ˈtwɪstɪd ˈæŋkəl/
umpire (n) /ˈʌmpaɪəʳ/
unconscious (adj) /ʌnˈkɒnʃəs/
vary (v) /ˈveəri/
vet (n) /vet/
well-trained (adj) /wel treɪnd/
What is more (exp)
wound (n) /wuːnd/

CURRICULAR CUTS 4: Science (p. 100)

carbohydrates (n) /kɑːʳboʊˈhaɪdreɪts/
cereals (n) /ˈsɪəriəlz/
fatty acid (n) /ˈfæti ˈæsɪd/
iron (n) /ˈaɪəʳn/
low-fat (adj) /loʊ fæt/
protein (n) /ˈproʊtiːn/

149

Word List

serving (n) /ˈsɜːrvɪŋ/
vitamin (n) /ˈvɪtəmɪn/

UNIT 9

abyss (n) /ˈæbɪs/
action-packed (adj) /ˈækʃən pækt/
actually (adv) /ˈæktʃuəli/
admire (v) /ədˈmaɪər/
admission (n) /ədˈmɪʃən/
advertise (v) /ˈædvərtaɪz/
alien (n) /ˈeɪliən/
art lover (n) /ˈɑːrt lʌvər/
award-winning production (n) /əˈwɔːrd wɪnɪŋ prədʌkʃən/
background (n) /ˈbækɡraʊnd/
behind the scenes (exp)
betray (v) /bɪˈtreɪ/
box office (n) /ˈbɒks ɒfɪs/
break down (phr v) /breɪk daʊn/
break the record (exp)
broadcast (v) /ˈbrɔːdkɑːst/
browse the Net (phr)
bug (n) /bʌg/
cameraman (n) /ˈkæmrəmæn/
capture (v) /ˈkæptʃər/
cashier (n) /kæˈʃɪər/
celebrity (n) /sɪˈlebrɪti/
channel (n) /ˈtʃænəl/
charity (n) /ˈtʃærɪti/
chat show (n) /ˈtʃæt ʃoʊ/
chopstick (n) /ˈtʃɒpstɪk/
classified ad (n) /ˈklæsɪfaɪd æd/
colleague (n) /ˈkɒliːɡ/
compete (v) /kəmˈpiːt/
computer animated (adj) /kəmˈpjuːtər ænɪmeɪtɪd/
corruption (n) /kərˈʌpʃən/
crazy (-crazier-craziest) (adj) /ˈkreɪzi/
cultural mix (n) /ˈkʌltʃərəl mɪks/
currently (adv) /ˈkʌrəntli/
date (v) /deɪt/
deal with (phr v) /ˈdiːl wɪð/
digital surround sound (n) /ˈdɪdʒɪtəl səraʊnd saʊnd/
disagree (v) /dɪsəˈɡriː/
documentary (n) /ˌdɒkjəˈmentri/
dreadful (adj) /ˈdredfʊl/
exhibition (n) /ˌeksɪˈbɪʃən/
experience (v) /ɪkˈspɪəriəns/
famine (n) /ˈfæmɪn/
fancy (v) /ˈfænsi/
fascinating (adj) /ˈfæsɪneɪtɪŋ/
fight (v) /faɪt/

fully booked (adj) /ˈfʊli bʊkt/
fundraising (adj) /ˈfʌndreɪzɪŋ/
gladiator (n) /ˈɡlædieɪtər/
graffiti (n) /ɡrəˈfiːti/
grand (adj) /ɡrænd/
grapes (n) /ɡreɪps/
greet (v) /ɡriːt/
guaranteed (adj) /ˌɡærənˈtiːd/
hilarious (adj) /hɪˈleəriəs/
historical (adj) /hɪˈstɒrɪkəl/
illegal (adj) /ɪˈliːɡəl/
image (n) /ˈɪmɪdʒ/
imaginary (adj) /ɪˈmædʒɪnəri/
impressive (adj) /ɪmˈpresɪv/
in common (exp)
in need (exp)
in the mood (exp)
include (v) /ɪnˈkluːd/
issue (n) /ˈɪsjuː/
it's up to sb (exp)
jelly (n) /ˈdʒeli/
keep up with (phr v) /kiːp ʌp wɪð/
laugh-a-minute (exp)
laughter (n) /ˈlɑːftər/
law firm (n) /ˈlɔː fɜːrm/
lawyer (n) /ˈlɔɪər/
makeup artist (n) /ˈmeɪkʌp ɑːrtɪst/
material (n) /məˈtɪəriəl/
matinee performance (n) /ˈmætɪneɪ pərˈfɔːrməns/
miss the chance (phr)
monster (n) /ˈmɒnstər/
movement (n) /ˈmuːvmənt/
moving (adj) /ˈmuːvɪŋ/
multicultural (adj) /ˌmʌltɪˈkʌltʃərəl/
must (n) /mʌst/
mystery (n) /ˈmɪstəri/
nation (n) /ˈneɪʃən/
neither (conj) /ˈnaɪðər/
newsreader (n) /ˈnjuːzriːdər/
novel (n) /ˈnɒvəl/
on display (exp)
on sale (exp)
on time (exp)
oversleep (v) /ˌoʊvərˈsliːp/
particularly (adv) /pərˈtɪkjʊlərli/
perform (v) /pərˈfɔːrm/
performance times (n) /pərˈfɔːrməns taɪmz/
performance (n) /pərˈfɔːrməns/
picture strip (n) /ˈpɪktʃər strɪp/
plot summary (n) /plɒt sʌməri/
poverty (n) /ˈpɒvərti/
profession (n) /prəˈfeʃən/
put across (phr v) /pʊt əˈkrɒs/

put on (phr v) /pʊt ɒn/
quizmaster (n) /ˈkwɪzmɑːstər/
raise (v) /reɪz/
release (n) /rɪˈliːs/
revenge (n) /rɪˈvendʒ/
review (n) /rɪˈvjuː/
running time (n) /ˈrʌnɪŋ taɪm/
samurai (n) /ˈsæmjʊraɪ/
science fiction (n) /saɪəns fɪkʃən/
scissors (n) /ˈsɪzərz/
screen (n) /skriːn/
screening (n) /ˈskriːnɪŋ/
senior (n) /ˈsiːnjər/
sensation (n) /senˈseɪʃən/
series (n) /ˈsɪəriz/
set up (phr v) /set ʌp/
setting (n) /ˈsetɪŋ/
settle in (phr v) /ˈsetəl ɪn/
shave (v) /ʃeɪv/
shore (n) /ʃɔːr/
showing (n) /ˈʃoʊɪŋ/
signature (n) /ˈsɪɡnətʃər/
sitcom (situation comedy) (n) /ˈsɪt kɒm/
slogan (n) /ˈsloʊɡən/
soap opera (n) /soʊp ɒpərə/
solve (v) /sɒlv/
spray paint (n) /spreɪ peɪnt/
stalls (n) /stɔːlz/
star (v) /stɑːr/
state-of-the-art (adj) /steɪt əv ði ɑːrt/
station (n) /ˈsteɪʃən/
superb (adj) /suːˈpɜːrb/
support (v) /səˈpɔːrt/
surface (n) /ˈsɜːrfɪs/
sweat (v) /swet/
tag on (phr v) /tæɡ ɒn/
talent (n) /ˈtælənt/
technique (n) /tekˈniːk/
the authorities (n) /ði ɔːˈθɒrɪtiz/
the pick of sth (exp)
the public (n) /ðə pʌblɪk/
throughout (prep) /θruːˈaʊt/
top (adj) /tɒp/
touching (adj) /ˈtʌtʃɪŋ/
troupe (n) /truːp/
turn down (phr v) /tɜːrn daʊn/
turn off (phr v) /tɜːrn ɒf/
turn on (phr v) /tɜːrn ɒn/
turn out (phr v) /tɜːrn aʊt/
turn to (phr v) /tɜːrn tə/
turn up (phr v) /tɜːrn ʌp/
TV guide (n) /tiː viː ɡaɪd/
unbelievable (adj) /ˌʌnbɪˈliːvəbəl/
unite (v) /juːˈnaɪt/
unoriginal (adj) /ˌʌnəˈrɪdʒɪnəl/

unreal (adj) /ʌnˈriːl/
upper circle (adj) /ˈʌpər sɜːrkəl/
valid (adj) /ˈvælɪd/
vote (v) /voʊt/
weather forecaster (n) /ˈweðər fɔːrkɑːstər/
wizard (n) /ˈwɪzərd/
15-minute interval (n) /ˈfɪftiːn mɪnɪt ɪntərvəl/

UNIT 10

access (n) /ˈækses/
accurate (adj) /ˈækjʊrət/
advanced (adj) /ədˈvɑːnst/
air conditioning (n) /ˈeər kəndɪʃənɪŋ/
answering machine (n) /ˈɑːnsərɪŋ məʃiːn/
attend (v) /əˈtend/
attitude (n) /ˈætɪtjuːd/
average (adj) /ˈævərɪdʒ/
blurred (adj) /blɜːrd/
built-in (adj) /ˈbɪlt ɪn/
button (n) /ˈbʌtən/
capacity (n) /kəˈpæsɪti/
carrying case (n) /ˈkæriɪŋ keɪs/
cash (n) /kæʃ/
CD-ROM (n) /siː diː rɒm/
cell (n) /sel/
chat (v) /tʃæt/
chat room (n) /tʃæt ruːm/
communicate (v) /kəˈmjuːnɪkeɪt/
computer file (n) /kəmˈpjuːtər faɪl/
connection (n) /kəˈnekʃən/
craze (n) /kreɪz/
damage (v) /ˈdæmɪdʒ/
delete (v) /dɪˈliːt/
density (n) /ˈdensɪti/
designer gear (n) /dɪˈzaɪnər ɡɪər/
designer label (n) /dɪˈzaɪnər leɪbəl/
desktop (n) /ˈdesktɒp/
digital camera (n) /ˈdɪdʒɪtəl kæmrə/
disc tray (n) /dɪsk treɪ/
disk drive (n) /dɪsk draɪv/
display (n) /dɪˈspleɪ/
dissatisfaction (n) /ˌdɪssætɪsˈfækʃən/
distorted (n) /dɪˈstɔːrtɪd/
divide (v) /dɪˈvaɪd/
educational system (n) /ˌedʒʊˈkeɪʃənəl sɪstəm/
enclosed (adj) /ɪnˈkloʊzd/

Word List

entitle (v) /ɪnˈtaɪtəl/
entry (n) /ˈentri/
excuse (n) /ɪkˈskjuːs/
experiment (n) /ɪkˈsperɪmənt/
expert (n) /ˈekspɜːrt/
eyesight (n) /ˈaɪsaɪt/
face to face (exp)
fast forward (phr)
faulty (adj) /ˈfɔːlti/
flash (n) /flæʃ/
flickering (adj) /ˈflɪkərɪŋ/
floppy disc (n) /ˈflɒpi dɪsk/
frequently (adv) /ˈfriːkwəntli/
gadget (n) /ˈgædʒɪt/
garage music (n) /ˈgærɑːʒ mjuːzɪk/
Gb (gigabyte) (n) /ˈgɪgəbaɪt/
GCSE (n) /dʒiː siː es iː/
grade (n) /greɪd/
graduate (v) /ˈgrædʒueɪt/
gravity (n) /ˈgrævɪti/
guarantee (n) /gærənˈtiː/
hairstyle (n) /ˈheərstaɪl/
hard drive (n) /hɑːrd draɪv/
headphones (n) /ˈhedfoʊnz/
hear from (phr v) /hɪər frəm/
hip-hop (n) /hɪp hɒp/
hurricane (n) /ˈhʌrɪkən/
I haven't a clue (exp)
I haven't the faintest idea (exp)
install (v) /ɪnˈstɔːl/
invent (v) /ɪnˈvent/
invoice (n) /ˈɪnvɔɪs/
jam (v) /dʒæm/
kbps (kilobyte per second) (phr)
keep in touch with (exp)
keypad (n) /ˈkiːpæd/
lab (laboratory) (n) /læb/
lead to (v) /liːd tə/
lens (n) /lenz/
log on (phr v) /lɒg ɒn/
majority (n) /məˈdʒɒrɪti/
mate (n) /meɪt/

Mb (megabyte) (n) /ˈmegəbaɪt/
meet up with (phr v) /miːt ʌp wɪð/
midday (n) /ˈmɪdeɪ/
modem (n) /ˈmoʊdem/
national curriculum (n) /ˈnæʃənəl kəˈrɪkjʊləm/
no wonder (exp)
nu-metal (n) /njuː metəl/
occasionally (adv) /əˈkeɪʒənəli/
online (adv) /ɒnˈlaɪn/
option (n) /ˈɒpʃən/
overheated (adj) /oʊvərˈhiːtɪd/
own (v) /oʊn/
parachute (n) /ˈpærəʃuːt/
parking ticket (n) /ˈpɑːrkɪŋ tɪkɪt/
password (n) /ˈpɑːswɜːrd/
PC (personal computer) (n) /piː siː/
plug in (phr v) /plʌg ɪn/
pocket calculator (n) /ˈpɒkɪt kælkjʊleɪtər/
portable stereo (n) /ˈpɔːrtəbəl sterioʊ/
processor (n) /ˈproʊsesər/
properly (adv) /ˈprɒpərli/
protest march (n) /ˈproʊtest mɑːrtʃ/
purchase (n) /ˈpɜːrtʃɪs/
qualification (n) /kwɒlɪfɪˈkeɪʃən/
qualify (v) /ˈkwɒlɪfaɪ/
question (v) /ˈkwestʃən/
range (n) /reɪndʒ/
refund (n) /ˈriːfʌnd/
reliable (adj) /rɪˈlaɪəbəl/
remote control (n) /rɪˈmoʊt kənˈtroʊl/
replacement (n) /rɪˈpleɪsmənt/
research (v) /rɪˈsɜːrtʃ/
researcher (n) /rɪˈsɜːrtʃər/
result (n) /rɪˈzʌlt/
scientific experiment (n) /saɪənˈtɪfɪk ɪkˈsperɪmənt/
scroll (v) /skroʊl/
secondary school (n) /ˈsekəndri skuːl/
seismograph (n) /ˈsaɪzməgrɑːf/
select (v) /sɪˈlekt/
set up (phr v) /set ʌp/
share (v) /ʃeər/
site (n) /saɪt/
slide (n) /slaɪd/
socialise (v) /ˈsoʊʃəlaɪz/
software (n) /ˈsɒftweər/
split (v) /splɪt/
spokesperson (n) /ˈspoʊkspɜːrsən/
state (n) /steɪt/
statistical (adj) /stəˈtɪstɪkəl/
sth is out of order (exp)
stuck (adj) /stʌk/
submarine (n) /sʌbməˈriːn/
sum (n) /sʌm/
surf the Net (phr)
survey (n) /ˈsɜːrveɪ/
switch on (phr v) /swɪtʃ ɒn/
take a place by storm (exp)
take after (phr v) /teɪk ɑːftər/
take off (phr v) /teɪk ɒf/
take on (phr v) /teɪk ɒn/
take out (phr v) /teɪk aʊt/
take out (phr v) /teɪk aʊt/
take up (phr v) /teɪk ʌp/
teenager (n) /ˈtiːneɪdʒər/
text (n) /tekst/
text messaging (n) /tekst mesɪdʒɪŋ/
tidal wave (n) /ˈtaɪdəl weɪv/
trend (n) /trend/
trendy (-trendier -trendiest) (adj) /ˈtrendi/
turn up (phr v) /tɜːrn ʌp/
typical (adj) /ˈtɪpɪkəl/
unplug (v) /ʌnˈplʌg/
unreliable (adj) /ʌnrɪˈlaɪəbəl/
unsuitable (adj) /ʌnˈsuːtəbəl/
virus (n) /ˈvaɪərəs/
walkie talkie (n) /ˈwɔːki tɔːki/
windscreen wiper (n) /ˈwɪndskriːn waɪpər/

You're welcome. (exp)

CURRICULAR CUTS 5: Art & Design (p. 124)

basic (adj) /ˈbeɪsɪk/
blend (v) /blend/
characterise (v) /ˈkærɪktəraɪz/
Cubism (n) /ˈkjuːbɪzəm/
daylight (n) /ˈdeɪlaɪt/
emphasise (v) /ˈemfəsaɪz/
especially (adv) /ɪˈspeʃəli/
image (n) /ˈɪmɪdʒ/
imagine (v) /ɪˈmædʒɪn/
Impressionism (n) /ɪmˈpreʃənɪzəm/
inspire (v) /ɪnˈspaɪər/
introduce (v) /ɪntrəˈdjuːs/
messy (adj) /ˈmesi/
mind (n) /maɪnd/
outdoors (n) /aʊtˈdɔːz/
Post-Impressionism (n) /poʊst ɪmˈpreʃənɪzəm/
reality (n) /riˈælɪti/
represent (v) /reprɪˈzent/
subject (n) /ˈsʌbdʒɪkt/
Surrealism (n) /səˈriːəlɪzəm/
through (prep) /θruː/
unexpected (adj) /ʌnɪkˈspektɪd/
unreal (adj) /ʌnˈriːl/
view up (phr v) /vjuː ʌp/s

American English–British English Guide

American English	British English
A	
account	bill/account
airplane	aeroplane
anyplace/anywhere	anywhere
apartment	flat
B	
bathrobe	dressing gown
bathtub	bath
bill	banknote
billion=thousand million	billion=million million
busy (phone)	engaged (phone)
C	
cab	taxi
call/phone	ring up/phone
can	tin
candy	sweets
check	bill (restaurant)
closet	wardrobe
connect (telephone)	put through
cookie	biscuit
corn	sweetcorn, maize
crazy	mad
D	
desk clerk	receptionist
dessert	pudding/dessert/sweet
downtown	(city) centre
drapes	curtains
drugstore/pharmacy	chemist's (shop)
duplex	semi-detached
E	
eggplant	aubergine
elevator	lift
F	
fall	autumn
faucet	tap
first floor, second floor, etc	ground floor, first floor, etc
flashlight	torch
French fries	chips
front desk (hotel)	reception
G	
garbage/trash	rubbish
garbage can	dustbin/bin
gas	petrol
gas station	petrol station/garage
grade	class/year
I	
intermission	interval
intersection	crossroads
J	
janitor	caretaker/porter
K	
kerosene	paraffin
L	
lawyer/attorney	solicitor
line	queue
lost and found	lost property
M	
mail	post
make a reservation	book
motorcycle	motorbike/motorcycle
movie	film
movie house/theater	cinema
N	
news-stand	newsagent
O	
office (doctor's/dentist's)	surgery
one-way (ticket)	single (ticket)
overalls	dungarees

American English	British English
P	
pants/trousers	trousers
pantyhose/nylons	tights
parking lot	car park
pavement	road surface
pedestrian crossing	zebra crossing
(potato) chips	crisps
public school	state school
purse	handbag
R	
railroad	railway
rest room	toilet/cloakroom
S	
sales clerk/sales girl	**shop assistant**
schedule	timetable
shorts (underwear)	pants
sidewalk	pavement
stand in line	queue
store, shop	shop
subway	underground
T	
truck	lorry, van
two weeks	fortnight/two weeks
V	
vacation	holiday(s)
vacuum (v.)	hoover
vacuum cleaner	hoover
vest	waistcoat
W	
with or without (milk/cream in coffee)	black or white
Y	
yard	garden
Z	
(pronounced, "zee")	(pronounced, "zed")
zero	nought
zip code	postcode

Grammar

He just went out./ He has just gone out.	He has just gone out.
Hello, is this Steve?	Hello, is that Steve?
Do you have a car?/ Have you got a car?	Have you got a car?

Spelling

aluminum	aluminium
analyze	analyse
center	centre
check	cheque
color	colour
honor	honour
jewelry	jewellery
practice(n,v)	practice(n) practise(v)
program	programme
realize	realise
tire	tyre
trave(l)ler	traveller

Expressions with prepositions and particles

different from/than	different from/to
live on X street	live in X street
on a team	in a team
on the weekend	at the weekend
Monday through Friday	Monday to Friday